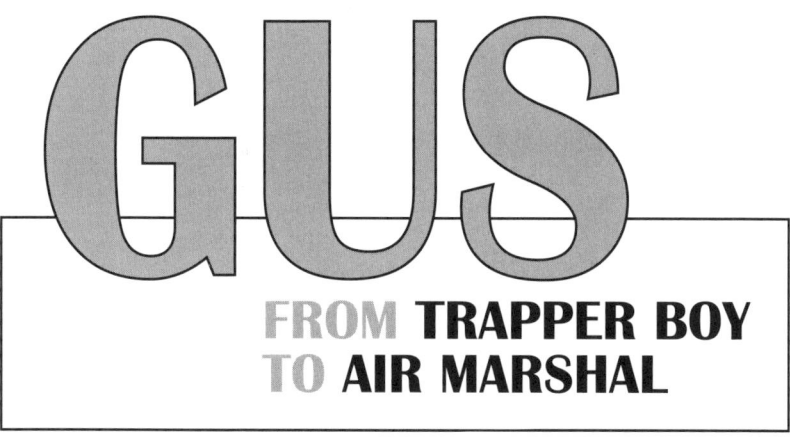

FROM TRAPPER BOY TO AIR MARSHAL

Air Marshal Harold Edwards,
Royal Canadian Air Force
A LIFE

By his daughter,
Suzanne K. Edwards

Published by

GENERAL STORE
PUBLISHING HOUSE

499 O'Brien Rd., Box 415
Renfrew, Ontario, Canada K7V 4A6
Telephone (613) 432-7697 or 1-800-465-6072
www.gsph.com

ISBN 978-1-897113-74-5
Printed and Bound in Canada

Cover design and formatting by Robyn Hader
Printing by Custom Printers of Renfrew Ltd.

No part of this book may be reproduced, stored in a retrieval system or transmitted in any form or by any means, without the prior written permission of the publisher or, in case of photocopying or other reprographic copying, a licence from Access Copyright (Canadian Copyright Licensing Agency), 1 Yonge Street, Suite 1900, Toronto, ON M5C 1E6.

Library and Archives Canada Cataloguing in Publication

Edwards, Suzanne K., 1931-
      Gus : from trapper boy to air marshal / Suzanne K. Edwards.

Includes bibliographical references.
ISBN 978-1-897113-74-5

      1. Edwards, Harold. 2. Canada. Royal Canadian Air Force--Biography.
3. Marshals--Canada--Biography. 4. Canada. Royal Canadian Air Force--History--World War, 1939-1945. I. Title.
UG626.2.E37E37 2007   358.40092   C2007-905531-1

© Copyright Suzanne K. Edwards 2007

*In memory of my mother
Beatrice Coffey Edwards
—Gus's darling Bea—
whose love and support sustained
him throughout their life together.*

CONTENTS

FOREWORD	1
ACKNOWLEDGEMENTS	3
PROLOGUE	5

1 **THE EARLY YEARS**   7
Immigration to Canada; growing up in Cape Breton; educating himself while working in the coal mines.

2 **THE BEGINNING OF THE GREAT ADVENTURE**   12
1915–1916
Able seaman in RCN; acceptance as a RNAS pilot; training in England.

3 **FIGHTER PILOT**   19
1916–1917
Fighter pilot in France with 3 (Naval) Wing; shot down and captured.

4 **CAPTURE—ESCAPE—RECAPTURE**   27
1917–1918
Imprisonment; attempted escapes; successful escape; recapture; prison life.

5 **FROM WAR TO REVOLUTION**   35
1919–1920
Death sentence; six weeks' leave; fighting the Bolsheviks in South Russia.

6 **THE PEACETIME AIR FORCE PART I**   41
1920–1926
Return to Cape Breton and acceptance in the newly formed CAF; posting to Ottawa; marriage; posting to Winnipeg; aerial mapping of Manitoba.

7	**THE PEACETIME AIR FORCE PART II** **1926–1933** *Liaison officer in London; attendance at Schneider Cup Air Race in Venice; staff course at Royal Naval College; return to Ottawa; effects of Depression on RCAF.*	52
8	**THE PEACETIME AIR FORCE PART III** **1934–1938** *CO of RCAF Station Dartmouth; the Moose River Mine disaster; the Beryl Markham flight; coronation of King George VI; Unemployment Relief Project No. 153; return to Ottawa and preparation for war.*	62
9	**THE SECOND WORLD WAR PART I** **1939–1941** *Royal tour; British Commonwealth Air Training Plan; Clayton Knight Committee; air member for personnel; posting to London.*	84
10	**THE SECOND WORLD WAR PART II** *Canadianization.*	105
11	**THE SECOND WORLD WAR PART III** **1942** *Overseas and the Home Front: wartime Ottawa; next of kin; visit to Chorley; trip to Canada; Battle of the Bloody Nonsense; Peter the dog; WDs at HQ; one airman's story; trip to Middle and Far East.*	123
12	**THE SECOND WORLD WAR PART IV** **1943–44** *Investiture at Buckingham Palace; trips to Canada in June and November; "Highdale" the official residence; East Grinstead; posting to Ottawa; surgery and hospitalization; retirement.*	157
13	**RETIREMENT** **1945–1951** *Ottawa; Victoria; letters to author; St. Sauveur des Monts; car accident and Sir Archibald McIndoe; visitors.*	183

14 THE LAST TRIP 195
1951–1952
South to Arizona; death; back to Ottawa; funeral parade.

15 AFTERWARDS 203
Letter to A/M W.A. Curtis; return to St. Sauveur des Monts; letter to author from M/Gen H.F.H. Hertzberg.

EPILOGUE 207

APPENDIX A 208
"Halifax-Dartmouth and the Royal Canadian Air Force 1918–1939"

APPENDIX B 212
"They Toil Without Glory." In praise of ground crews—CBC broadcast 20 July 1942.

APPENDIX C 217
"Unite the Fighting Forces." Article published in *The Ottawa Citizen* in 1946 advocating unification.

APPENDIX D 225
Letter from A/M John Plant

APPENDIX E 227
RCAF Organization, Operations, and Rank Structure in 1942–43

APPENDIX F 229
Career Summary

APPENDIX G 232
Abbreviations

ABOUT THE AUTHOR 235

FOREWORD

In September 1944, Harold "Gus" Edwards, at the age of fifty-one and at the peak of his career, retired from the Royal Canadian Air Force with the rank of Air Marshal. The punishment he had inflicted on his body in the grinding climb to the top had finally caught up with him, and that body could no longer respond to the demands he placed upon it. But what a journey it had been: from a young boy in the coal mines of Cape Breton, through war, revolution, peace, and yet another war, to the highest rank in the Service. He had been an integral part of its extraordinary growth from its inception in 1924 with a total strength of 375 to the nearly quarter of a million men and women who enlisted during the Second World War, almost 94,000 of whom served overseas. Between the wars, in that tiny force, he had served as an administrative officer in Ottawa, commanded the air stations at Victoria Beach and Dartmouth, taken the air force contingent to King George VI's coronation, and with his drive and personality left his mark on the RCAF, its standards, discipline, and morale.

At the outset of the Second World War, it was he who directed the effort to overcome the enormous number of personnel problems arising from its own phenomenal growth and its participation in the British Commonwealth Air Training Plan (BCATP). Perhaps his reputation as a controversial figure in the RCAF had its origin during this early part of the war, for it was in the spring of 1941 that he initiated the process to change the racist enlistment policy that excluded non-whites and required applicants to be of "pure European descent." If, indeed, that was the origin, then the article he wrote in retirement in 1946 advocating the unification of the armed services—twenty-two years before the actual event—could only have added fuel to the fire that had raged during the war over his passionate defence of "Canadianization."

As Air Officer Commanding-in-Chief, RCAF Overseas in London in 1942–43, he battled long and hard with the British Air Ministry and the

RAF to meet their obligations under Article XV of the BCATP to keep Canadian air crews (and later ground personnel as well) together in their own squadrons. A sailor in the navy served with other Canadians in his ship; a soldier in the army served with other Canadians in his regiment; but not so in the air force. Nearly sixty percent of Canadian airmen were scattered throughout 700-odd RAF units, some individually, some in twos and threes, and others in small groups. It was the championing of this Canadianization policy, in which he believed so profoundly, that would be the final blow to his health, leaving him partially disabled in retirement, and result in his death seven years after the end of the war.

But just as the air force was the beneficiary of his talents, it was the air force that provided him with the means to develop those talents. Between the wars, it continued his education by sending him on courses both in Canada and England, watched over his development, and gave him ample opportunity to expand his horizons—truly, a perfect match. Whether he would have succeeded as well in another profession or in the corporate world is an interesting question; perhaps, perhaps not. There were many offers presented to him after the war, none of which he could pursue, due to ill health. Certainly he thrived in the military world and never regretted his decision to dedicate his life to the air force and to the service of his country.

ACKNOWLEDGEMENTS

That this book should ever see the light of day is due in no small measure to a wide array of individuals and institutions. I gratefully acknowledge their contribution and will be forever in their debt. They smoothed the path of a neophyte biographer who stumbled her way through five years to complete the project.

Unknown to each other, Brenda Turner Norris and Wayne Ralph set me on the journey by convincing me that I, rather than an historian, should tell my father's story. Along the way I was fortunate to have the support, encouragement, and assistance of many others: Tanya Belliveau; Margaret Davidson; Roger and Suzanne Easton; Duggan Gray; Archie and Shirley Hood; Maurice MacDonald; Peter R.D. Mackell; Nancy Wilson MacNeil; Dagmar Hertzberg Nation; Michael and Suzanne Nolan; Barbara Reardon Smith; and Richard and Joan Winchester.

I was blessed with the wise counsel of Dr. Stephen J. Harris, Chief Historian, Directorate of History and Heritage, Canadian Department of National Defence; Professor Norman Hillmer, Carleton University; and Professor Desmond Morton, McGill University. Critical information and/or photographs were provided by Glenn Curtis, Col. Norman H. Jeffries (Ret'd), John Smith, B/Gen W. Don Stewart (Ret'd), and historical researchers Col. Ernest S.C. Cable (Ret'd) and Owen Cooke. My long-suffering cousins deserve special mention for answering my never-ending questions: Martha Coffey; Frank C., Harold G., and Robert B. Edwards; Louise Coffey Hastings; Marjorie Edwards MacLeod; and Jane Dalton Ready. My thanks also to Mark Amirault, *père et fils*, for their magical work with old photographs; and to Michael Cleaves, the computer wizard.

The extraordinary co-operation accorded me by the guardians of the nation's history, the men and women of the country's museums and archives, never ceased to amaze me: at Library and Archives Canada: Timothy Dubé, Military Archivist, and Diana Gibson, Access to Information & Privacy

Analyst; at CF Joint Imagery Centre, "A" Squadron: Pam Goulet, Lucie Ethier and Major A.W. Farrell; at Shearwater Aviation Museum: Christine Dunphy, Librarian/Archivist; at RCAF Memorial Museum, Trenton: Earl Hewison, former Curator; at Maritime Command Museum: Marilyn Gurney, Curator; at Highland Village Museum: Pauline MacLean, Genealogist; at Glace Bay Historical Society: Howard MacKinnon; at Trinity College School: Reneé Hillier; at City of Ottawa Archives: Hariette Fried, Reference Archivist, and Ian Cross; at *Maclean's* Magazine: the Librarian; and at CBC Radio Archives: Norbert Boily.

Special thanks must go to my nephew Bogart Edwards and my niece Amadea Edwards Andino, for Gus's letters to his mother. Equally important were the reminiscences of Michael Belcher, Julia Hibberd, Jill Wigg Kennedy, and Alan M. Mann, MD.

Of all those who contributed to the book, I am most grateful to Hugh Halliday for his meticulous review of the first draft, Thea Hertzberg Gray for her reminiscences, encouragement, and sound advice, and Eileen O'Dea Kelleher, who, for two long years, read every word and every rewrite with unfailing good humour.

But the help and encouragement of all these wonderful people would have been for naught without my editor, Jane Karchmar, who, with wit and wisdom, turned the manuscript into a book. My gratitude to her knows no bounds, and if any errors remain, I alone am responsible.

PROLOGUE

At exactly 10:30 a.m. on 27 February 1952, the 412 Squadron Dakota aircraft carrying his casket taxied to a stop in front of a hangar at RCAF Station Rockliffe. After a fifteen-hour journey from Arizona to Ottawa, his last flight had landed. Forty-eight hours later, on a crystal clear, bitterly cold day, his beloved air force would bury him. One last time, the columns of troops would gently sway to the cadence of the slow march, the drums beat, the band play, the rifles crack, the trumpets sound—one last time, but this time for him.

So ended the life of my father, Harold "Gus" Edwards, CB, Air Marshal, RCAF. It is evident from his early years, as he struggled to educate himself, and from the intensity and passion he later brought to his military career, that this had been a life unlike most. Indeed, he seems to have personified the air force motto: *Per Ardua ad Astra*—Through Adversity to the Stars.

* * *

In August 1944, as a mark of his affection, Gus gave a beautiful, leather-bound edition of *Nuttall's Standard Dictionary of the English Language* to his great friend, Major General H.F.H. Hertzberg. One day I chanced on the definition of "hero" in that dictionary. It reads: "A clear-seeing, self-reliant, self-sufficient, valiant man"—what a fitting description of both these men. Canada has produced many heroes in all walks of life, both civilian and military, but Canadians often seem reluctant to tell their stories, and our country's history is the poorer for it. Casting aside my own reluctance, but with more than a little trepidation, I have put together my father's story, part biography, part memoir—one more addition to our historical mosaic.

1

THE EARLY YEARS

Canada is a nation of immigrants. They come for many reasons: some to escape political or religious repression; some to escape the ravages of war or famine; and some, unable to support themselves or their families, to seek employment opportunities. Like the tens of thousands who preceded them and the millions who followed, the Edwards family came to Canada because of unemployment in their native country. The father, William, or Will as he was known, had been the underground manager of a coal mine, but the mine closed, leaving him and his brothers, James and George, unemployed. Will was born in Chorley, Lancashire, England, in 1863 and married Katherine Louisa Warburton in 1888. Kate gave birth to two sons: Benjamin on 13 June 1891 and Harold on 24 December 1892.

In the summer of 1903, Will and his family left England, following James, who had immigrated to Canada several years earlier. George struck out for South Africa, only to find he missed his brothers so much that he and his family later moved to Canada as well. All three brothers and their young families settled in the mining town of Glace Bay on Cape Breton Island, Nova Scotia.

In those early years of the twentieth century, the life of a coal miner in Cape Breton was not an easy one. Labour and management were constantly at odds. There were bitter clashes over safety, wages, and working conditions, with the inevitable result that layoffs, shutdowns, and strikes were the norm rather than the exception. The Company exercised almost total control over the miners' lives, both at work and at home. Because it owned the houses in which they lived and the infamous "Company Store" where they were forced to buy their supplies, miners were virtually indentured servants.

Will found work not as a manager but as an ordinary miner. By working at odd jobs after school, his two young sons, aged twelve and ten, did what they could to help supplement his income. It was a hard, constant struggle to keep afloat.

Harold attended the New Aberdeen Public School until 1907 and then, at the age of fourteen, and despite his mother's protests, left school and followed his father and brother into the mines. His job as a trapper boy was to open the ventilation door for the ponies as they pulled the wagons filled with coal to the surface and then returned below for another load. For ten hours a day, he opened and closed that door in dark, dripping, rat-infested surroundings. Yet his situation was not unique. There were many other boys his age, and some much younger, even as young as eight, working in those conditions. However, Harold's obsession was always to escape from the mine. The route for that escape lay in education, and he followed it with dogged determination. Frederick Griffin's newspaper article describes how he achieved his goal:

> He and his mother worked out a system. It was six o'clock of an evening and often dark when he got home from the mine. By seven he had washed and finished his supper. Then he went to his room to work in a dim light for two hours over his books. At nine sharp his mother made him lay them away . . . But at 3 o'clock, at his own insistence, this devoted woman called her son and he got up and studied for three hours before it was time to leave for the mine. . . . For seven years through summer and winter he kept up that routine of study. . . .
>
> In the meantime during those years young Edwards was climbing. He ceased to be a miner. At 18 he was chief electrician of the British Empire Steel Corporation, Glace Bay mines. He built the first radio set in Nova Scotia. He was already a boy of education far beyond his fellows with a working knowledge of liberal arts and sciences, wide reading of classics, ranging vocabulary, and questing, if haphazard, acquaintance with a number of technical subjects, including aviation.[1]

Harold's interest in both electricity and aviation is not surprising. While he worked and studied, events of enormous importance in these two fields were

---

[1] Frederick Griffin, "Apostle of Canadianization," *The Star Weekly* (24 October 1942).

1 - THE EARLY YEARS

The Silver Dart in flight. 23 February 1909
DND photo courtesy Shearwater Aviation Museum

taking place nearby. In 1907, almost in his backyard, Guglielmo Marconi established the first transatlantic wireless service between Glace Bay and Clifden, Ireland. Another event, which would also change the world, occurred two years later, not sixty miles away, in Baddeck. Under the direction of Dr. Alexander Graham Bell, the first powered flight by a British subject in the Empire took place when the *Silver Dart*, piloted by J.A.D. McCurdy, lifted off the ice of Bras d'Or Lake and flew for half a mile. Certainly Harold was fascinated by the inventor and his experiments, but whether he actually met him is not clear. He did become a deck hand on a racing yacht in the summers, but again it is unclear who owned the vessel.

As the years went by and he grew into a young man, the family's financial situation improved when both he and Ben held more responsible and better-paying positions in the mines. Growing up with a large circle of friends and relations, they revelled in playing tricks on them, one of which is described in a letter by Ben's daughter:

> [Y]our Dad and my Dad aspired to be electricians so we had two chairs that had nails attached into the seats (underneath). They would wire the whole thing up, invite their friends in and treat them to an electric shock when they sat down. They and their friends were full of tricks.[2]

---

[2] Letter of 29 September 2002 from Margerie Edwards MacLeod.

Kate ensured her boys were exposed to classical music, opera, and poetry. There were other activities as well, baseball and fishing among them. It was on the Mira and Margaree Rivers that Harold developed a love of fishing, a sport he avidly pursued for the rest of his life.

Harold, Kate, Will, and Ben Edwards. c. 1907

1 - THE EARLY YEARS

In the summer of his twenty-first year, bursting with youthful enthusiasm and ambition, the future seemed bright. It was also the summer of 1914, the summer of *The Guns of August*, when the events in Europe would propel him on a journey not even he could have imagined.[3]

Harold on fence at left; Ben standing at right. c. 1914

---

[3] *The Guns of August* is the title of Barbara W. Tuchman's account of the causes of the First World War.

2

THE BEGINNING OF THE GREAT ADVENTURE

1915–1916

Harold volunteered as a naval pilot but faced a difficult situation.

In 1915, when the Royal Navy began recruiting Canadians for the Royal Naval Air Service, young Edwards was one of the hundreds who applied and was accepted as a candidate. In those days both the R.N.A.S and the Royal Flying Corps expected a recruit to be in possession of his pilot's ticket (the F.A.I. certificate) before being enrolled. Applicants who had the necessary physical and educational requirements were accepted for the service on condition that they obtain this certificate at their own expense, before being appointed to a commission. There was at that time only one school in Canada capable of giving pilot's training. This was the Curtiss School at Toronto, directed by J.A.D. McCurdy, and it was flooded with applications far beyond its limited capacity. Edwards was one of those who enrolled in the school but he was far down the list (No. 227) and when winter came on the school closed before his turn came to begin training.

The Department of the Naval Service at Ottawa, concerned at the plight of the number of young Canadians who were left with their pilot's training unfinished, or unstarted, devised the plan of enrolling those who interested them in the R.C.N. ("Niobe") at Halifax, giving them room and board and some elementary naval

2 - THE BEGINNING OF THE GREAT ADVENTURE: 1915–1916

training until the Admiralty could send them to Britain in groups to complete their air training.[4]

Harold's formal application, dated 15 August 1915, lists his occupation as "Operating and Repairing Electric Engines and Equipment; also Electrician in Charge." On 3 December, he was accepted as a candidate for the RNAS and sent a warrant for the transportation costs from New Aberdeen to Halifax. On the 14th, he joined the RCNVR as an aviator candidate, with the equivalent rating of able seaman.[5] That is the official version of events, but there is a far more colourful version that appeared in an undated local newspaper article.

HMCS *Niobe*.
Harold Edwards far left back row (with hat— partially hidden behind man with signal flags). December 1915
(In December 1917, several of her crew were killed when *Niobe* was damaged in the Halifax explosion.)

---

[4] From an unattributed and undated typed summary of a handwritten manuscript titled *Air Marshal Harold Edwards CB* included with copies of some 2,000 documents contained in Gus's personnel file forwarded from Library and Archives Canada. All dates and facts in the article agree with those that appear in *The Official History of the Royal Canadian Air Force—Volume I—Canadian Airmen and the First World War*, by S.F. Wise, but it focuses exclusively on Gus's participation in the events, providing many details not included in the published work. It may possibly have originated in the Air Historical Section of the Department of National Defence. It is reproduced with the permission of the Minister of Public Works and Government Services, 2006.

[5] Ibid.

A LOCAL BOY TO JOIN THE FLYING CORPS

Harold Edwards, chief electrician at Nos. 2 and 9 collieries, has resigned his position and leaves on Sunday evening for Halifax, where he commences the preparatory course in aviation.

Mr. Edwards who has been a skilled and highly esteemed official at the biggest colliery has volunteered his services in the Canadian Flying Corps and his patriotic offer has been accepted by the Canadian military authorities. He will spend two or three months at the capital city receiving preliminary instructions in gunnery and signalling, before sailing for England, where he will begin to learn the art of a bird-man.

Mr. Edwards leaves a lucrative position with the Dominion Coal Co. to do his share for the Empire, and as he is a very popular young man, his host of friends will wish him every success in his new career.

The *bird-man* was out of the mines and on his way, joining that powerful agent of Empire, the mighty Royal Navy.

On 7 February 1916 he sailed for England and received his orders on 25 February.

> BY COMMAND OF THE COMMISSIONERS FOR EXECUTING THE OFFICE OF LORD HIGH ADMIRAL OF THE UNITED KINGDOM OF GREAT BRITAIN AND IRELAND, &C.
> PROBATIONARY FLIGHT SUB LIEUT. HAROLD EDWARDS, R.N.
>
> THE Lords Commissioners of the Admiralty hereby appoint you Probationary Flight Sub Lieutenant of His Majesty's Ship *President* additional for Royal Naval Air Service; to be lent *Victory* for short course of navigation and direct you to report yourself to the Commanding Officer, H.M. Navigation School, Portsmouth, on the evening of Sunday, February 27th, 1916.
>
> Your appointment is to take effect from 3rd February, 1916.
> By Command of their Lordships

2 - THE BEGINNING OF THE GREAT ADVENTURE: 1915–1916

LAC PMR 71-682
Group of F/S/Ls in England 1916. H.S. Murton second from left; Harold (Gus) Edwards second from right.

It was at Portsmouth, when introduced in the mess as Mr. Edwards, someone asked if he was any relation to Gus Edwards, the American songwriter and vaudeville legend.[6] Harold replied, "I am Gus Edwards," and the nickname stuck.[7]

The next six months were anything but uneventful. He attended various courses at White City, Eastbourne, Cranwell, and East Church, interspersed with leave in London. One cannot help but marvel at the derring-do of those young pioneer pilots. Exposed as they were to the elements, they wrestled to manoeuvre a machine with an unstable airframe or an unreliable engine, but the thrill of exploration, going where none had gone before, the sheer mystique of flight could only have spurred them on. For Gus, learning to fly resulted in at least two forced landings, records of which have survived through photos he took of the scenes.

---

[6] Two of his biggest hits were "School Days" and "By the Light of the Silvery Moon."
[7] L.S.B. Shapiro, "To Air Marshal the Hard Way," *Maclean's* (15 March 1943). Corroborated by H.S. Murton in a letter of 3 November 1964, who added, "Gus, when you knew him, was quite a comic."

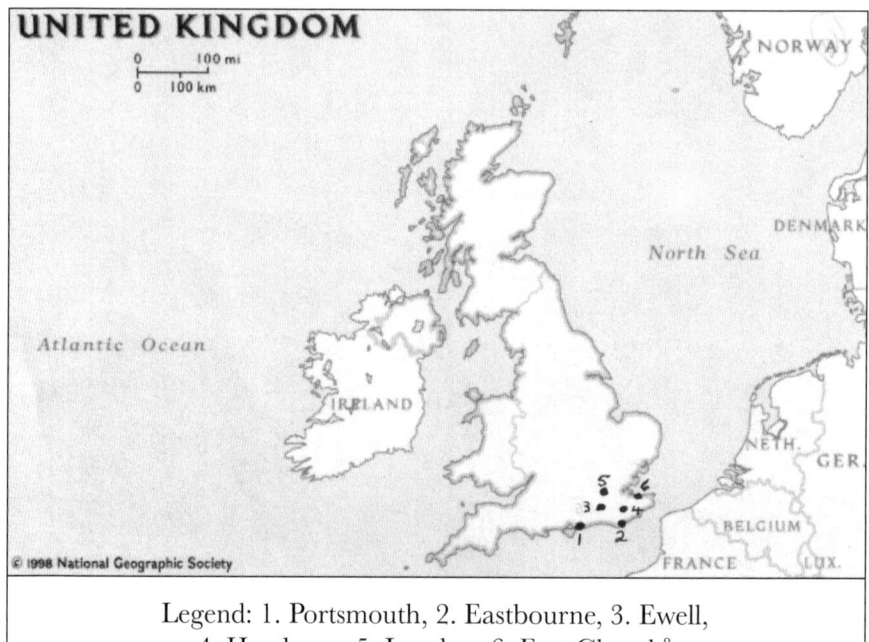

Legend: 1. Portsmouth, 2. Eastbourne, 3. Ewell, 4. Headcorn, 5. London, 6. East Church[8]

Either the crash at Ewell or the forced landing at Headcorn was the cause of the amputation of the little toe on his left foot, requiring a stay at the RN Hospital at Haslar. In any event, he recovered quickly and at the end of August, with only fifty-three minutes with an instructor and less than six hours overall in the air—including the time it took him to fly his plane to France—he went to war, joining millions of others to fight the war that was to end all wars.

---

[8] All hand-numbered maps, are used with permission of the National Geographic Society.

2 - THE BEGINNING OF THE GREAT ADVENTURE: 1915–1916

Photos of crash scenes at Ewell and Headcorn and recovery at RN Hospital. 1916

EWELL

AEROPLANE DAMAGED.—Many people in the parish possess one or more pieces of an aeroplane, souvenirs of an accident to an aircraft on Wednesday. Flight Sub.-Lieut. Harold Edwards was flying in a machine from Eastbourne, when, on reaching this district, he experienced trouble with his engine. He decided to alight, and commenced to make a descent, on what looked like a very suitable piece of ground at Priest Hill Farm, but as he was reaching the earth he found there was underneath him a sunken road. To have attempted to bring his machine to a standstill in that would have been courting disaster; and the airman, in rising again, caught the telegraph post and wires on the railway embankment. The result was that the machine was badly damaged, though fortunately the airman escaped injury. There was considerable damage to the planes, and the propellor was broken to pieces. Help being obtained, the machine was removed from the railway bank into the field, and later in the day was taken away. The airman was shown much hospitality by Mr. W. C. Joyce-Meade, whose residence on the Reigate-road is not far from the scene of the accident. A large number of people visited this spot during the afternoon, and took away some of the pieces broken off the machine as relics of the occasion.

3

FIGHTER PILOT

1916–1917

On 29 August 1916, F/S/L Harold Edwards was posted to 3 (Naval) Wing at Luxeuil-les-Bains in northeastern France near the German border. The official history describes the operation:

> By using the French base it would be possible to bomb German targets without flying over neutral territory—this was why the wing did not operate from southeast England, which would have meant flying over Holland. . . . [9]

> Aircraft of the naval wing carried out all their raids between 30 July 1916 and 14 April 1917. For much of the time Nancy or Ochey, rather than Luxeuil, served as the base—a development that played an important part in target selection. From Luxeuil aircraft could easily fly to the Belfort Gap, which opens up between the Jura and Vosges mountains. Beyond lay the Black Forest, and only on the other side of that inhospitable terrain were the factory towns of the German homeland. From Ochey and Nancy, in contrast, situated as they are in the heart of Lorraine, it was easily possible to reach any number of targets in the highly industrialized valleys of the Saar and Moselle rivers. The targets to be attacked from Luxeuil in the ensuing months—Mülheim, Oberndorf, and Freiburg—were farther away, more difficult to reach and of lesser industrial significance. The raids from Luxeuil were carried out at ranges between sixty and a hundred miles; those from the more

---

[9] S.F. Wise, *The Official History of the Royal Canadian Air Force—Volume I—Canadian Airmen and the First World War* (Toronto: University of Toronto Press in co-operation with the Department of National Defence and the Canadian Government Publishing Centre, Supplies and Services Canada, 1980), p. 263.

northerly airfields were carried out at ranges between thirty and seventy miles. . . .[10]

Although the wing is very much a part of Canadian air history, as with virtually every other instance of Canadian participation in the war in the air the airmen involved were masters of their fate only at the tactical level. The policy that placed them at Luxeuil, and indeed the entire debate about strategic bombing, was British, and it deeply divided opinion, whether public, political, or military-professional. At the level of policy, men were torn between moral scruples and the belief that German air raids upon England demanded retaliation from a proud people. Among the military, some took the view that bombing was a weapon of high potential that should be exploited to the maximum extent, possibly as a way to circumvent the stalemate on the Western Front, while others were dubious about the weapon and believed, in any event, that tactical needs and [British Field Marshal] Haig's often desperate shortage of aircraft should be given primacy.[11]

In pursuance of the Admiralty's plan for systematic attacks upon German industrial centres in the Rhineland, the Wing might be called the first strategic bomber force in history. Delays in delivery of the necessary aircraft however, kept the Wing from beginning major operations until October . . .and the cold and bad weather of the winter that followed greatly hampered the Wing's work. Nevertheless, 19 raids were carried out, most in Sopwith 1 1/2 Strutters of which there were two versions: the single-seater bomber which could carry two 112 lb. or four 65 lb. bombs, and the two-seater fighter escort.

Approximately two-thirds of the pilots in 3 Wing were Canadians and F/S/L Edwards made his first operational sortie (from Ochey) on 3 December, when he took part in a seven-aircraft offensive fighter patrol over enemy lines. Edwards' gunlayer got in some shots at 300 yards, then Edwards manoeuvred the enemy in front of his Sopwith and opened fire into its tail. The German machine was much faster than the British, and got away.

---

[10] Ibid , p. 264.
[11] Ibid., p. 260.

3 - FIGHTER PILOT: 1916–1917

On 25 February 1917, Edwards flew one of the Sopwith bombers in an attack on the iron works and blast furnaces at Saarbrucke-Burbach. The formation of fourteen bombers and six fighters flew in two squadrons, keeping very good formation throughout. The target was small and difficult, and any damage done by the 65 lb. bombs was not easily observed. There was a heavy barrage of flak over Burbach and enemy aircraft made many attacks on the Sopwiths. Two of the enemy were shot down, and one Canadian pilot was killed.

A week later, Burbach was bombed again by ten Sopwiths escorted by five fighters, one of which was piloted by Edwards. The Germans were now strengthening their defences in the Saar Valley and the second squadron of British aircraft tangled with ten enemy aircraft over the objective. In a series of spirited combats the Sopwith fighters fended off thrusts at the bombers and forced down two of the enemy. A German aircraft with which Edwards engaged was seen to make a forced landing in a field.

On 22 March, a small force of six bombers and three fighters set out to attack the blast furnaces at Burbach. Weather conditions en route were very bad; heavy banks of clouds covered the sky and above 8,000 feet the cold was so extreme that compasses froze and pilots' faces were frost-bitten. Bombing was carried out on the target, but again results were difficult to observe. Eight of the formation of nine had to land at French airfields on the way home. The only pilot to regain his home base at Ochey was F/S/L Edwards—and he came back on five cylinders.[12]

By the end of March, the days of 3 Wing were numbered. The decision had been made to cease long-distance bombing in order that more aircraft could be supplied to the Royal Flying Corps for operations in support of the army on the Western Front. However, the Wing remained at Luxeuil another three weeks to carry out a special raid on Freiburg, in reprisal for the torpedoing of the hospital ship *Asturias* on 20 March.[13] The raid took place

---

[12] The foregoing five paragraphs were compiled from the unattributed and undated manuscript titled *Air Marshal Harold Edwards CB*.

[13] The British public was infuriated over what were deemed a series of German atrocities. It demanded revenge for the sinking of the *Asturias* and other incidents such as the execution of Edith Cavell, the sinking of the passenger ships *Lusitania* and *Sussex*, and the neglect of allied prisoners of war suffering from typhoid fever.

on 14 April when two formations were dispatched: "A" flight in the morning at 1100 hours and "B" flight in the afternoon at 1530 hours.

> In addition to the 3,900 pounds of bombs dropped, the aircraft carried leaflets explaining the purpose of the raid. F/S/L Edwards flew in the second formation comprised of seven bombers and three fighters—all piloted by Canadians, with three British naval gunlayers in the fighters. As did the first formation, the second encountered strong opposition from anti-aircraft batteries and enemy fighters. Edwards was engaged by a very fast type of fighter, which hit his Sopwith with several bursts and killed the gunlayer. Another fighter came to his assistance and shot down his opponent in a spinning nose dive. But Edwards' aircraft had been so badly damaged that it steadily lost height as he struggled to reach friendly territory. Finally, he crash landed behind enemy lines near Schlettstadt.[14]

Gus in front of a "Curtiss." June 1916

---

[14] Compiled from the unattributed and undated manuscript titled *Air Marshal Harold Edwards CB*.

3 - FIGHTER PILOT: 1916–1917

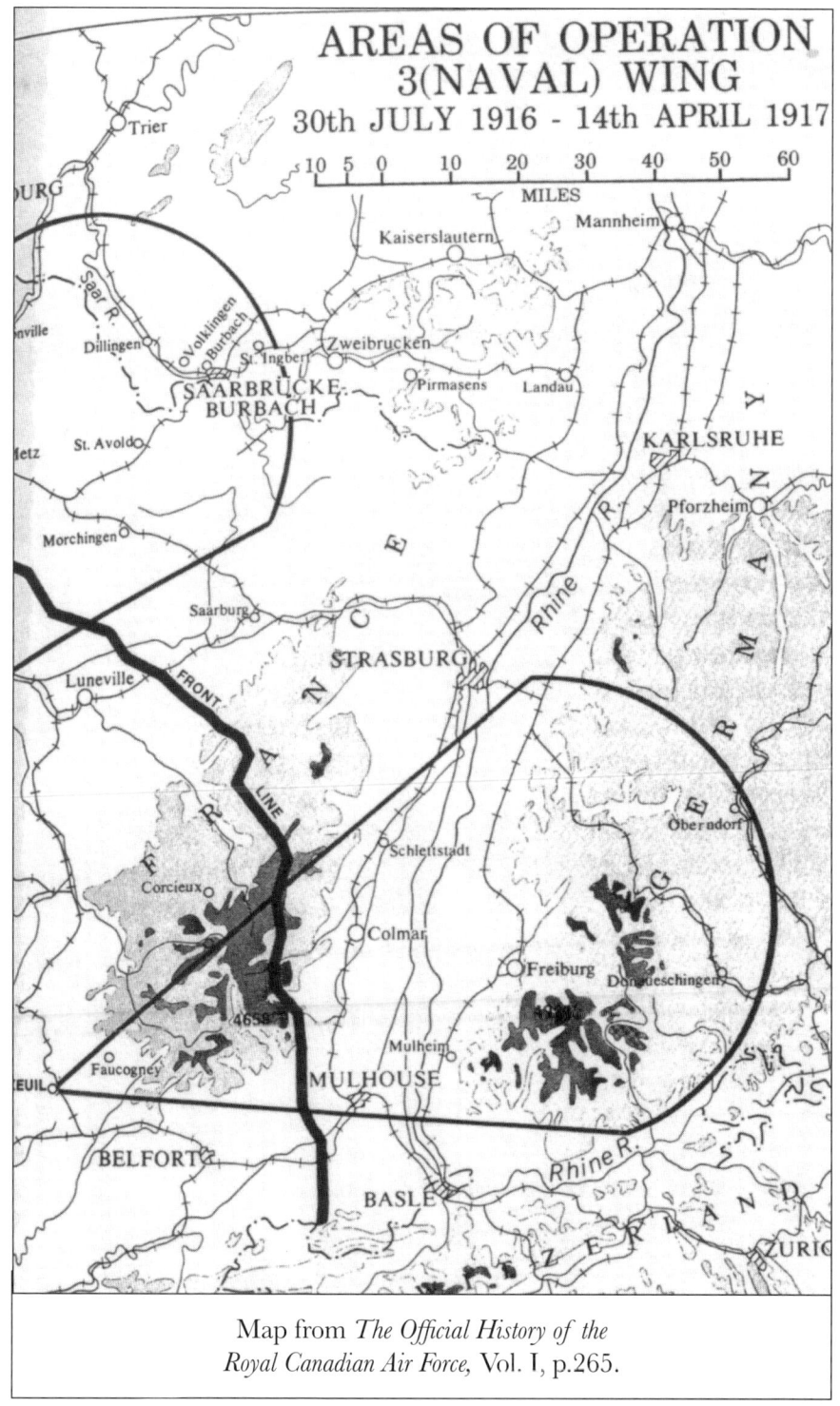

Map from *The Official History of the Royal Canadian Air Force*, Vol. I, p.265.

In a letter to a friend, Gus describes, in more vivid detail, how his Sopwith Strutter No. N5117 was shot down:

> . . . I am a prisoner at Karlsruhe. I was shot down after lengthy engagement with several enemy machines. My Observer [Air Mechanic] (J.L. Coghlan) was wounded in about 15 places and died a few minutes after we came down. My controls were shot away and I fell all the way completely out of control. Luckily we struck the ground in such a way that I was unhurt. Since then I have sombered away with a gnawing in my stomach like many others who have shared this fate.[15]

The German aircraft, an Albatross DIII, was piloted by nineteen-year-old Vzfw Rudolph Rath of Jagdstaffel 35. This was Rath's only victory. He was killed ten days later, on 24 April 1917, his twentieth birthday.[16]

On 25 April, Captain W.L. Elder, Gus's CO, wrote to Will Edwards. Amidst the appalling carnage of that war, his letter includes a reference to an act of great courage and human kindness by an enemy pilot.

> Dear Sir,
>
> It is with deep regret that I write to tell you, your son Harold has been made a prisoner.
>
> He was carrying out a raid on the town of Freiburg as a reprisal for the sinking of the hospital ship *Asturias* and did not return.
>
> I have today received information dropped by a German airman that he is a prisoner and unwounded.
>
> Your son was a favourite with us all and we deeply regret his loss, but hope he will before many months be at liberty again.

Captain Elder, in his report to the Admiralty, commented that the Sopwith

---

[15] Abstract of letter of 25 August 1917 to J. Murphy, Esq.; obtained by Allan Snowie from the Public Records Office in Kew Gardens, London.

[16] Information obtained by Allan Snowie from *The Jasta Pilots* by N. Franks, F. Bailey, and R. Duiven, Grub Street, London 1996.

fighters ". . . are now quite outclassed by the German type of machines, and no longer perform adequate protection to the bombing machines. It is only through the self sacrifice of the three missing Fighter Pilots and their Gunlayers that all our bombing machines returned safely.[17]

And for Gus he had a special word of commendation: ". . . always a conspicuous fighter pilot who has always realized the great importance of protecting his flight . . ."

Walker, HE, Sheriff, Whealey, Wallace, and Lemon.

"Our Cabin."

---

[17] Compiled from the unattributed and undated manuscript titled *Air Marshal Harold Edwards CB*.

Sharman, Lemon, Collishaw.

Fall, Glover, and HE.

Members of 3 (Naval) Wing in France. December 1916

4

CAPTURE—ESCAPE—RECAPTURE

1917–1918

Another description of being shot down and captured appeared in *Maclean's*.

> With its elevators shot away, the plane went into a spectacular series of loops and spins. Only a gust of wind and a prayer saved him. As the plane plunged toward a field, it miraculously straightened out and young Edwards found himself careening across farmland. The last thing he remembered of the incident was a farm horse on a dirt road suddenly bolting at the sight of the plane and upsetting a man and girl in the cart. He fainted—"likely from fright," he recalls. When he came to he was a prisoner.[18]

L/Col C.F.N. Rathbone, who had been shot down in the morning raid and then shut in a cell in the Military Detention Barracks at Colmar, describes what happened next:

> I looked through the peep-hole in the door of the cell and soon discovered that somebody in the opposite cell was trying to signal to me by means of Morse code by flashing his hand across the peep-hole. The occupant turned out to be F/S/L Edwards, a stout-hearted Canadian who had also been shot down a little later than myself. I was glad to have company and most of the time was spent in communicating by means of signals when the phlegmatic warder was not about. During the next eight days we

---

[18] L.S.B. Shapiro, "To Air Marshal the Hard Way," *Maclean's* (15 March 1943).

> were frequently marched to the Intelligence Officer who put us through the well-known process of pumping. He was, however, unable to obtain any information from us and although they kept Edwards and myself apart, we always managed to communicate on our return through the peep-holes in the cell. At the end of eight days, when pumping was supposed to be over, Edwards was allowed to come into my cell during the day. My cell was larger than his and being a Lieutenant-Colonel I was given a bed to sleep on whereas Edwards had the ordinary cell boards. . . . The meals of the men consisted of two plates of thin soup and half a piece of bread per day; no soap was allowed them.[19]

In addition to Colmar, Gus spent time in four other prison camps: Freiburg, Karlsruhe, Holzminden, and Schweidnitz. There are no records to indicate the length of time spent at Freiburg and Colmar, but, according to a Red Cross list, he was at Holzminden on 3 December, and at his last prison, Schweidnitz, just north of Leipzig, on 31 January 1918.

Official documents make mention of escape attempts, but curiously no details are provided. The only available description of these attempts is contained in newspaper articles. The accuracy of these articles is of course open to question, but they are the only surviving record of what may have occurred.

> His first attempt was at Freiburg. He was one of three optimists who sought to get out of a third story window by a frayed clothesline. But the rope snapped before the first man was down, which ended that attempt.
>
> The second was from a prison that had been a Catholic poorhouse and still held a few monks. Edwards and another fellow spent a long time digging a tunnel under the stone floor to a wine cellar door which led to a crypt and freedom. The trouble was that a monk occupied the crypt and he prayed all night. Impatiently they waited hours for his vigil to cease. But it didn't. So towards dawn they attacked the door. Alarmed, the monk fled, and when they got through the door into the crypt it was to be captured by waiting Germans.[20]

---

[19] Compiled from the unattributed and undated manuscript titled *Air Marshal Harold Edwards CB*.
[20] Frederick Griffin, "Apostle of Canadianization," *The Star Weekly* (24 October 1942).

4 - CAPTURE—ESCAPE—RECAPTURE: 1917–1918

But he was to be successful on the third attempt, from Colmar, which he described in some detail in an interview in 1940.

> A cake of toilet soap was traded to a guard for a hacksaw blade. Maps and a tiny compass were smuggled in by friends.
>
> As an armed German sentry paced around three sides of the wing of the university that served as a prison, the group captain sawed at the window bars. His own sentries, placed at other windows, relayed the position of the sentry to him, so he could stop when the sentry approached.
>
> With the bars cut through, discipline came into play. Eager as the three British prisoners were to escape, only one at a time slipped through the window to freedom. As each one left, the bars were put back in place until the sentry passed again on his rounds.
>
> Just as a military column would move through hostile country, so the fugitives filed silently through the night. The centre man or "main body" held maps, compass and food. One man scouted ahead and the third acted as a rear guard.
>
> For ten days the trio tried to reach a neutral country. They travelled swiftly by night along the side of the road, slept all day in the underbrush. Unfortunately the escape attempt failed.
>
> Three days of heavy rain left the fugitives cold, wet, hungry and dispirited. Their caution relaxed and they started moving too early one night and walked around a corner into the arms of a military provost marshal.
>
> They were unsuccessful in trying to convince their captor they were Russians heading for home.
>
> "He bought us beers in the nearest pub," chuckled the 47-year-old Lancashireman who grew up near Halifax. "Then he turned us over to his colonel, who bought us dinner and had the local jail carefully swept out for us."
>
> The prisoners, back at Kolmar, were punished by two weeks' solitary confinement . . .[21]

---

[21] *Hamilton Spectator* (5 February 1940).

The three had shown considerable resourcefulness throughout the planning and execution of the escape. They had tricked the guard into supplying the hacksaw blade on the pretext of doing some woodcarving, and then covered up the filings in brown shoe polish. Once free of the prison, eating only stolen eggs and raw vegetables, they managed to avoid detection for ten long days and nights, travelling an amazing 175 miles on foot—*in the dark*. If they were headed for neutral Holland, they came heartbreakingly close to reaching their objective. Had they succeeded, and somehow managed to avoid internment, they might have been able to get a boat to England. Instead, recapture meant return to the miseries of prison and solitary confinement.

Conditions varied widely from prison to prison, with treatment more abusive in some than in others, depending on the commandant. Persistent escapers were sent to more repressive camps, Holzminden being one. Other ranks were sometimes subjected to atrocious treatment: vicious beatings from guards' rifle butts, torture, and forced labour in the salt mines. Officers, on the other hand, were treated more humanely. They were not required to work and indeed were free to fill their time pretty well as they wished. This is not to imply life was pleasant for them. They could be shot trying to escape; their quarters were cramped, cold, and damp; the food was sometimes inedible; and long stints in solitary confinement tested the best of men.

> I am sure that people then and since have no concept of the demoralizing nature of "barbed wire" disease. Indeed, even now people somehow assume that imprisonment is a neutral experience.[22]

The Red Cross and other organizations provided library services, food parcels, tobacco, and clothing, all a godsend to those "behind the wire." The library service gave Gus access to the books he needed, and imprisonment the luxury of uninterrupted time to study. He gave up attempting to escape and dug into the books. In the year and half he was a captive, he taught himself German, increased his command of French, and read his way to what must have been close to the equivalent of a university education. A lasting reminder of this period was the day he shaved his head in the hope

---

[22] Letter of 1 April 1993 from Prof. Desmond Morton, which includes: "I was unaware that your father was among approximately 377 Canadian aircrew prisoners of war, though the description of his experience and his escape attempts seems to share a common thread." Much of the above description of camps is taken (with permission) from Professor Morton's *Silent Battle—Canadian Prisoners of War in Germany 1914–1919*, which gives a detailed account of camps and treatment of prisoners.

4 - CAPTURE—ESCAPE—RECAPTURE: 1917–1918

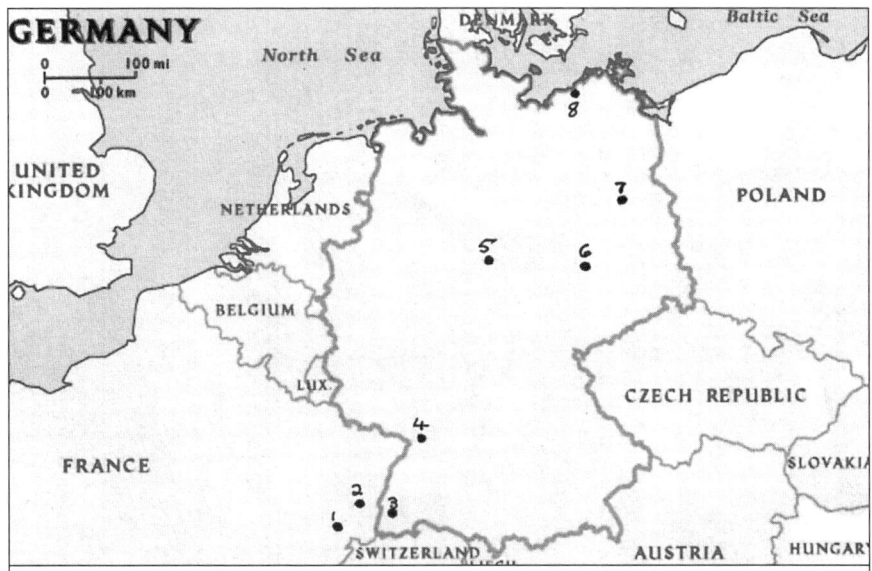

LEGEND: 1. Luxeuil-les-Bains, 2. Colmar, 3. Freiburg, 4. Karlsruhe, 5. Holzminden, 6. Schweidnitz, 7. Berlin, 8. Warnemünde

Seated second from left: L/Col C.F.N. Rathbone, with whom Gus communicated by Morse code, in military detention barracks at Colmar.

DND RE 17201 Frostbitten faces.

Gus and Barclay McPherson (third and fourth from left) were two of the escapees. Perhaps one of the others in the photo was the third member. Note greatcoats worn indoors.

Prisoner-of-War camps 1917-1918

of getting his thinning hair to grow again. That was the last he saw of his hair—he was bald thereafter.

In October 1918, he was posted to Berlin as repatriation officer, and in January sent to Warnemünde on the Baltic Sea as embarkation officer in charge of the evacuation to Britain of former prisoners.[23] On 16 December 1919, he was "Mentioned for valuable services whilst in captivity" (*London Gazette*).

---

[23] The number of prisoners evacuated is in doubt; some documents show the figure 2,500; others have 25,000.

Capt. Edwards. H
R. A. F.

BUCKINGHAM PALACE

1918.

The Queen joins me in welcoming you on your release from the miseries & hardships, which you have endured with so much patience & courage.

During these many months of trial, the early rescue of our gallant Officers & Men from the cruelties of their captivity has been uppermost in our thoughts.

We are thankful that this longed for day has arrived, & that back in the old Country you will be able once more to enjoy the happiness of a home & to see good days among those who anxiously look for your return.

George R.I.

5

FROM WAR TO REVOLUTION

1919–1920

On his return to England in mid-January 1919, Gus, now a captain in the RAF[24], found himself in yet another desperate situation: during a physical examination, the medical officer told him he suspected tuberculosis and that he had months, perhaps a year to live. Despondent, he had no idea what to do next. A newspaper article picks up the story:

> So—that was the result of more than two years of German prisons and German wartime food. A fine outlook for Edwards, facing discharge into a post-war world ill and with no job ahead.
>
> "The bottom of things dropped out for me," he recalls. "I walked down the street in blackness. Just then I heard my name called and saw Seton Broughall of Toronto."
>
> Seton had been with Edwards in Germany. He was one of the devil-may-care gifted flyers in which early aviation abounded. He listened without comment to Gus' tale of despair. Then: "How much money you got?" he asked.
>
> Edwards judged: "About 300 quid lying around London."
>
> "Fine," cried Seton. "I've got about 350. If you're going to die let's enjoy ourselves while you've time."
>
> Avoiding all mention of Edwards' condition, the pair spent six weeks in primrose travel. It was actually the first good time

---

[24] On 1 April 1918, those serving in the Royal Naval Air Service and the Royal Flying Corps were transferred to the newly formed Royal Air Force.

Edwards had ever had. It opened doors to new horizons and made a marked change in his character. Before that, his stern life of work and study had left him no time to be social. He was far from being a mixer. Up to those fateful six weeks in 1919, he confessed today, he would stammer before strangers and cross a street rather than meet a girl. During those weeks of carefree companionship with Broughall, when he learned to laugh in the face of fate, he found the beginning of those qualities of easy self-possession and ready charm which have of recent years won many friends and influenced many people.

Thus, out of this adversity a new Edwards was born, for one day a Harley St. specialist, called into consultation, pronounced the first doctor a nincompoop, and said there was nothing wrong with his lungs.[25]

But everything was wrong with his bank account. He was not merely broke and unemployed, but letters from Cape Breton told him that things did not look promising either in Canada or Britain. Many good electricians were being demobilized from the army, and young fighter pilots were a dime a dozen. But some fighter pilots were needed to risk their necks on what turned out to be an ill-starred expedition to Russia. It was a chance of employment and Edwards went.[26]

* * *

In the spring of 1919 while David Lloyd George, Georges Clemenceau, and Woodrow Wilson were in Paris wrangling over German reparations, redrawing borders, and creating new countries, the Bolshevik revolution continued unabated in Russia. For over a year, the Allies had sent both troops and enormous quantities of munitions and supplies in the hopes of shoring up the counter-revolutionary forces, but the Allied governments now had to decide on their policy in the confused Russian situation. The original purpose of intervention, to revive an Eastern front against Germany, was now meaningless. Russian exiles argued that, since the pre-Bolshevik governments

---

[25] The exact date doctors discovered there was nothing wrong with his chest is open to question, as the *Maclean's* cover story of 15 March 1943 states it was *after* his service in Russia.

[26] Frederick Griffin, "Apostle of Canadianization," *The Star Weekly* (24 October 1942).

5 - FROM WAR TO REVOLUTION: 1919–1920

of Russia had remained loyal to the Allies, the Allies were bound to help them. To this moral argument was added the political argument that the Communist regime in Moscow was a menace to the whole of Europe, with its subversive propaganda and its determination to spread revolution.[27]

The British had sent military missions to both North and South Russia. It was to this latter mission, which supported General Deniken's White forces in the Kuban steppes, that Gus and Broughall, after their six-week spree, volunteered for duty. On 12 April they joined "C" flight of 47 Squadron, commanded by Major Raymond Collishaw at Krasnodar. During the next year, while an active service pilot participating in the fighting, Gus had two other duties: motor transport officer to the Aviation Section, and, in December, adjutant of "A" Detachment (47 Squadron having been disbanded in October and replaced by "A" Detachment).

On the open steppe, this mobile war depended entirely on the railway net.

> [I]n the vast country over which we were fighting, the lateral supply of stores and ammunition would be so complicated that military operations were practically always confined to areas extending ten or fifteen miles on each side of the railway system along which the groups of troops moved. The intervening spaces between were occupied and watched by small forces of cavalry living entirely on the country and, because of the distances, seldom in contact with similar enemy formations.

wrote one of the British advisers. "C" flight adapted to these conditions, living, moving and working in its own special train, and using the open steppe as an enormous aerodrome.[28]

The conditions existing there were atrocious. Death seemed to be the only penalty for any crime. Typhus scourged the country.[29]

In September the White forces [under Deniken] moved northward from Ukraine and from the lower Volga toward Moscow. On

---

[27] www.onwar.com.

[28] Owen Cooke, *Canadian Airmen and Allied Intervention in Russia, 1918–1921*, background piece for S.F. Wise, *The Official History of the Royal Canadian Air Force—Volume I* (Directorate of History, c. 1973), p. 34, with quote from H.N.H. Williamson, *Farewell to the Don* (London: Collins, 1970), p. 111.

[29] "Man of the Week," *The Montreal Standard* (10 February 1940).

October 13th they took Orel. At the same time General Yudenich advanced from Estonia to the outskirts of St. Petersburg. But both cities were saved by Red Army counterattacks. Yudenich retreated into Estonia and Deniken, his communications greatly overextended, was driven back from Orel in an increasingly disorderly march, which ended with the evacuation of the remnants of his army, in March 1920, from Novorossisk.[30]

Raymond Collishaw's memoir gives a chilling account of "A" flight's withdrawal to the Crimea in the early days of January 1920.

Conditions on the railways were almost indescribable. There was neither fuel nor water for the locomotives. The people along the route had become intensely hostile and anxious to welcome the Reds. Forces of hostile irregulars were operating freely across the lines of communication. . . . The normal train crews had gone over to the Reds and airmen served as engineers and firemen on the two locomotives that pulled our train. As an act of mercy we had taken aboard several hundred Russian officers' wives and children and they now became a source of embarrassment to us. Typhus had broken out and they hid their dead on the train. . . .

Officers stood on guard, fully armed, night and day, in the locomotive cabs and on the roofs of the cars. . . . As we passed through the towns we had to send out armed parties to commandeer wood for fuel. Water for the locomotive was obtained by the women holding out their skirts to be filled with snow, and then dumping it into the water tanks. The rail lines were congested and progress was slow. . . .

While our train was halted for fuel at Balshoi Tokmak the enemy managed to release a run-away locomotive down an incline and it smashed into the rear of our train at high speed. Our train was turned into a shamble. . . . Herculean efforts were required to thrust the smashed trucks off the rails and to join up the surviving steel coaches.[31]

---

[30] www.onwar.com. See also S.F. Wise, *The Official History, Vol. I*, Appendix A "Canadian Airmen and the British Intervention in Russia, 1918-20," pp. 626–7.

[31] Owen Cooke, *Canadian Airmen and Allied Intervention*, p.41, with quote from Raymond Collishaw, "Memoirs of a Canadian Airman"; *Roundel* 16 No. 6 (July-August 1964), pp. 23–4.

5 - FROM WAR TO REVOLUTION: 1919–1920

LEGEND: 1. Moscow, 2. Orel, 3. Tsaritzin (Volgograd),
4. Krasnodar, 5. Novorossisk, 6. Crimea

In Gus's own words he was ". . . fighting in the vicinity of Taritzin at the time of the Bolshevik rush in the Fall of 1919 and the Spring of 1920."[32] Their unit remained in the Kuban until they also were evacuated from Novorossisk in March. They beat a very hasty retreat, in great disorder, because he goes on to say ". . . I cannot produce my Flying log book, because, at the time of the Bolshevik Advance, I, together with the other British Officers serving there, lost my kit, which fell into their hands."

For his service in South Russia, he received three awards:

Order of St. Stanislaus w/sword and bow on 19 January 1920
Mentioned in Despatches on 15 March 1920
Order of St. Anne 3rd class w/sword and bow on 23 March 1920

On 5 July 1920, he was demobilized and returned to Canada. His financial situation was anything but satisfactory, and once again he found himself unemployed, but he did have one thing in his favour: the death sentence no

---

[32] Letter to H.R. Stewart, Secretary, Canadian Air Force Association, Maritime Provinces Branch, 29 July 1920. There are several different spellings of Taritzin, the city that would later be renamed Stalingrad and become notorious as the scene of the titanic battle between the German and Soviet armies during the Second World War. It had a second name change in the latter half of the twentieth century and is now known as Volgograd.

The War of 1914-1918.

Royal Air Force.

Flt./Lt. H. Edwards.

was mentioned in a Despatch from
Major General H.C. Holman, K.C.B., C.M.G., D.S.O.
dated 15th March. 1920.
for gallant and distinguished services in the Field.
I have it in command from the King to record His Majesty's
high appreciation of the services rendered.

Winston S. Churchill

War Office
Whitehall, S.W.
1st March 1919.

Secretary of State for War.

longer hung over his head.

6

THE PEACETIME AIR FORCE PART I

1920–1926

It was a far different family that Gus returned to in Glace Bay from the one he had left five years earlier. During his absence, the family had been devastated. While still a prisoner of war, he received word that his father had died on 13 June 1918 at the age of fifty-five. Another, even more tragic death, had occurred just a month before he came home. His brother Ben, with whom he had been so close growing up, was killed in the mine on 12 June 1920, a day short of his twenty-ninth birthday and the second anniversary of their father's death. Ben's death left his wife, Josephine Boutilier, whom he had married in 1916, with three children under four years of age: Harold, Marjorie, and Robert.

The effect on his mother of losing both a husband and a son within two years is hard to imagine. Coping with their deaths on an emotional level would have been difficult enough, but the financial impact of the loss of two wage earners had to be dealt with as well. After Will's death, she lived with Ben and Josie, and after Ben's death—and indeed for the rest of her life—lived with Josie and her children until they were grown, married, and moved away.

The disastrous state of the family finances was certainly not lost on Gus, and he wasted little time seeking employment. On 29 July, he applied to be a member of the recently formed Canadian Air Force. He also had an offer of a position in the Maritimes, because he pressed for an early reply to his application, stating: "I will be extremely glad if you will consider this matter as urgently as possible, as I expect to take up employment here at an early date, and should I do so, I should feel loath to relinquish it, once commenced."[33]

---

[33] Letter to H.R. Stewart, Secretary, Canadian Air Force Association, Maritime Provinces Branch, July 29th, 1920.

The sense of urgency increased with each passing day. He obviously preferred the air force to the other offer but could not get a firm commitment until regulations for the new CAF received Privy Council approval. The days dragged on while the family's financial situation worsened. As time ran out and he had to make a decision, he pleaded for a firm offer. Telegrams flew back and forth. He had a brief period of hope when the position of adjutant at Camp Borden became available, but another candidate received the appointment. Toward the end of August, in a desperate effort to press his case, he decided to go to Toronto in the hope of being taken on as part of the Ontario quota. But Mr. Stewart, who had championed his cause from the beginning, managed to have him accepted from the Maritime Provinces and, finally, on 9 September as a flight lieutenant with service number C30, he was ordered to proceed the following week to Camp Borden for a short course of flight training.[34]

His instructor's report to the CO of the school summed up his less-than-stellar performance.

> This Officer while under my instruction has completed 5 hours and 5 minutes dual and 1 hour and 50 minutes solo flying. At the beginning of his course this Officer showed poor all round flying ability. He was erratic in the air due principally to being very heavy on the rudder.
>
> His flying lately has improved greatly and if put on heavy machines should make a creditable pilot. His main trouble is inconsistency, one day flying well, the next rather erratic.
>
> He is keen, fond of stunting and has good judgment. In my opinion he wouldn't do well on scouts nor do I consider him suitable for an instructors course.
>
> He should make a good war pilot.

The CO's evaluation was equally reserved: "I have flown with this officer, he flies only moderately well and is extremely keen. He would make a fair war pilot."

---

[34] F/L W.A. Curtis was also on the course, and the medical officer was F/L H. Norman Bethune. W.A.B. Douglas, *The Creation of a National Air Force: The Official History of the Royal Canadian Air Force*, Volume II (Toronto: University of Toronto Press in co-operation with the Department of National Defence and the Canadian Government Publishing Centre, Supplies and Services Canada, 1986), p. 52.

6 - THE PEACETIME AIR FORCE - PART I: 1920–1926

He may have been a "conspicuous" pilot in France, but these results were definitely disappointing. In any event, he was posted to headquarters in Ottawa on 15 October. This was to be the first of three- or four-year postings that alternated between HQ and assignments elsewhere. These rotations were standard procedure for all officers and would continue until the beginning of the Second World War.

He took up his position as staff officer in charge of Records, then Pay and Records, and finally Personnel. It was in this posting that he began what was to be a life of travel in connection with his duties. Trips in later years would be mostly by air, but in those early days of the fledgling air force, travel was primarily by train, or sometimes even by ship, as was the case in 1921 when he went from Ottawa to Quebec by rail and from there to Halifax by boat.

Here, too, began his lifelong financial commitment to his mother. Each month an amount was deducted from his pay and sent to her, the amount increasing when a promotion occurred. Nor did he forget his niece and nephews, as he wrote in a Christmas letter to his mother in 1921:

> Twenty thousand wishes for a Merry Xmas & Brighter new year. I have just posted a parcel of stuff for the kids a train for young Harold brick farmhouse arrangement & a monkey for the wee ones . . .
>
> I am enclosing for you a cheque for $150.00 & for Josie $25.00. I would have bought something but I don't know what you would be best suited with.

But the life of this young, unattached officer was not all work and financial worry—far from it. He received invitations to various social events, including one to Government House, where he "had fairly good time of course every thing is formal. It is like going to court as they did in olden times & makes you laugh."

* * *

Whether at a skating party he attended a year later at Rideau Hall, or on some other occasion, Gus's life was to take a radical turn for the better when he met and was totally captivated by a vivacious, brown-eyed Ottawa belle by the name of Beatrice Coffey.

Bea was the sixth of eight children born to Patrick Joseph Coffey and Mary

Beatrice Coffey. c. 1917

Ann Tierney on 29 March 1901. Her paternal grandfather, Thomas Coffey, "a native of Tipperary,"[35] flourished in the grocery business, owning and operating a store in Ottawa's ByWard Market and leasing several blocks of fruit and vegetable stands that he had contracted with the City to maintain. He was also active in civic affairs as a waterworks commissioner.

> [T]he first Water Works Commissioners were elected in March 1872. Their duties were set by an Ontario provincial statute. Early municipal board positions were held by men who were financially comfortable and of independent means as the board positions were unsalaried. The first Board Chairman was Francis Clemow and the Board members were Thomas Coffey, J.T.C. Beaubien, John P. Featherston, and Jas. Cunningham.
>
> Their first order of business was to hire a Chief Engineer (Thomas C. Keefer). Following that, they selected the site for the Water Works, construction supplies were purchased and the Works were

---

[35] This phrase is carved on the monument in the Coffey family plot in Ottawa's Notre Dame Cemetery and is testament to the fierce attachment Irish immigrants had to their native land.

built (By-law 317-1872). In other words, the first Water Works Commission was responsible for the initial water infrastructure system for the City of Ottawa.[36]

Her maternal great-grandfather, Dennis Tierney, had been a successful farmer in Ireland and immigrated to Canada in 1824, settling in Fallowfield, just west of Ottawa. Despite an appalling episode of sectarian violence some thirty years later, in which one of his sons was beaten to death, his other descendants continued to earn a prosperous living from farming for the next hundred years.[37]

Bea's father, educated at the University of Ottawa, was the registrar of the County of Carleton. He was also a well-known member of the Liberal Party and a staunch supporter and neighbour of its leader, Sir Wilfrid Laurier, who lived just two blocks away. She and the other children grew up at 271 Stewart Street, a large, three-storey brick house that had been built in 1902 in the new district of Sandy Hill in Ottawa. While not wealthy, they were well enough off financially to enjoy the amenities their father's position provided: servants, music lessons, and tennis and skating parties with their friends. It was a comfortable and pleasant upbringing until it all came to an abrupt end on 15 June 1917 when their father suffered a heart attack in his office, collapsed, and died.

Her father's death severely reduced the family income so that Bea, at the age of sixteen, left Ottawa Normal School where she was a student, enrolled in a commercial course, and from then on, until her marriage to Gus, earned her living as a secretary at the National Harbours Board, a division of the Department of Fisheries.

The marriage almost didn't take place. Bea had been brought up in the Roman Catholic Church, Gus in the Church of England. The point at issue was the religious faith of any children of the marriage. Bea's Roman Catholicism was unbending in its tenet that all children, regardless of sex,

---

[36] E-mail of 2 June 2005 from Hariette Fried, City of Ottawa Archives.

[37] "Following a local election in Nepean on January 8, 1856 about 30 men were returning to the Richmond area on sleighs. Their route went by a local drinking establishment. . . . The men on sleighs belonged to the Protestant Orange Order whereas the patrons of the hotel were Catholic. It is not clear what caused the events that followed but given the religious tension which existed at the time it would have taken very little to create a disturbance. The men from the sleighs entered the hotel, savagely beat the patrons and wrecked the hotel. Dennis Tierney . . . died from his injuries. After many delays, a Justice of the Peace issued warrants for the arrest of nine men. . . . The case dragged on for several months and eventually was dismissed for lack of concrete evidence as to who actually struck the fatal blow." Manning Monaghan, *The Monaghans of Fallowfield* (Toronto: Self-published, 2004), p. 49. Reprinted with permission.

be baptized and raised in the Church. Gus, on the other hand, thought it only reasonable that girls could be Catholics, boys Anglicans. Religious convictions were strongly held in the 1920s, and Bea, with her strict Irish Catholic background, was immovable on this point. For his part, Gus was unable to accept what he considered an unfair condition, and after much anguish and heartbreak, they broke their engagement.

But near midnight a few weeks later, the telephone rang in the Coffey house. It was a distraught Gus, unable to face his future without Bea, surrendering to her wishes by saying, "I don't give a damn if you bring them all up as *monkeys*, I *have* to marry you!" My brother and I, for obvious reasons, were particularly thankful that he made that call. Of all the decisions he made in his life, this one certainly had the happiest result, and they were married on 21 May 1924 in the rectory of St. Joseph's Church in Ottawa. As for religion, they worked out a *modus vivendi* so that we were never conscious of its being a contentious issue between them. In fact, it was from their respect for each other's views, so often tinged with humour, that we learned the meaning of tolerance.

* * *

With Gus's personal life now happily settled, his professional one began to show the first signs of advancement. In August 1923, he was transferred to Winnipeg, spending most of his time at the sub-station at Victoria Beach. No sooner had he settled in than he was selected to attend a three-month staff course at the Royal Military College in Kingston. Some of the subjects covered—such as Military Law and Staff Duties—would apply to any branch of the armed services, but one cannot help but wonder at the relevance for an airman of some of the others, such as "India and Frontier Warfare" or "Employment of Tanks in the Field." The cavalry was still a vital component of the army, so naturally there was a lecture on its deployment and "Veterinary and Remount Services." Gus even earned a Certificate of Equitation, but failed miserably in his attempt to have a pair of breeches paid for by the CAF. The report of the commandant, however, showed he was anything but a failure at the course: "*This officer worked very hard and showed extraordinary keeness: results very satisfactory.*"

Next, it was off again to Camp Borden for more flight training. This time, though, as he was the only officer under instruction, he would receive intensive training for over a month and benefit enormously from the individual instruction. The report on this course shows how much his performance had

6 - THE PEACETIME AIR FORCE - PART I: 1920–1926

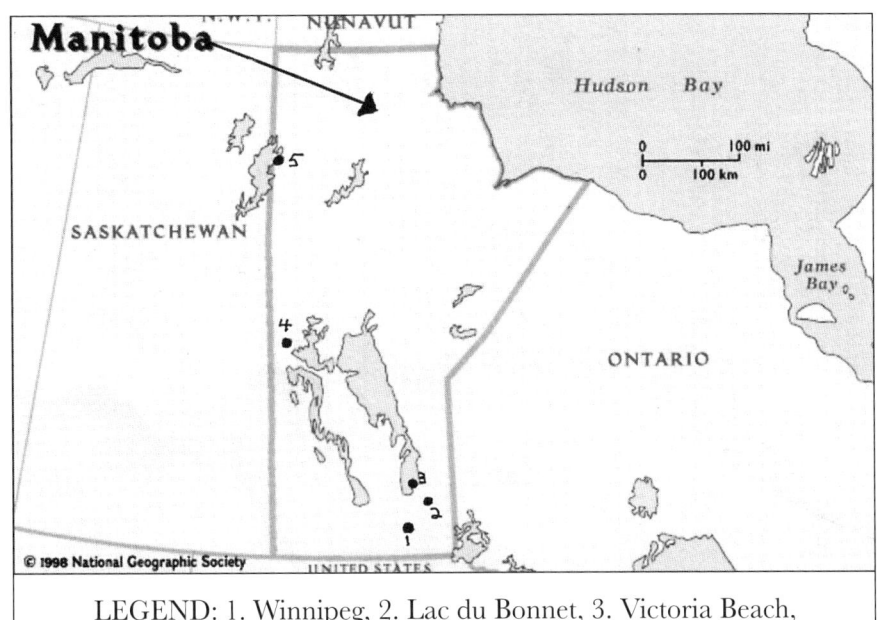

LEGEND: 1. Winnipeg, 2. Lac du Bonnet, 3. Victoria Beach, 4. The Pas, 5. Reindeer Lake

improved, needing only more practice on forced landings. The report states: "*Very keen, has been anxious to learn and perfect every manouvre [sic] possible with an aeroplane.*"

With these two courses successfully completed, he returned to Fort Osborne Barracks in Winnipeg in February, and there, on 1 April 1924, the date the Royal Canadian Air Force officially came into being with a total strength of sixty-eight officers and 307 other ranks, he swore the Oath of Allegiance:

> I, H. Edwards, do make Oath (or do solemnly declare), that I will be faithful and bear true Allegiance to His Majesty KING GEORGE the FIFTH, His Heirs and Successors, and that I will as in duty bound honestly and faithfully defend His Majesty, His Heirs and Successors, in Person, Crown and Dignity, against all enemies, and will observe and obey all orders of His Majesty, His Heirs and Successors, and of all the Generals and Officers set over me. So help me GOD.

In May, he was granted a month's leave and left for his wedding in Ottawa, returning with his new bride in mid-June to take up his duties once again as adjutant, operational pilot, and OIC Victoria Beach.

What an interesting time it was for aviation, those early years after the war. In the early 1920s, the government began to realize the merits of using aircraft for forest surveys, fire patrols, mineral exploration, and mapping the vast expanses of the country. By the middle of the decade, the system was in full swing, with flying boat bases established at strategic points across the country, Victoria Beach being one. As open water was necessary for takeoff and landing, operations were restricted to when lakes and rivers were free of ice in the spring, and before freeze-up in the autumn. Aerial mapping was carried out by means of a camera mounted in place of a machine gun.

Just as during the war, the crews were in open cockpits, exposed to the elements, and, since wireless communication had not yet been introduced, homing pigeons were carried on board to send distress signals from downed aircraft. Flying could be undertaken only during daylight hours, so crews had to set up camp each night, making it necessary to carry on board provisions and camping equipment. Equipment included such items as a tent, an axe, a shotgun, and a folding canoe—paddles included. Due to the limited amount of fuel on board, extra fuel had to be sent on ahead, usually in the winter, and stored in the bush along proposed flight paths.

An epic flight to map Reindeer Lake and its environs is an example of the truly extraordinary feats these airmen accomplished.[38] The pilot, S/L Basil D. Hobbs (Gus's CO), with a crew of three set out from Victoria Beach on 18 July 1924 and returned four weeks later. At an altitude of 5,000 feet and a ground speed of sixty mph, they flew nearly 3,000 miles, took 1,700 photographs, and mapped 15,000 square miles.

Gus later wrote a report recommending the reduction of crews from four to three to allow more stores and safety equipment to be carried on board; and another outlining how the photos were taken.

> In the 1925–26 annual report, F/L H. Edwards, OIC at Victoria Beach, described the art at that time of map-making from aerial photographs:
>
>> An aerial photographic traverse is made beginning at some place whose geographical position has been exactly located, following a suitable watercourse in a large loop of 200 to 400 miles, and ending at another point whose position has

---

[38] S. Bernard Shaw, *Photographing Canada from Flying Canoes* (Burnstown, Ont.: General Store Publishing House, 2001), pp. 63–8, provides a detailed description of this historic flight.

6 - THE PEACETIME AIR FORCE - PART I: 1920–1926

The Viking IV chosen by the Canadian Air Force as a replacement for the Curtiss HS-2L in 1923 had a 50 foot, 15 section wing. The crew was housed in open cockpits, but an additional camera position was provided in the nose by the RCAF. The Rolls-Royce engine version was chosen, primarily for reasons of economy. This caused the Viking IV to be considerably underpowered for an Aircraft of its size and weight.
CF Photo

been exactly determined. An altitude of 5,000 feet is held and photographs are taken in groups of five every three miles, one straight ahead and two to either side, covering an arc of 90 degrees on each side of the line of sight. (In previous seasons, only three pictures were taken, one ahead and one on each side. The additional two pictures are found to give better control of the side pictures through the larger overlap.) These pictures and a rough plot from them of the waterways are then given to the surveyor, who, using them as a guide, makes a ground traverse over the course already flown fixing stations along the route by instrumental observations and marking his course and the stations occupied on the pictures. This gives complete control along the loop of the traverse. The area lying within the loop is then filled in by parallel photographic flights beginning, in this case, on the shore of Lake Winnipeg and ending on the controlled traverse. No groundwork is necessary in the interior of the blocks bounded by the traverse.

Experience, F/L Edwards maintained, had demonstrated that the aerial photography method was equally accurate to ground-based surveys. He forecast the technique being used for a survey of the whole of Northern Canada by small ground parties transported and supplied by aircraft that would also take the photographs: "The infinite amount of time and labour a survey of this nature will save is only realized by those who have had experience of travel in Northern Canada."[39]

* * *

Many different types of transport were sometimes required to reach one's destination. On one occasion, Gus was ordered to preside over a court of inquiry into the crash of an Ontario government aircraft near Savanne. Nowadays it would be a quick flight followed by a short helicopter ride to the crash site, but in 1924 it required over forty-eight hours and several different conveyances. His expense account shows that he left Victoria Beach at 3:15 p.m. by air to Selkirk; then a streetcar ride to Winnipeg, a CNR train overnight to Port Arthur, arriving at 10:00 a.m., a CPR train departing the following morning at 2:30 a.m. arriving in Savanne at 4:30 a.m., and finally renting a motorboat for $5.00 to reach the actual site.

His official reports may have helped improve flying conditions, but his sense of humour was sometimes lost, and for good reason, on one member of the station, W/C Tommy Cooper, then a sergeant, who described an incident:

> There were the inevitable inspection visits from senior officers even in those days and it meant best dress and medals. I well remember one occasion. We had been dressed in our number one blues and S/L G.O. Johnson was taxiing an aircraft away from

---

[39] Ibid., pp. 83–4. Reproduced with permission of the publisher.

the dock. To prevent the wing from being damaged I walked to the end of the dock, holding the wing, and as the tailplane was passing I bent forward to make sure everything was clear. "Gus" Edwards could not resist the temptation to put his foot behind me and pushed me in, thereby demonstrating a sense of humour not fully appreciated by me at the time![40]

* * *

Three happy years were spent at Victoria Beach, Lac du Bonnet, and Winnipeg. Thankfully for his career, Gus's skills as a pilot had improved considerably, for he was deemed "A very capable pilot and efficient officer in every respect—keen and energetic. A good organizer and Commander."[41]

In late August 1926, he and Bea took the train to Ottawa and then on to Montreal, where they boarded the SS *Montcalm* for England and his new post as RCAF liaison officer at the Air Ministry in London. Bea, seven months pregnant, was described by the medical officer to be "in a delicate state of health; and should be provided with special accomodation [sic] on the train. . ."[42]

---

[40] W/C Thomas F. Cooper, "Jack of All Trades," *Airforce*, 75th Anniversary Issue (Fall 1998). Reprinted with permission.

[41] 1925 Annual Confidential Report.

[42] Letter from Col. A.E. Snell to OC RCAF Winnipeg, 21 August 1926.

7

THE PEACETIME AIR FORCE PART II

1926–1933

I do not know whether Bea was actually in a "delicate state of health," or this was simply a euphemism for pregnancy; nor what effect, if any, the roughness of the eight-day crossing may have had on her condition. In any event, shortly after settling in London, she was—as Royal Proclamations so describe childbirth—safely delivered of a son. William John Robert, forever after known in the family as Billy, was born on 23 October 1926. This significant event happily coincided with another milestone: Gus's promotion to squadron leader.

A year later, Gus's official duties took him to the Schneider Cup Air Race in Venice. This competition had been instituted in 1913 to encourage the development of seaplanes. Over the years, it had grown into an international event, with Service teams participating as well, and in 1927 the RAF team included two of his friends from the ill-fated Russian intervention. Following the trip, he wrote a lengthy letter to his mother. This was one of many he wrote, always letting her know what he was up to, even during the hectic period in London during the Second World War.

This particular one is typical of Gus, constantly in motion, eager to see and learn new things, calling a spade a spade, and describing events in detail so that she had a clear picture of his life. Rather than quoting snippets here and there, it is reproduced in its entirety, including the curious combination of English and French for a place name.[43] The "travelogue" of the first several paragraphs may be boring, but some interesting observations and fascinating details emerge as the letter goes on.

---

[43] It is dated 8 October, and considering he was just learning to type, it is remarkably free of errors. Of the many letters he wrote to his mother during her lifetime, eighteen of them—written between 1918 and 1944—have survived. Unfortunately, however, such is not the case with those he wrote to Bea during long absences from home and from London in 1942–43. These she destroyed just prior to her death.

7 - THE PEACETIME AIR FORCE - PART II: 1926–1933

55 Hervey Road
Blackheath,
London, S.E.3
8/10/27

My dear Mother:

I find that to pursue the course properly which I am now taking it is necessary to do a lot of writing, and since my writing is so bad and loses me a lot in consequence, I have got a typewriter and have made up my mind that to do the thing properly will take a lot of practice and so I am going to type nearly all my letters for some time to come. I do not think this will worry you very much because you too have probably had a bit of trouble making out some of my hand-written ones. The typing will probably be very bad for a little while, but at worst it can never be as bad as my ordinary writing.

We got home safely last saturday night after having been away almost two weeks. Our journey took us first to Paris, via Dover and Calais, where we stayed the afternoon and night. We had a short drive through the city, mostly looking for an hotel as the place was packed with The American Legion. We saw the unknown soldiers tomb under the Arc de Triumph, the Seine, Notre Dame cathedral, the Champs Elysee and nearly all the points of interest that can be seen from a taxi-cab. That night we had dinner at Maxim's which is a pretty famous place, stayed at the Pennslyvania hotel, a little place, and pushed off next morning for Switzerland.

Our route took us through Dijon and Vallorbe. It was our idea to cover as much territory as we could, and thus see as much as we could, without getting off the beaten track in the general direction of Venice. We had our tickets routed therefore to go one way and come back the other. If you have a map you will probably be able to trace them by the places I mention. We got into the foothills of the Alps towards the afternoon, they were very beautiful, but we saw the real Alps about an hour later when we climbed the tops of the foothills. The railways have evidently been put through the most beautiful part of the country, and I should think it has paid them well to have done so on account of the extra traffic which it has brought to the railways.

That night we stayed at a small "Pension" hotel at Lausanne on Lake Geneva. It is a wonderful spot on the edge of the lake looking out across it to the mountains which climb out of the lake on all sides, and rise to very great heights. The people are particularly pleasant and seem to have the idea of giving service without being servile.

Next morning we set off for Milan. The journey took us again through mountain scenery, through Montreux, St. Maurice and finally the greatest tunnel in the world called the "Simplon" from the name of the town nearest to it. When we emerged from the tunnel we were in Italy. Continuing on we came to Stressa on Lake Maggiore. This place, while being quieter and less majestic in beauty, was very nice to see. Continuing on we arrived at Milan about noon where we had a wait of an hour and a half. We took the opportunity to see the Cathedral and the famous painting by di Vinci of the Last Supper. The cathedral is the best I have ever seen, but of course I am no judge of such things, and would not venture a comparison with any other. The painting was to me pretty good, but of these things again I know nothing. Outside of the above there is practically nothing further in Milan. It is much like any other continental city, quite dirty and uninteresting. In fact to see one of them is to see the lot.

Next we passed Lake Garda, slipped through Verona (of Shakespeare's "Three Gentlemen"), through Padua and arrived at Venice at about nine o'clock at night.

Before starting to tell you what happened at Venice I had better give you some idea of how it got there.

Hundreds of years ago the rivers brought down from the Alps a lot of debris, (which they do still) and dumped it into the Adriatic Sea. This deposit formed little mud islands, on which, the people of the time, who were very warlike, sought protection from their enemies. They built their first houses on piles like many natives of the East do at present, and finally as the deposit of earth increased, they erected stronger houses on the islands, which are called "Lidos."

This accounts for the present canals which are the only system of transport in Venice today. There is one central artery called the "Grand Canal" and miles of smaller ones connected with it.

7 - THE PEACETIME AIR FORCE - PART II: 1926–1933

Gondolas are still the normal means of conveyance, but motor boats are gradually taking their place, just as the taxis have taken the place of the horse cab.

Unfortunately the place is filthy. The canals are used for sewers as well as the purpose for which they were intended. Nevertheless it is an interesting old place and I am glad to have seen it once. I never want to go again however.

We saw the "Doges Palace" and all the things connected with it, such as the bridge of sighs, the prisons and so forth. St. Marks cathedral, with its four bronze horses, also came into the picture, but the race for which we went was the cream of the lot.

The course for the race was laid at the Lido beach, a fashionable summer resort across the lagoon from Venice. Only two nations competed for the cup i.e. Great Britain and Italy, the latter being in possession of the cup, having won it from the U.S.A. last year. The British won hands down, reaching a speed of 281 miles an hour. Kinkhead and Slatter who you will remember were with me in South Russia, were two of the pilots. It was a beautiful sight. About 250,000 people were there.

Unfortunately Bea got a touch of ptomaine poisoning which, though she saw the race, gave a miserable time during the day.

We left Venice on Tuesday, not a bit too soon for either of us, retracing our steps to Milan. Here we changed routes to go through the St. Gothard tunnel, and as you will see, saw both places you mention in your letter.

We edged Lake Como and took a picture of it. I hope it turns out alright. Further on we passed Lugano and in the distance Locarno. That night we came to and stopped at Lucerne. Feeling pretty tired we stayed there two nights. It is a lovely spot and we certainly hated to leave it. We next came the following morning to Bale and changed trains for Colmar.

I had always hoped to go back and see the place where I was shot down and my gunlayer [Air Mechanic J.L. Coghlan] is buried. We saw the actual places and even talked to a couple of women (one was then a small child) who actually saw me as I landed and recognized me. They pieced up the story of what happened to my gunlayer after I was taken away to jail; the story of his burial and so forth. By permission of the French commandant who is now in charge of the barracks we saw the cell where they kept me in solitary confinement for several weeks. It was all very interesting.

We reached Strasbourg the same evening and spent the night there. We ran out by street car to Kehl and to see the Rhine as Bea of course had never seen it before. We stepped for a moment into Germany. Strasbourg is very much like any other town of its size on the continent and is of no particular interest.

The next day we took train for Lille. This took us along the Saar basin where we used to bomb the factories during the war. At one place, two chimneys which I remember quite well were blown down by one of our bombs, are standing up straight again and quite new. It was dark when we came into Lille. We spent the night there and set out by train across the old battlefields early the next morning. The whole of the country is now all built up again. New and clean looking villages have taken the place of the ruins left in 1918, in fact it is hard to realize a war had ever been fought there at all. Every thing is clean except for here and there a branchless tree or the remnants of an old German "Pill-box" which are blockhouses made of thick concrete. The better ones are evidently occupied for here and there a stove pipe sticks through the roof. . . .

We got home early in the evening which gave me time to get ready for the college on Monday. So far I find the course very pleasant, but I think before it is finished fifteen months hence, they will have knocked a lot of work out of us.

We did not take the baby with us and consequently were glad to get back to him again. He is as fat and as healthy as can be. Bea enjoyed the trip very much and is feeling a good deal stronger than she was both before and during it.

That is all this time. Please give my love to Jo and the children, as well as to any others you may think fit.

Ever your Loving son,
Harold

7 - THE PEACETIME AIR FORCE - PART II: 1926–1933

Gus in Full Dress.
London 1927

Gus with Bea and Billy.
London 1927

For the next fifteen months, Gus attended the staff course at the Royal Naval College at its magnificent site in Greenwich on the Thames River.

An exceptional opportunity arose in September 1928 when the course included joining the Atlantic Fleet for ten days on board HMS *Argus*, the first aircraft carrier

> . . . to have a full-length flight deck upon which wheeled aircraft could land and take off with relative safety. As such, she established the general pattern for future aircraft carriers.
>
> *Argus* was commissioned in September 1918, shortly before the end of the "Great War". She spent much of her first decade on the vital work of developing carrier techniques and training aviators in the demanding work of operating aircraft at sea.[44]

---

[44] www.history.navy.mil

St. Mark's Square. Venice 1927

At the completion of the course in December, Gus received this report:

> Squadron Leader Edwards has taken a very great interest in the course.
> He appears to be a thoroughly capable and level headed officer, he is quick to grasp essentials.
> He expresses himself clearly and concisely both verbally and in written work.
> Unassuming to a fault almost and well adapted to co-operate with officers of another Service in a combined operation.[45]

---

[45] Confidential report of 20 December 1928 transmitted by The Secretary, Office of the High Commissioner, on 9 January 1929.

7 - THE PEACETIME AIR FORCE - PART II: 1926–1933

After the Christmas holidays, it was back to Canada, sailing from Southampton aboard the SS Ascania, which docked in Halifax on 11 January 1929. Gus took a week's leave to visit his mother, while Billy and Bea went on by train to Ottawa. From the time of his birth until leaving England, Billy had been looked after by a nanny with the inevitable result that this loquacious two-year-old had a strong English accent. On seeing snow for the first time in his young life, he delighted nearby passengers on the train by chirping brightly, "Owe Mummay, look at all the shugah!"

* * *

Although the two years in London had been a fascinating and eventful experience that both Bea and Gus had enjoyed immensely, his posting to Ottawa was a particularly happy event for Bea. Apart from the brief stopover on their way to England, she had not seen her family since her marriage in 1924. During the next five years they lived in Sandy Hill, the neighbourhood in which she had grown up and where many of her family and friends still lived. Summers were spent at a cottage, the last one at Constance Bay on Lac Deschênes.[46]

* * *

In addition to fishing and golf, racquet sports were an important part of Gus's life, and he was an enthusiastic squash, tennis, and badminton player. Bea also played spirited games of badminton and tennis and, much to Gus's occasional humiliation, ran him ragged on the court at the Rideau Lawn Tennis Club. She accomplished this very effectively by countering his long flowing strokes from the baseline with the classic tactic of slicing the ball just over the net. Recounting one of these games in a tone mixed with both admiration and resignation, but at the same time implying this strategy should be outside the bounds of fair play, he sighed, "Well, of course, your mother *cuts* the ball." Bea just smiled and winked.

Another episode he described with much amusement was his attempt to teach Bea how to drive a car equipped with a manual gear shift. Having become proficient at driving "on the flat," he judged her ready to tackle the dreaded operation of "starting on a hill." The spot chosen for this exercise was Range Road, adjacent to Strathcona Park. Sandy Hill came by its name

---

[46] The author was born on 4 January 1931 and baptized Suzanne Katherine.

honestly, and Range Road provided the perfect incline as it approached Laurier Avenue. As instructed, Bea stopped the car in the middle of the hill, applied the hand brake, and turned off the ignition. She then turned on the ignition, released the hand brake, let out the clutch *too quickly*, and the engine stalled. Undeterred, she tried again . . . and again . . . and again, with the same unfortunate result. On the fourth try, Gus totally lost patience with her inability to coordinate the clutch and accelerator. Happily, the exact words that next passed between them have not survived, but Bea, furious, got out of the car, slammed the door, and proceeded to walk home. By the time she reached the top of the hill, Gus had caught up with her in the car, and driving slowly beside her, doffed his hat, saying, "How do you do, Mrs. Edwards, may I offer you a lift?" Bea ignored him and kept on walking. But Gus persisted, driving beside her, doffing his hat and repeating his greeting, until finally, after two blocks, her anger melted into laughter and she got into the car—on the passenger side.

* * *

Gus took up his appointment as a staff officer at headquarters with responsibility for organization and personnel. These two categories covered a wide range of activities, one of which, as a member of a development committee, took him on an inspection of US Naval and Army airports. He travelled to the northeastern states, the legation in Washington, Florida, Louisiana, St. Louis, and finally home via Chicago. Several years later, this tour was to serve him well when he was sent to Halifax to oversee the development of the Dartmouth Air Station. While in Ottawa from 1929 to 1934, he took more than fifty trips over a period of four and half months; some were day trips to Trenton or Montreal, while others were to the USA or the Maritimes and lasted several days or weeks.

In his annual performance reports of the period, his energy, keenness, and organizing ability are emphasized over and over again. With the diversity of duties from chairman, Airmen and Boys Selection Committee, to drill instruction of all RCAF in Ottawa, to courts martial, to flying—certainly life was never routine or dull.

Paperwork was another matter; submitting an expense account that varied in any way from the norm brought down the wrath of the finance department gods. With the amount of travelling involved, inevitable differences of opinion arose between amounts claimed and those approved for payment. Tariffs had been established for every eventuality and woe betide anyone who

7 - THE PEACETIME AIR FORCE - PART II: 1926–1933

claimed an amount above the tariff! One such incident occurred with the claim covering the move to England. The tariff for a taxi in Montreal from Windsor Station to the Ritz Hotel was fifty cents. Due to excess baggage, Gus paid and claimed $1.00. This item, and a similar one for $2.50 for the taxi from the hotel to the dock—an amount "considered excessive for the distance travelled"—generated five lengthy memos and took almost three months to resolve—in Gus's favour. Certainly the public purse was zealously guarded.

Not having the resources to invest in the Stock Market in 1929, its collapse in October had no effect on Gus's finances. The state of the government's finances, however, was an entirely different matter and what effect the weakened economy would have on the military establishment was a question all members of the Services asked themselves. The answer was not long in coming.

> By 31 Mar 30 the R.C.A.F. had increased to 175 officers and 669 airmen and a programme was under way to train university science students as provisional pilot officers during their summer vacations. By the beginning of 1932 it was obvious, however, that the economic depression was not going to disappear rapidly. The Canadian Government slashed its defence expenditures and almost one-fifth of the R.C.A.F.—78 officers, 100 airmen and 110 civilians—had to be released. The concomitant major reorganization was to convert the R.C.A.F. into a military organization however, and action finally was taken to form a Non-Permanent Active Air Force.[47]

Though total strength was reduced by one-fifth, the officer component was decimated—from 175 to 97, a reduction of 45%—and those who remained lived with the gnawing fear that further cuts would follow. Military personnel shared these fears with civilians, and as the Depression deepened, the next several years were desperate times for the country and its air force. Strangely, it was this very Depression, which caused so much misery, that was the catalyst for one of Gus's most challenging postings.

---

[47] Report No. 67, Historical Section (G.S.) Army Headquarters (15 Jan 1954), p. 2. Reproduced with the permission of the Minister of Public Works and Government Services, 2006.

8

THE PEACETIME AIR FORCE PART III

1934–1938

In September 1934, Gus was posted to Halifax to oversee the development of RCAF Station Dartmouth and assume command of No. 5 (Flying Boat) Squadron, consisting of five detachments: Dartmouth, Sydney, Rimouski, Gaspé and Shediac.[48] While Bea and I travelled down by train, Gus and Billy went by car, visiting RCAF (MP) detachments on the way. Since no married quarters existed at what was then a remote station in Eastern Passage, the district officer commanding assigned a house in Halifax. And what a perfect house it turned out to be: part of the Glacis Barracks complex situated on the side of Citadel Hill, a brick structure surrounded by a fenced garden. The army had obviously spent some time and effort to spruce it up prior to our arrival, which prompted Ottawa to order the OIC to have "cartage unpack furniture and place in house taking care not to damage new lawns and walls in process."[49] Interestingly, the zeal headquarters displayed in protecting government property did not seem to extend to the family furniture, as no such cautionary order was issued for it.

It was in Halifax that Gus first met Brigadier "Dane" Hertzberg who, as District Officer Commanding Military District No. 6, was Gus's commanding officer.[50] In 1936, largely as a result of the Brigadier's recommendation for accelerated promotion, Gus became a wing commander. Part of his letter of recommendation contained a prescient comment: "This recommendation is made not only in the nature of a reward for his past services, but particularly

---

[48] For a brief history of Dartmouth Air Station between the wars see Appendix A, an undated paper by the RCAF Air Historian titled *Halifax—Dartmouth and the Royal Canadian Air Force 1918–1939*.

[49] Telegram from S/L G. Mercer dated 19 September 1934.

[50] Major General H.F.H. Hertzberg CB, CMG, DSO, MC had two familiar names: "Dane" and "Hertz." In 1934 he was a Brigadier.

8 - THE PEACETIME AIR FORCE - PART III: 1934–1938

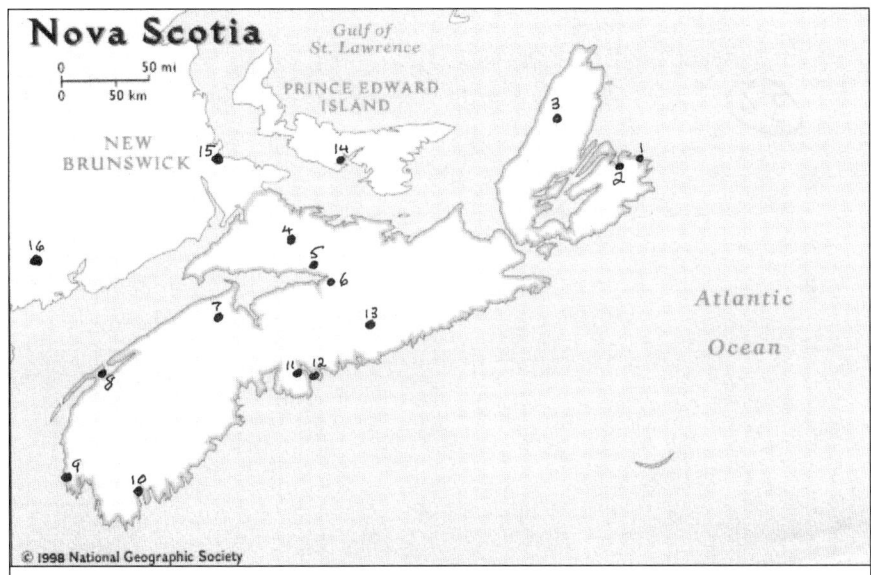

LEGEND: 1. Glace Bay, 2. Sydney, 3. Margaree, 4. Westchester, 5. Debert, 6. Truro, 7. Kentville, 8. Digby, 9. Yarmouth, 10. Shelburne, 11. Halifax, 12. RCAF Station Dartmouth, 13. Moose River Mine, 14. Charlottetown, 15. Shediac, 16. Fredericton

Maritime sites visited by Gus as CO of RCAF Station Dartmouth.

in anticipation of the usefulness of this officer in his future employment."[51]

Over the course of the Halifax years, the close working relationship they established evolved into a lasting friendship, as did a similar one between their wives.

*   *   *

Personnel at the station consisted of fourteen headquarters staff and twenty-two involved in flying operations, for a total of thirty-six, all ranks. The Flying Boat Squadron was engaged in a number of tasks, one of which provided two aircraft to the RCMP for preventative reconnaissance in support of their counter-rum-running and illegal immigration activities. Curtailing the importation of rum was a controversial programme that did not sit well with many Nova Scotians.

---

[51] Letter of 13 January 1936 from Brigadier Hertzberg to The Secretary, Department of National Defence.

Members of the RCMP, transferred to the Maritime Provinces in the 1930s, were somewhat surprised and in some cases dismayed to find that the main thrust of their duties consisted of enforcing the Customs and Excise Act and Provincial Liquor regulations. The importation of illicit spirits into the Maritime Provinces from the West Indies or via the French islands of St. Pierre and Miquelon had been an active industry for a number of years and considered a worthwhile investment by many prominent business and professional people. With the repeal of the United States Prohibition Act in 1933, smuggling activities were greatly reduced and confined to the Maritime Provinces and the St. Lawrence River area in Quebec.

The most popular importation was 40 percent overproof Demerara rum, known as "Black and Dirty," in five-gallon kegs. Belgium Alcohol in two and a half gallon cans was favoured in the Gulf of St. Lawrence area.[52]

The two aircraft, with an RCAF pilot and an RCMP observer, patrolled the coasts, working in consort with the RCMP Marine Section in an effort to thwart the ships landing their forbidden delights in hundreds of small Nova Scotia coves and harbours. The introduction of wireless communication between aircraft and vessels increased the number of intercepts, but with just two aircraft and a long coastline, limited success could be expected. Also, aerial surveillance could be carried out only during daylight hours, and it was easy for the rum ships to avoid detection by simply laying up 70 to 80 miles offshore, waiting for darkness, then sailing in to shore and offloading their precious cargo.

* * *

In April 1936, the Squadron played a crucial, though secondary, role in the famous Moose River Mine Disaster. The owners were considering selling a gold mine located in a remote area some sixty miles northeast of Halifax. Two of them, Dr. David E. Robertson, chief of staff of the Hospital for Sick Children in Toronto, and Herman R. Magill, a lawyer, also from Toronto,

---

[52] Col. Ernest S.C. Cable OMM, CD (Ret'd), *No. 5 (Flying Boat) Squadron Counter Rum Running Operations at RCAF Station Dartmouth* (Undated).

descended into the mine with Alfred Scadding, the mine timekeeper, on Easter Sunday, 12 April. Hours later, they were trapped underground by a cave-in, and rescue efforts began. It took endless hours to reach the mine over dirt roads, so flying supplies and equipment in and out was a much faster method of transport. The premier appointed Gus "to co-ordinate the efforts in respect of supplies and communication."[53] Millions in North America and Europe heard the rescue described on the radio:

> The men are in the mine on an inspection tour when the ceiling collapses. Townspeople hear the noise and within minutes Moose River miners begin rescue work. Within days, several hundred miners from throughout Nova Scotia—from Westville, Caribou Mines, Montague Mines, Springhill, Goldenville, Waverly and Stellarton—and as far away as Ontario arrive to help. But no one knows whether there are any survivors.

> After six agonizing days, Billy Bell, a diamond drill operator with the Nova Scotia government, breaks into an open space at the 43-metre level with his drill. He shouts down the pipe but there is no response. Officials decide to abandon rescue operations. Bell refuses to leave. Eleven hours later, a steam whistle arrives and a piercing note is sent down the pipe. Bell hears a faint tapping in response. The men are alive.[54]

> Rescuers quickly fed a garden hose through the pipeline, a simple tube which would represent the lifeline of the trapped men. For five days, down the tube went candles, matches, chocolate, brandy and hot soup. MT&T sent down a miniature telephone, designed especially for the survivors. The prisoners now had food, communication and perhaps most important, a reason to believe they might survive.[55]

> It is now Sunday, April 19. The next morning, mine co-owner Herman Magill dies of pneumonia. Fatigue, weather and continuous rockfalls hamper the rescue. There's only one hope left—reopening the adjacent Reynolds Shaft, which had earlier

---

[53] Letter from Premier Angus L. MacDonald to S/L H. Edwards, 22 April 1936.
[54] www.archives.cbc.ca; reprinted with permission from CBC.
[55] www.shirleycollingridge.com. Reprinted with permission.

been condemned as too dangerous. Experienced miners from Westville and Stellarton are brought in to deal with this extremely unstable environment.

As the rescue operations drag on, newspaper reporters descend on Moose River. At this time, newspapers are the primary source for news from around the world. Radio is considered an entertainment medium. Which is one reason why officials of the Canadian Radio Broadcasting Commission, a precursor to the CBC, will not allow their only reporter east of Montreal to go to the scene.

Twenty-eight-year-old J. Frank Willis is the CRBC's Regional Director for the Maritimes. When he finally receives permission to go to Moose River, it's already Monday, April 20. He makes his first broadcast at 6 p.m. that day. For two minutes every half-hour Willis is live on air throughout North America. He continues for 56 hours straight. An estimated 100 million people are listening. It is North America's very first live 24-hour news event, changing forever the perception of what radio can do.

- Willis used improvised equipment, including an old table microphone from a Halifax hotel, and a borrowed car as a studio.

- Before Willis could make any broadcasts, he had to convince everyone on the 18-mile-long party-line phone circuit to put down the phone and listen to his reports on the radio. Otherwise, the signal was so weakened that his voice came through no louder than a thin whisper.

- Mine co-owner Dr David Robertson was brought up from the mine at 12:45 a.m., Thursday, April 23. Willis broadcast his last report at 2 a.m. the same day.

- Willis's broadcasts were carried on 58 Canadian stations and about 650 stations in the United States. The BBC picked up the broadcasts for Great Britain and Europe.[56]

It was during these broadcasts that Gus's name first became known across

---

[56] www.archives.cbc.ca; reprinted with permission from CBC.

the country as he explained the rôle the RCAF was playing in support of the rescue mission. Overall, the Squadron acquitted itself well, as the text of a highly complimentary letter from the Minister of Public Works and Mines, Nova Scotia, indicates:

> Halifax, Nova Scotia,
> April 28, 1936
>
> Hon. Ian Mackenzie, Minister of National Defence
> Ottawa
>
> Dear Mr. Mackenzie,
>
> I wish to express to you Sir, my appreciation for the services rendered in the effort to rescue the entombed men at Moose River by your Flying Squadron Leader H. Edwards and Staff from Dartmouth Headquarters.
>
> Squadron Leader Edwards was indefatigable in transmitting messages and made his planes available for carrying material and conveying the rescued men from the mine to the Hospital in Halifax. This latter service enabled them to obtain full hospital treatment several days earlier than would have been possible if it had been necessary to remove them by car.
>
> I feel you should know how much the assistance rendered by your Department has been appreciated by all, and that Squadron Leader Edwards left nothing undone.
>
> Yours faithfully,
> Michael Dwyer
> MINISTER

Another well-publicized event was the first non-stop solo flight from London to New York that Beryl Markham attempted in September 1936. Flying against the prevailing winds, unfortunately she fell just short of her goal. After a difficult flight in bad weather, engine trouble forced her to crash land in a bog close to the small village of Baleine Cove near Louisbourg. Still, this was an amazing feat, and she received a hero's welcome in Halifax and then, as co-pilot on a US Coast Guard aircraft, flew on to New York and a tumultuous welcome there.

Several days later, Gus was asked to inspect the damage and found that souvenir hunters had taken various items, the loss of which prevented the aircraft from flying without extensive repairs. After this initial assessment, Harry Bruno authorized him to "get ship under shelter earliest" and [advise] "best method putting ship flying condition" and ended his telegram with "Mrs. Markham and I appreciate all you have done to help."[57]

* * *

Two German Naval vessels visited Nova Scotia in the 1930s. In 1936 the *Schwabenland* docked in Sydney in October, and in March of the following year the *Schlesien* paid a courtesy call in Halifax.

The *Schwabenland* had a catapult mounted on the deck for launching aircraft and was of considerable interest to the air force. Gus was not certain he would be permitted on board, but such was not the case, and he and his nephew Harold spent some time visiting the ship, with Harold afterwards taking some of the crew duck hunting on the Mira River.[58] In 1938–39 this was the vessel that was a key component of Germany's expedition to the Antarctic.

Unlike the *Schwabenland*, there were no such suspected restrictions on visiting the *Schlesien*. On the contrary, the *Schlesien* welcomed visitors. It was a pre-war Deutschland Class battleship, which had fought in the Battle of Jutland and had been converted to a cadet training ship. During her time in the harbour, many Halifax families went on board, our family being one. Captain Thile Seebach had been a gracious and charming host to his many guests, and we were all stunned when, two years later, Gus told us the *Schlesien*, together with the *Schleswig-Holstein*, had fired some of the first shots of the Second World War as they bombarded the Hela Peninsula in Poland.

As anyone who has served in the nation's armed forces knows only too well, the accumulation of wealth was never an incentive to enlist. In Gus's case, it wasn't even a question of saving a little money, but rather trying to keep his financial head above water. As he rose in rank, the demands of each new position required more and more entertaining. Although entertainment allowances were provided, they often were less than the sums expended, with differences made up from his own pocket. Being a CO brought increased responsibilities, worries, and stress, but it had its rewards as well, not the

---

[57] Mary S. Lovell, *Straight on Till Morning* (New York: St Martin's Press, 1991), pp. 198–9. Harry Bruno was a New York public relations consultant hired by Beryl Markham.

[58] Telephone interview with Harold G. Edwards on 14 January 2004.

8 - THE PEACETIME AIR FORCE - PART III: 1934–1938

Schwabenland.

Schlesien and *Schleswig-Holstein* in a German port.
Note pre-Nazi-era national ensign. c. 1934

least of which were two important perquisites: a batman and a staff car and driver.[59]

There was another privilege of rank, one in which he took great pleasure: the use of "The 158," an inboard motorboat whose actual identification was RCAF *M158*. Its primary purpose was as a rescue craft to fish pilots out of the water if they had been careless enough to crash in the harbour. I do not know how often, if ever, it was used for this purpose, but Gus would take it to save time crossing from Halifax to the Station. Bridges over the harbour were but a dream in those days; the only way to drive to Eastern Passage was around the basin through Bedford, a considerable distance. On other occasions, it was used for entertaining. What a delight to the eye it was with its varnished deck, shining brightwork, white leather cushions, and the air force ensign, stiff in the wind, flying from the stern as its Rolls-Royce engine powered it effortlessly through the water. No wonder he loved to be on board.

Just as living in Ottawa had brought Bea close to her family, so too the move to Nova Scotia brought Gus nearer to his, and he took advantage of every opportunity he could to see them. There were many flights to the Sydney Detachment that provided the opportunity to slip over to Glace Bay. In addition to the flying visits, he took leave to indulge in his favourite pastime of salmon fishing. His niece Marjorie remembered two such visits.

> My memories of "White Uncle Harold." They are all a bit vague but I remember most his deep concern for Grama Edwards and my Mom . . .
>
> The first visit I remember was when you were in Halifax. He was a Squadron Leader then and had opened the Air Force Base at Eastern Passage. He came one weekend to see us . . . 1935 maybe. I remember how the hall down the centre of our apartment there echoed when he walked down it in those heavy brogues he wore and how his eyes would flash with humour but become so piercing when he was serious. Then in 1937 (maybe) he brought Billy with him and he took Grama, Mom & me up to Margaree so he could go fishing. He installed us, Mom and me & Grama, in some cottages there where we went up to a big house for meals.

---

[59] The car was for official use only and was never used by the family. As far as I know, Gus adhered to this regulation religiously except for one occasion when he broke the rule and took me with him on my first day of kindergarten, delivering me to the Convent of the Sacred Heart on Spring Garden Road.

RCAF Crash Boat—"The 158."
D.ND photo courtesy Shearwater Aviation Museum

He went off at 4 a.m. to fish with Lawrence [the local blacksmith] and they were gone until maybe 10:00 a.m. Then he would take us on the wildest car ride throughout the country lanes (unpaved) in the Margaree Valley singing at the top of his lungs his favorite songs "Her Name was Mary, Mary, Plain as any name can be" "Let me call you Sweetheart." He also knew a lot of songs from old operas . . .

In 1937 he treated Grama and me to a trip to Halifax by train for a visit. . . . I remember how gracious they were to us . . .[60]

---

[60] Letter of 29 September 2002 from Marjorie Edwards MacLeod. "White Uncle Harold" was the name Marjorie's son Hugh Allan gave to Gus, his great-uncle. This was to distinguish him from his other uncle Harold, Marjorie's brother. It was a clever way to identify Gus—the "white" referring to the colour of what little hair he had left on his head.

When Mom was wondering what to do with Harold . . . your Dad said "Put him in the Air Force. He won't make much money but will end up with a trunk full of curtains that will fit any window in Canada." Of course the war changed everything for all of us. Bob went right into pilot training but dear Harold started at the bottom in 1935 or 36.[61]

Bea, too, experienced the horrors of drives on Nova Scotia roads with Gus at the wheel. She had spent the most terrifying time of her life, most of the trip with her eyes covered, as he drove merrily over the one-lane dirt track of the Cabot Trail in Cape Breton. At that time it was aptly named a trail. It had no such comforting feature as a guardrail, and with the ocean, in some places hundreds of feet below, crashing over the rocks, it could be an unnerving experience to meet an oncoming car on a hairpin turn with no room to pass, forcing one driver to back up to a point wide enough for the other to proceed.

Bea had other favourite stories from Halifax; one concerned the nightmare. It seems one night she was awakened by Gus tossing and turning, obviously in the throes of a bad dream. Her verbal attempts to wake him brought no result and the more she tried, the more he thrashed about. Finally, in desperation, she pinched his shoulder and with that he sat bolt upright and shouted:

"Jesus Christ, he *got* me."

"Don't swear, dear—who got you?"

'The *tiger*, I was being chased by a *tiger*.'

"Go back to sleep, dear, it wasn't a tiger. *I* got you, and I've had you for *years*."

Another was the parade. Gus was to lead an air force parade and I, at the tender age of four, told him we would wave and he could wave back. Evidently I was bitterly disappointed when it was carefully explained to me that waving was not possible in these circumstances, but perked right up when told he would find some way to indicate he had seen us. The solution turned out to be an almost imperceptible wink of his right eye as the parade marched past.

---

[61] In the summer of 1935, Gus's nephews Harold and Bobby were eighteen and fifteen years old, while their sister Marjorie was sixteen. Both boys would go on to have successful careers in the RCAF, retiring in 1968. During the war they both served overseas: Harold, aka "Curly," in 1944 as a pilot in Mosquito fighter bombers in England with 487 NZ Squadron completing a tour of fifty operations, including participating in D-Day action; and Bobby, aka "Joe," for two years as a fighter pilot in Hurricanes with 136 RAF Squadron in India and Ceylon. Marjorie married Dr. Lloyd MacLeod and lived a great part of her life in Liverpool, NS.

8 - THE PEACETIME AIR FORCE - PART III: 1934–1938

The final one was an account of a train trip to Ottawa. She and Gus had left Billy and me in the compartment, in our pyjamas ready for bed, while they went to the dining car to enjoy a peaceful dinner. They told the porter where they would be and off they went. No sooner had they gone than a dispute arose as to who would occupy the coveted upper berth. Billy argued that, being the elder, he was entitled to it—an argument similar to the doctrine of the Divine Right of Kings—and I, aged six, put forward what I hoped was an equally compelling case in favour of being the younger.

Unable to resolve the dispute ourselves, Billy, ever the wise older brother at the advanced age of ten, decided to take the matter to arbitration. Putting on our slippers and dressing gowns and carefully taking me by the hand, we paraded through the cars to the dining car to present our respective cases to Gus, the fount of all knowledge and arbiter of all disputes in our world. Why our porter permitted us to leave the car or why no one stopped us on the way, seems curious; but not until we reached the dining car were we challenged by anyone. As we entered the car, we could see Bea with a look of sheer disbelief on her face, mouthing the words "Oh, dear God," and Gus turning around to see what was causing the laughter from their fellow diners.

Billy carefully explained to the steward that we had urgent business to discuss with our father, and, as if our appearance were routine, he ceremoniously ushered us to their table. Gus listened gravely as we presented the insoluble problem. Trying to keep a straight face, he handed down the obvious decision: since there were two nights on the train, one could have the upper birth one night and the other could have it the next, leaving it up to us to decide who got it the first night. Such a solution had not occurred to either of us and we happily returned to our car. History does not record who got the first night.

* * *

Dogs were always an integral part of our family life, and the first one I remember was Brucie, the Newfoundland. Now Newfoundlands are one of the larger breeds, blessed with a sanguine disposition, and will happily accept any amount of playing young children can inflict upon them. That was why Gus bought us Brucie. He came to us as a four-month-old bundle of black fluff, and for the entire family it was love at first sight.

Only two things bothered him: heat, which he detested; and the noise of the noon gun, which terrified him when fired from the Citadel just above us. The first he solved quite easily by spending the majority of his life outside

RCAF Station Dartmouth c. 1935. Note submerged vessel in upper right-hand corner— the scene of Brucie's heroic rescue.
DND photo courtesy Shearwater Aviation Museum

the house, preferring to sleep in his kennel, even in the depths of winter. The second, however, took him a little longer to sort out, but in time he resolved that as well. Each day everyone knew when it was ten minutes to twelve, because exactly at that time, in anticipation of the dreaded boom, he would amble nonchalantly through the kitchen into the hall, as if looking for someone, and then sneak into the dining room and cower under the table until the gun was discharged. Once fired, he would amble out again, bravely returning outdoors (shades of the Cowardly Lion in *The Wizard of Oz*).

The breed is known for its life-saving capabilities, and on one memorable occasion Brucie proudly upheld the tradition. He loved the water, as long as he was doing the swimming. One day on a picnic, Billy decided to swim out to a half-submerged vessel that had run aground not far from shore. Brucie watched warily as Billy waded into the water. As long as Billy was just wading, Brucie permitted him to do so, but the minute he started to swim, Brucie hurled himself into the water, paddling furiously to catch up to him. Reaching him, he grabbed his trunks and triumphantly dragged him back to shore, half drowning him in the process—but he had made his point: there

8 - THE PEACETIME AIR FORCE - PART III: 1934–1938

was to be *no* swimming on *his* watch.

When the time came to move back to Ottawa, Gus decided Brucie would have to remain behind. There were two reasons for this devastating news: first, he felt the dog, with his thick coat, would suffer too much in the summer heat of Ottawa; and second, there was a housing shortage in Ottawa and he had no idea where we were to live. Naturally, we were very upset by this decision and tears flowed, but Gus was adamant Brucie remain in Nova Scotia. He arranged with a sergeant who lived on McNab's Island in the harbour to take the dog to live with him there.

Off they went on the ferry to the island. To the sergeant's horror, Brucie jumped overboard and swam back to shore. Everyone was frantic with worry, but three days later, dirty and covered with burrs, he appeared at the kitchen door. How he had found his way home from the docks and through the downtown area always remained a mystery, but even his valiant effort to return home didn't weaken Gus's resolve and, heartbreaking though it was, he was sent off again, this time successfully, to live out his days in the outdoors on the island.

* * *

In 1937, Canada sent a contingent of 351 military and RCMP personnel to join thousands of their counterparts from all over the Empire to take part in the parade following the coronation of King George VI and Queen Elizabeth. The RCMP, RCN, and RCAF squads each consisted of about thirty members, with the army providing the balance. Gus commanded the RCAF contingent of eight officers and twenty-two other ranks, leaving Halifax on 11 April for two weeks' training at Camp Borden, then sailing from Montreal at the end of the month.[62]

The previous December, the abdication of Edward VIII, the enormously popular Prince of Wales, had thrown the British government and people into turmoil. There were those who thought it might be the end of the monarchy; others that his younger brother, the shy and retiring Duke of York, lacked the training for the position and was not "up to the job." History was to prove the naysayers wrong, but at the time the coronation provided a much-needed boost to the public morale. Hundreds of thousands lined the parade route to watch the pomp and pageantry, a superb spectacle of carriages, bands,

---

[62] Members of the contingent included: the commanders of the five senior non-permanent squadrons, two of whom were S/Ls W.A. Curtis and F.S. McGill; also Sgt. T.F. Cooper, the unfortunate recipient of Gus's push off the dock at Victoria Beach ten years earlier.

troops, and horses. Gus's handwritten letter to his mother not only reflects the mood of the time, but also his personal attachment to the monarchy and the pride he felt in his own achievements.

Royal Air Force Club,

Parade following the Coronation of King George VI, 12 May 1937. Gus is just visible leading the RCAF contingent, directly behind the RCMP.
Photo courtesy Glenn Curtis

8 - THE PEACETIME AIR FORCE - PART III: 1934–1938

> 128, Piccadilly, W. 1.
> 16/5
>
> My dear Mother,
>
> Well the show is over. It was the most gorgeous display I have ever seen or ever will see. I am writing a complete account of it & sending it . . . to Bea. We will send it on to you after.
>
> The King presented us with medals on the fourteenth. I saw them both with the two Princesses & the two Dukes. What a sight! We were at Buckingham Palace. Whatever may be said to the contrary, he is "every inch a King" & she "every inch a Queen."
>
> My thoughts turned to you Mother. How I wished that you could have been there to see it as I saw it all. My thoughts also went elsewhere: to Chorley; to the Hub; to the little back room in the house No.1 in the first row & I gave due & fervent thanks for my great fortune. For out of an Empire of over four hundred million people, there were only a few hundred similarly honoured. It is not often that I feel emotional but I do feel that: "the prayers of a righteous woman have availed much" . . .
>
> This morning is the first in a month that I have had a breather. I feel relieved that all has gone well. I have been complimented on all sides for our turn-out . . .[63]

What he failed to tell his mother, but laughingly told us, was how he had spent most of the parade trying to avoid stepping in the droppings from the RCMP horses and ruining his highly polished shoes.[64]

* * *

The Dartmouth Air Station began as a U.S. Naval Base in 1918 under the command of Richard E. Byrd, later famous as the admiral who led the expedition to the South Pole. It had been on a "care and maintenance" basis

---

[63] Chorley was his birthplace in England; "the Hub" was a district of Glace Bay, and "house No.1 in the first row" was the company house in which he lived growing up and working in the mine.

[64] After Gus attended the Imperial Conference, which followed the coronation, my recollection is that he spent a short time in Germany visiting Luftwaffe bases. Unfortunately, I have been unable to unearth any corroborating evidence to substantiate this childhood memory.

for several years and required upgrading from a strictly seaplane base to a fully operational unit including land-based aircraft. This upgrade was carried out under the Unemployment Relief Scheme.

The Scheme began in 1932 as a well-intentioned plan to house, clothe, and feed single homeless men during the Depression. Some projects evolved as the plan intended, while others did not, with disastrous results. The voluntary program paid men a meagre twenty cents per day to work at their own trades, and they were supposedly free to join or leave as they saw fit. In practice, however, this was not always the case. Some were forced to join or forfeit the benefits they received from the community in which they lived, while others might be dismissed if they brought forward a complaint.

In 1935, grievances at some remote camps in British Columbia led to strikes, which in turn developed into the On-to-Ottawa Trek, when thousands of the unemployed, led by Arthur (Slim) Evans, boarded freight trains to present their demands to the government for better wages and living conditions. Prime Minister Bennett ordered the march stopped in Regina and offered to meet with the leaders in Ottawa. Then, like the collapse of a house of cards, one event precipitated another. The meeting deteriorated into a shouting match that led to Bennett's decision to crush what he perceived to be a budding communist revolution. This led to the brutal attack by Regina police and the RCMP on 1,500 mostly local residents. They had gathered in support of the trekkers and the attack soon caused them to riot. All these events contributed to Bennett's defeat and the election of the Liberals under Mackenzie King.

In the case of Dartmouth, there appears to be only one reference to Gus's management of the Project:

> In addition to his duties as Sqr. Leader he has been in charge of U.E.R. Project No. 153 (Dartmouth Air Station) where his sound judgement and untiring energy have been the main factor in carrying on this work under considerable difficulties.[65]

"Considerable difficulties" were not defined, nor have statistics surfaced that could provide details as to the number of men employed, where they were housed, how they were treated, man hours worked etc. Some indication of the magnitude of the project is the amount of the increase in appropriations to the RCAF which resulted in expenditures of over $200,000 from 1934

---

[65] Annual Confidential Report dated 30 December 1935.

8 - THE PEACETIME AIR FORCE - PART III: 1934–1938

to 31 March 1938, and a further $410,000 the next fiscal year—enormous sums during the Depression. In addition to expanding the seaplane facilities, the funds were used to acquire land and construct runways, hangars, and buildings.[66]

Old meets new as Acadia Construction builds the Shearwater Airport in the winter of 1938. Oxen work alongside early cable-driven bulldozers and the first scraper used in Nova Scotia.

DND photo courtesy Shearwater Aviation Museum

* * *

Travel continued to occupy a considerable amount of Gus's time, as it had during the previous posting in Ottawa. He was constantly on the move with a host of different activities: the opening of Provincial Legislatures in Charlottetown or Fredericton, inspections of detachments, reconnaissance of the three Maritime provinces to select sites for the development of new aerodromes, and meetings in Ottawa, to say nothing of the trip overseas to the coronation. Out of the forty-three months spent in Nova Scotia, the time away from Halifax was an astonishing seven and half months. All this travel, together with his duties as CO of the Station and manager of the Relief Project, made for a heavy workload. But make no mistake, he revelled in it. Annual Reports repeatedly mention his eagerness to accept

---

[66] See Appendix A: *Halifax-Dartmouth and the Royal Canadian Air Force 1918–1939*.

new responsibilities and his seemingly boundless energy and enthusiasm to tackle the ever-increasing demands of his position.

No matter how much he enjoyed it all, it was just a matter of time before his body would rebel against the pace he set for himself. "The terrific stress and strain of dealing with relief projects" was the cause of his first attack of auricular fibrillation in August 1937, at the age of forty-four.[67] He was hospitalized for three weeks; other than rest, there seemed little or no treatment for the condition. Had the benefits of modern medicine been available, it could easily have been controlled with medication or a pacemaker, but such was not the case, and he would be incapacitated again and again in the years to come.

In February 1938, it was time once again to be posted back to headquarters in Ottawa, but not before one last swing from one end of Nova Scotia to the other to select the site of new aerodromes at Yarmouth, Sydney, Truro, and Westchester. All these trips were by train, but at the last one he found the road from the station to the site impassable by car due to a heavy snowfall. Undaunted, and in true pioneer spirit, he reached the site—by hiring a horse and sleigh.

* * *

The Ottawa we returned to in the spring of 1938 was a city of just under 200,000, double the size it had been when Bea was born there at the beginning of the century, but still not a large city. The housing shortage, which was to become so acute two years later, had begun to manifest itself, and there was great difficulty in finding a place to live. The search continued throughout the summer, but Bea, unable to find a suitable house, hit upon the next best thing: an upper duplex located at the end of Rideau Street just before it crossed the river. It suited our needs perfectly, and in September we finally settled in.

While the house hunting continued, we spent that summer, and three more to follow, at the cottage "up the Gatineau," local parlance for the Gatineau River and environs north of Ottawa. Along its banks as far up the line as Wakefield, the river was dotted with cottages, with our particular one located at Larrimac Links, a group of a dozen or so cottages with a nine-hole golf course. The cottage was newly built and we were its first occupants; but that did not mean it was blessed with mod-cons. There was no electricity, nor a

---

[67] Gus's description on a Medical Board Report of 25 July 1944.

8 - THE PEACETIME AIR FORCE - PART III: 1934–1938

Sandy at the cottage. 1938

telephone, nor indoor plumbing, but it did boast one luxury: the pump, rather than outdoors, was at the kitchen sink.

No sooner were we installed at the cottage than Bea and Gus left one morning and when they returned, out of the car sprang "Sandy," a two-year-old spaniel of somewhat questionable ancestry. They had picked him up from the Ottawa Humane Society in the hope he would fill the void created by Brucie's absence. Well, he did that in spades, for what an affectionate, clever dog he turned out to be. Like all dogs, he loved the country, but even the city didn't restrict his movements. When not lying on the back step surveying his kingdom, he followed us everywhere or roamed far and wide on his own. One day from the streetcar I even saw him trotting purposefully past the Château Laurier Hotel, apparently on his way to investigate the Parliament Buildings.

* * *

Gus was now stationed at headquarters as Senior Staff Officer, Air Personnel and Records, and this position did not entitle him to a batman or staff car; these perks would only return a few years later after several promotions. So, when not on leave in July, he would drive the family car into Ottawa each day. This was not today's pleasant, easy drive on a scenic parkway in an air-conditioned car, but rather a hot, tedious one over gravel roads or bumpy pavement eventually winding through the streets of Hull, which seemed to have a stop sign at every corner. But the drive was always worth it when he returned in the late afternoon for golf and a swim, or to sit on the verandah after dinner listening to the bullfrogs and whippoorwills during the long summer evenings.

It was here, too, that Gus taught Billy and me the fundamentals of golf.

Declaration of War. 10 September 1939
Courtesy of Historical Section, Department of Foreign Affairs and International Trade.

8 - THE PEACETIME AIR FORCE - PART III: 1934–1938

At the age of seven I received three wooden-shafted clubs that he had cut down for me: a putter, a brassie (my driver), and a mashie (my club for everything else). These I carried on my shoulder that first summer until the next Christmas, when I was given a small white canvas golf bag, which I proudly sported from then on.

Gus's teaching method was very basic: one was shown how to hold the club, how to swing it, instructed to count every stroke and not cheat, and then sent on one's way to discover for one's self the joys and sorrows of that most difficult and seductive of games. Golf balls were acquired by searching the rough. However, it did not take wise old Billy—now aged eleven—long to figure out an easier way than spending hours searching through long grass on a hot muggy day. He knew that, on one particular hole where Gus and his partners often had difficulty—with their drives falling short of the fairway and landing in a long gully—rather than waste time looking for the errant shots, or risk breaking a leg by descending into the gully, they would simply hit another. So, by positioning himself strategically in the gully behind some bushes, and waiting for their drives to fall virtually into his lap, my brother had an endless supply of golf balls.[68]

Like most cottagers, we returned to the city after Labour Day. Ottawa in 1938 was a slow-paced government town emerging from the Depression and gradually, if reluctantly, gearing up for the war.

On Saturdays we could accompany Gus on his rounds, which sometimes included Rockliffe Air Station, or the hardware store to surpass all hardware stores: Trudel's. Many an hour was spent watching with fascination as the Trudel sons reached the uppermost shelves by scrambling up ladders that rolled on tracks from one end of the store to the other; and all the while happily listening to Gus and Mr. Trudel discussing in great detail the merits of which fly, attached to which line, reel, and rod, would best attract which species of fish, under what climate condition.

---

[68] During those summers, G/C Lloyd S. Breadner (later Air Chief Marshal) was Gus's frequent golfing partner. The Breadner cottage was nearby at Kirk's Ferry, and there were many visits back and forth.

9

THE SECOND WORLD WAR - PART I
1939–1941

In the spring of 1939, as Hitler edged ever closer to war, King George VI and Queen Elizabeth, crowned just two years earlier, arrived in Canada for a countrywide tour. They travelled by train and at every stop were greeted by enormous crowds who gave them tumultuous receptions. It was to be the last truly formal royal tour, with the military often in full dress uniform, complete with swords and all the trappings.

Gus, by now the recognized expert in Drill and Ceremonial, was also known throughout the Service as always being impeccably turned out. Billy and I were quick to point out that his success in this area was due in no small measure to *our* efforts, as we were the ones in those years responsible for that famous "spit and polish"—Billy for polishing his shoes and I for the buttons.[69] Notwithstanding our contribution, he was the logical choice to be placed in charge of air force arrangements for the tour and also the Guard of Honour at Government House.

The plan was for the horse-drawn carriage carrying Their Majesties to stop outside the gates, the Guard to Present Arms, the band to play "God Save the King," and then the carriage to proceed slowly up the drive to Rideau Hall. Stands had been erected for spectators, and due to an old-fashioned dose of nepotism, we had seats there. Gus had been training the troops for some time and had himself been practising with his gloves on so as not to commit the cardinal sin of dropping his sword.

Excitement was intense when the great day finally arrived. The crowds lining Sussex Drive cheered and waved miniature Red Ensigns and Union

---

[69] Anyone who has ever polished brass buttons on a military uniform will remember "the stick," which allowed several buttons to be done at one time and also prevented the polish or the brush from touching the tunic—a truly marvellous invention.

9 - THE SECOND WORLD WAR - PART I: 1939–1941

Jacks as the carriage approached. Gus gave the command "Preeeesent Arms!" and the band struck up the Anthem. Apparently the details of the plan had never been made entirely clear to the horses, or they had failed to understand their orders fully, for rather than stopping sedately, they took the music as their cue to increase the pace. They then pranced merrily off through the gates and up the drive, leaving the Guard in their wake and Gus with his sword glistening in the sunlight, while the band played on.

* * *

As the inevitability of war became more and more apparent, we came back to Ottawa from the cottage earlier than usual, and spent a good deal of time huddled around the radio, which had been moved into the dining room because so many news broadcasts were at mealtimes. At the age of eight I listened to some of these, but of course had no conception of what it all meant; yet I can remember quite clearly hearing Britain's Prime Minister, Neville Chamberlain, on Sunday, the third of September, as he spoke the words: "I have to tell you now . . . this country is at war with Germany." That same day, Gus sent the following memo:

> *In the event it is decided to send an expeditionary force overseas, may I please place on record that I am ready and available.*

* * *

In 1938 the total strength of the RCAF was 2,510. Scarcely a year later, the figure had risen to 4,061, but was still a mere drop in the sea of volunteers that would flood recruiting centres after 10 September 1939, the day the Parliament of Canada declared war on Germany. By the time the war ended six catastrophic years later, the RCAF had become the fourth largest allied air force and a *quarter of a million* men and women had served in its ranks: 232,632 men and 17,032 women. Of the quarter of a million, 93,844 served overseas and 17,100 lost their lives.

The rapid increase in strength brought a corresponding rapid rise in rank for many of those Permanent Force officers who had been in the Service since its inception. In Gus's case, where it had taken ten long years from 1926 to 1936 to receive one promotion from squadron leader to wing commander, he received four in thirty-eight months: on 1 April 1939 to group captain; on 1 February 1940 to air commodore; on 5 August 1941 to air vice marshal;

and on 20 June 1942 to air marshal.

At the outbreak of war, Britain was in desperate need of trained air and ground crews to match the vastly superior numbers of those in the German Luftwaffe. It was to help remedy this situation that the British Commonwealth Air Training Plan was conceived, and in the autumn of 1939 its terms were negotiated in Ottawa by the UK, Australia, New Zealand, and Canada, with final agreement reached on 17 December. For a country the size of Canada with a population of just over eleven million, it was a mammoth undertaking to build and staff training schools of all types: Air Navigation, Air Observer, Bombing and Gunnery, Elementary Flying Training, Service Flying Training, Technical Training, Army Cooperation, Ground Instructional, Wireless, Air Armament, and General Reconnaissance.

By the time it ended, the cost was a staggering $2.2 billion, of which Canada contributed $1.6 billion and later caused Winston Churchill to describe it as Canada's greatest contribution to the Allied victory in World War II.

> During its five-year life, "The Plan" involved almost 360 units and schools operating from approximately 230 sites, not including relief airfields. "The Plan" exceeded expectations: 131,553 aircrew from four nations were trained as well as some 80,000 ground crew, including approximately 17,000 in the Women's Division. While the purposes and the glory of the "Plan" was training aircrew, this training could not have been carried out without the ground crew. It is generally conceded that it took ten persons on the ground to keep one in the air. The training of ground crew was just as rigorous as that of the air crew but generally less appreciated by the general population. Ground crew consisted of everything from aero engine mechanics (fitters) and air frame mechanics (riggers), instrument technicians, administration, vehicle mechanics and drivers to cooks, service police and some in other trades and occupations. More than 100 new airfields were built and many more vastly improved and expanded.
>
> In terms of manpower involved, deadlines met and financial expenditure, the building of "The Plan" exceeded the building of the CPR. It was an undertaking whose success was underpinned by Canadian contractors, flying clubs, other government agencies and the ordinary person in the street. After the war and even today "The Plan's" legacy serves Canada. The accomplishments were both numerous and impressive:

- Some 8,300 buildings were erected of which 701 were hangars or of a hangar-type construction; fuel storage totalling more than 26 million gallons installed;

- 300 miles of water mains and a similar length of sewer mains laid; involving two million cubic yards of excavation;

- 100 sewage treatment and disposal plants and 120 water pumping stations completed;

- Steam generation approached 80,000 horsepower; and

- More than 2,000 miles of main power lines and 535 miles of underground electrical cable placed, servicing a total connected electrical power load of over 80,700 horsepower.

When the war was over many of the training bases were converted to civilian use thus providing several more airfields than would have been the case had the BCATP not existed.

The training establishment changed the social and economic conditions in many communities forever. . . . Hundreds of BCATP buildings became community halls, hockey rinks, housing and business structures.

Because young men & women from all parts of Canada came together during training, it was probably one of the greatest unifying forces in our history.[70]

* * *

While the BCATP was in its formative stages another recruitment scheme, The Clayton Knight Committee, was designed to encourage and facilitate Americans' coming to Canada to join the RCAF.

---

[70] www.airmuseum.ca/bcatp. Reprinted with permission. The Commonwealth Air Training Plan Museum located at Brandon Airport MB is a National Historic Site. BCATP refers to the British Commonwealth Air Training Plan (later known as JATP—Joint Air Training Plan).

During the bitterly cold January of 1940, Gus's nephew Bobby stayed with us while taking elementary training in the RCAF. Each morning, he and I would leave the house at eight o'clock and walk down Rideau Street together until our paths diverged five blocks later: his to earn his coveted pilot's wings in one of the first classes of the BCATP and mine to grapple with the mysteries of fractions and long division in grade four at Holy Cross School.

When President Franklin Delano Roosevelt declared on 3 September 1939 that the United States would remain neutral, he neither expected nor demanded that "every American remain neutral in thought." "Even a neutral has a right to take account of facts," he declared in his "Fireside Chat" to the nation. "Even a neutral cannot be asked to close his mind or conscience." The direction in which the president would be led by his conscience was no mystery. He was unambiguously anti-fascist, pro-French, and pro-British, but he could not easily translate his private feelings into public policy. Besides the significant opposition to American belligerency throughout the country, not the least in Congress, there were also those who did not agree that the preservation of the United States and its values depended upon an Allied victory. Roosevelt could, at best, hope only to make American neutrality as benevolent to the British and French as possible.

Other Americans, some perhaps no more than adventurers, some truly concerned about the survival of democratic values, had their own way of demonstrating their support for the Allies. Following in the footsteps of the thousands of US nationals who volunteered to fight against Germany in the First World War (including some 1,500 in the British flying services), recruits began to move north across the border into Canada shortly after the dominion declared war. The existence of this potential source of manpower for the RCAF and RAF had been recognized before the war, in particular by W.A. Bishop, the Canadian First World War fighter ace. Convinced there would be no problem with the numbers who would come forward, Bishop was concerned primarily with tapping the American talent pool as efficiently as possible without violating US law which forbade the recruiting of Americans into foreign armed forces. However, when a visit to the White House in March 1939 left him with the impression that these legal barriers might not be unsurmountable, Bishop began to work on problems of organization and administration.[71]

---

[71] William Avery (Billy) Bishop VC, CB, DSO and Bar, MC, DFC, ED, Légion d'Honneur and Croix de Guerre, was the Canadian hero who shot down seventy-two German aircraft (twenty-five of which occurred during twelve combat days) in the First World War. In 1938 he was appointed an honorary air marshal in the RCAF and head of the Air Advisory Board. From January 1940 until 1944 he worked tirelessly as director of recruiting, thereby making an enormous contribution to the RCAF and the nation's war effort.

Hon. Ian Mackenzie was Minister of National Defence from 23 October 1935 to 18 September 1939.

9 - THE SECOND WORLD WAR - PART I: 1939–1941

At some point—the date is not clear—Bishop contacted Homer Smith, a Canadian veteran of the Royal Naval Air Service who had fallen heir to an oil fortune, obtaining his promise of financial backing. Bishop also spoke to Clayton Knight, an American aviation artist who had flown with the British on the Western Front in the First World War. With his broad ties to the US flying fraternity, Knight would be a valuable asset in public relations work and in ascertaining the current of American opinion. Given the likelihood of an enthusiastic response, the three agreed, it would be important to impose order by screening all applicants before channelling them across the border.

On 4 September 1939, the day after Great Britain declared war and six days before Canada followed suit, Bishop telephoned Clayton Knight, who was attending the Cleveland air races, advising him that it was time to begin work. Despite the warning of his dinner companion, Ohio attorney general Thomas J. White, that a scheme to "smuggle" pilots to Canada was unquestionably illegal, Knight found general enthusiasm for the idea among his colleagues but cautioned Bishop that it would be wise to undertake a more general survey of opinion among American airmen before making any commitments. On 9 September defence minister Ian Mackenzie granted Homer Smith a commission as a wing commander in the RCAF, and charged him with responsibility for Knight's survey. Shortly thereafter Smith rented a suite of rooms at the Waldorf Astoria Hotel in New York as his main base, and then accompanied Clayton Knight on a tour of American flying schools.

The enthusiasm for the project displayed by Bishop, Smith, Knight (and perhaps by Ian Mackenzie) was not matched by official Ottawa. The government wished to avoid any activity which might embarrass President Roosevelt and, apart from Smith's appointment and some "cloak-and-daggerish" communications between Knight and "Mrs. Bishop" and "Mr. P. Jones" (the code name for Group Captain Harold Edwards, the RCAF's senior personnel staff officer), the Department of National Defence remained steadfastly aloof.

Throughout the period of the "Phoney War" there was still no sense of urgency in Air Force Headquarters about securing the services of American Flyers. . . .

The air battles that followed the German assault on France in May 1940 changed everything. The development of the BCATP was accelerated, creating a dire shortage of flying instructors in the dominion especially those with experience on twin-engined aircraft. Called to a special meeting of the Air Council, along with representatives of Canada's major airlines, Smith and Knight listened quietly as the air staff was informed that perhaps two dozen instructors could be made available from Canadian sources. They then broke the silence that followed this sombre disclosure with the announcement that they already had a list of 300 Americans, experienced pilots all, who were eager to come to Canada. Sceptical at first, the air staff eventually accepted this solution, and the Clayton Knight Committee was born. Its instructions were simple: to find qualified American pilots and direct them to Canada once it was settled that such activities would not upset the United States government. . . .

All the State Department asked was that US nationals not be forced to swear an oath of allegiance that would forfeit their citizenship. The Canadian Privy Council waived this requirement, substituting an oath of obedience to senior officers; then, in November, it was agreed that Americans in all British Commonwealth forces should have the right to transfer to their own services should the United States become a belligerent. . . .

By September 1940, 197 civilian pilots had been sent to Canada and accepted for service. . . By the end of the year the number of volunteers accepted by Canadian authorities had reached 321 . . .[72]

The significance of the Clayton Knight Committee's recruiting activities is told partially by statistics. According to its own estimates, the committee dealt with some 49,000 Americans, and by February 1942 had sent 900 experienced aircrew and 1,450 trainees, most with some aviation experience, to the RCAF.[73] An

---

[72] W.A.B. Douglas, *The Creation of a National Air Force Volume II*, Appendix C, pp. 632–5.

[73] One of these trainees was P/O John G. Magee Jr., the author of *High Flight*.

additional 300 pilots were sent to Canada for the RAF, and a few dozen more had been posted to flying schools in the United States before assignment to Britain. Perhaps more significantly, there were the hundreds of civilian flying instructors and staff pilots who allowed the BCATP to operate at greater capacity much sooner than anticipated.[74]

It would take some time before the Plan would start to produce the trained aircrews Britain needed so desperately. By mid-1940 she was fighting for her very survival, in danger of being overwhelmed by the force of the German attack. Dauntless in her determination to resist, somehow she managed to survive each crisis as it arose: the defeat of her army on the Continent and the evacuation from Dunkirk in June; the imminent threat of invasion during the summer; the Battle of Britain from July to October; and finally, the Blitz on London and other cities in the months that followed.

* * *

Added to the complexities of absorbing the Americans into the RCAF without violating United States neutrality were Gus's responsibilities, as the Air Member for Personnel, for solving the other myriad problems that arose from the influx of recruits into the BCATP. A memo recommending his promotion to Air Commodore in the winter of 1940 lists these responsibilities:

> An extremely efficient staff Officer. He is head of the personnel staff, a member of the Air Council, responsible for Manning of the Air Force, discipline, Pay, medical, chaplain services, appointments, promotions, retirements, postings, supervision of the Reserve, compilation of personnel Staff estimates and control of supervision of Divisional Appropriations.[75]

Even though Gus drew executives from all walks of life into the Service to help manage this growth, the enormity of the workload required long

---

[74] W.A.B. Douglas, *The Creation of a National Air Force Volume II*, Appendix C, p. 641.

[75] Undated memo from A/V/M/ G. M. Croil, CAS to the Minister of National Defence—approval date stamped 4 April 1940 but retroactive to 1 February 1940. Just in case that wasn't enough to do, he was also appointed president of the General Dress and Clothing Committee and, on 14 September 1940, Honorary Aide de Camp to the Governor General—a post he relinquished in November 1941 when posted overseas.

hours at the office and, together with trips to stations, recruiting centres, and the United States, had a predictable effect on his health. As he continued to suffer attacks of auricular fibrillation, cardiac specialists in Toronto and Montreal were consulted, both of whom prescribed the same medication, and which apparently provided only limited relief. Not surprisingly, in mid-October of 1940, he was ordered to take a month's sick leave; but the leave was mixed with duties, as this memo from the CAS to the Minister shows:

1. As you are aware, a semi-official recruiting organization has been established in the United States. It is becoming increasingly apparent that, in order to place this organization on an efficient basis, it should be inspected and re-organized by a senior R.C.A.F. officer familiar with all aspects of our requirements.

2. Moreover, there is a decided danger of subversive elements being taken into the R.C.A.F. from the same source, and the need for a definite and close liaison with the F.B.I. in Washington to counteract such activities has been indicated for sometime.

3. Action on these important questions has been delayed until an appropriate occasion presented itself. Air Commodore Edwards has been ordered on one month's sick leave by the Director of Medical Services, and he intends to convalesce in the Southern States during this period. Air Commodore Edwards is the logical officer to undertake the duties contemplated, and it has occurred to me that it would be of mutual advantage to himself and the Service if he could carry out this work during the time of the sick leave in question.

4. I have discussed this matter with Edwards and he has agreed to the arrangement, and it is, therefore, recommended for approval in principle.

5. Subject to authority being given, it is proposed to have Flight Lieutenant E.T. Atherton, who is the officer directly concerned with anti-subversive activities in the R.C.A.F., meet with Air Commodore Edwards at Washington when the consultations with the F.B.I. have been arranged.[76]

---

[76] Memo of 18 October 1940 from A/V/M/ L.S. Breadner, CAS, to the Minister of National Defence for Air.

9 - THE SECOND WORLD WAR - PART I: 1939–1941

Because of the secrecy surrounding the operation, it is difficult to establish the exact dates of the meetings in New York and Washington. However, what is clear is that he and Bea left Ottawa by car in mid-October and returned on 20 November. During that time, official duties were intermingled with leave. While in New York, they stayed at the Waldorf Astoria, the Committee Headquarters, saw Broadway shows, and attended a luncheon at Homer Smith's house in New Jersey. It was a rather large party and Bea, introduced to a number of people one after the other, didn't hear all the names properly. It was only *after* lunch that she was stunned to learn she had been seated next to the author Somerset Maugham during lunch. He, on the other hand, when asked by his host how he had enjoyed talking to Mrs. Edwards, replied, "Charming, absolutely delightful, never once asked me about my books!" Then it was off to spend two weeks as guests of the Smiths in Palm Beach.

* * *

Back in Canada and the realities of the war, Gus resumed his frantic pace in an effort to keep up with the heavy workload. His reputation as a controversial figure in the RCAF may have had its roots in a decision he made several months later: to eliminate racism from the enlistment policy of the Special Reserve. In 2006, a researcher at DND wrote,

> The research I was conducting related to racism in the enlistment policies of the three services during the Second World War. The policy of the RCAF was to exclude individuals who were not white; the regulations requiring that enlistees be of "pure European descent." In April 1941 your father became aware of this policy and started the process to change this, apparently on his own initiative. Regrettably, the policy change did not get beyond the Privy Council Office, and was thereby not implemented until much later.
>
> Considering the culture within the RCAF towards Blacks and Orientals, the stand taken by your father is quite remarkable. That he was able to convince others within the higher echelons of the RCAF of the need to change the policy attests to his integrity and

foresight, not to mention the fact that he apparently objected to this racist policy and was willing to take a stand.[77]

Perhaps the best description of those times is contained in two documents. The first is a letter Gus wrote to G/C Wilfred A. Curtis on 15 May 1941, following Curtis's departure from headquarters to command No. 2 Service Flying Training School at Uplands. In it he also reveals the great respect he has for Curtis's abilities and his "hope and plan" that they will have the opportunity of working together in the future.[78]

> My dear Wilf,
>
> Thank you for your letter. You always remember. I am sorry that I could not have been with you on Sunday although I thought of you and your command a great deal. Your drumhead service, by the look of the programme, must have been very impressive.
>
> Before I came down here, I gave you my material token of respect, gratitude and appreciation. Today my thoughts reach a little higher and rise, perhaps, to loftier levels. Our friendship has never been in question; our Service associations sprung queerly out of Borden in 1921, the Flying Clubs (which I never liked) and, finally, the Auxiliary Air Force and the Coronation.
>
> Together, for the past fifteen months, we have lived; worked; and striven. We have lost, won, compromised, failed, achieved and conquered. You and I, equally alike, have faced adversity, difficulty and, occasionally tragedy. Under this heavy load, there have been faltering hearts and worn-out nerves, but there has been no quivering of the spirit; no urge to quit.
>
> Many long days have gone by since you left me; many things, many

---

[77] Letter of 11 October 2006 from Major M. Joost, Department of History and Heritage, Canadian Department of National Defence. Paragraph 184 of Major Joost's report reads: "The situation was to change dramatically on 31 March 1942. On that date the RCAF issued an order that removed all restrictions on aircrew and groundcrew enlistments for the Special Reserve. The results were to be fairly dramatic, as members of visible minority groups began to be enlisted at ever increasing rates." Reprinted with permission.

[78] The "plan" definitely materialized, as Curtis would serve as DAOC-in-C with Gus in London from 1941–43. Curtis later went on to become Chief of the Air Staff from 1947–53 with the rank of Air Marshal.

events, many changes, have occurred; changes which show me the great value that you were to me...

One day I hope and plan that our courses will cross and join again. This war will end in time but, before it does, I do hope that we shall again be united, to think and do as we have done heretofore.

This Air Force, and this country, can but be proud of the product of your mind, heart and hands.

The second is a memo sent to the CAS on 5 June seeking permission to visit England to resolve with Air Ministry and RAF officials:

[A] number of things effecting [sic] my Division which require immediate settlement:

(a) administration and disciplinary aspect of R.C.A.F. Squadrons,
(b) personnel requirements for the 25 squadrons in process of formation,
(c) the Women's Active Auxiliary for the R.C.A.F.
(d) commissioning of the 17% of the Canadian products of the J.A.T.P. who have proceeded overseas, which seems to have bogged down,
(e) the interchange of the R.C.A.F. and R.A.F. personnel from the special schools in Canada,
(f) interpretation of the Visiting Forces Act which, from the queries received from overseas, seems to be a very obscure subject there,
(g) establishment of the records office,
(h) disciplinary control of J.A.T.P. graduates overseas,
(i) documentation and nominal rolls of drafts—incoming and outgoing.

At the end of June he was off to England and remained there almost a month, returning on 25 July. Despite the travails, another letter to Curtis shows that his sense of humour was still very much intact.

London, England,
July 4th, 1941.

My dear Wilf,

Thanks indeed for your "Bon Voyage" gift. It certainly helped to while away many of what otherwise would have been monotonous hours en route. As indicated, the trip by reason of your generosity was pleasant but uneventful.

There were only one or two small incidents—at Montreal I had to make a quick change from the Ottawa 'plane to the Liberator, and en route I overlooked the fact that oxygen was a necessity.

If you ever have the good fortune to be assigned to here I recommend this mode of transportation as it certainly cuts down the distance and prevents the submarines from getting a crack at you. Under present conditions it is not the most comfortable method as they pile in all sorts of baggage and the crew use your stomach as a stepping-stone to get from one part of the aircraft to another.

We are stopping at the Dorchester and while the service is good it is most expensive. However, we have hopes that the travelling allowance will cover. . . .

In the event, "immediate settlement" of some issues in his memo proved to be as elusive and slippery as quicksilver. Most would gradually be resolved in the coming months. However, the staffing of the twenty-five squadrons would prove to be the most elusive of all, consume an inordinate amount of time and energy, and only come close to resolution three long, arduous years later.

* * *

In the midst of all this activity, one day I found myself outside Gus's office in the Jackson Building on Bank Street.[79] It was a hot day and I deemed it a perfect opportunity to obtain the five cents needed to purchase an ice cream cone, so in I went.

---

[79] The summer of either 1940 or 1941—I was nine or ten.

"I'd like to see my daddy, please," I politely informed the corporal on duty.

"And who might your daddy be?" he asked, equally politely, and not unkindly.

"Air Commodore Edwards," I replied.

"Right," said the corporal, running his finger down a directory and picking up the telephone with his other hand.

Of course I heard only one side of the conversation which went something like this: "The Air Commodore's daughter is here and would like to see him . . . [pause] . . . yes, that's what I said, his *daughter* . . . [pause] . . . I know . . . [long, long pause] . . . very well."

This delightful man then told me to go up the stairs, giving me careful instructions as to how to reach Gus's office. I was greeted by his astonished secretary, who suggested I sit down and wait for a moment—presumably while she figured out what on earth to do with me. After a few minutes, while I sat swinging my legs, which did not quite reach to the floor, she knocked on his door and a murmured conversation took place. It was only then that it became clear why she had been so reluctant to act earlier: he was in the middle of a meeting with four other officers. With their backs to the door, their heads swung around in unison as I was ushered in. Gus, facing the door, was leaning back in his chair, looking at me, his eyes dancing with amusement.

"Well now, Sweetie, what brings you here?" he asked.

"Well, Daddy, I need five cents for an ice cream cone."

"Do you now; and what happened your allowance?"

"Oh, that—I *spent* that," I replied, dismissing out of hand his suggestion there was a connection between my weekly allowance of ten cents and this particular request.

"I see," he said, slowly reaching into his pocket and choosing a five-cent piece from a handful of change.

"Well, there you are; now off you go."

"Thanks, Daddy!" and off I went, down the stairs, past the grinning corporal.

Whatever possessed me to do such a thing is hard to imagine, and a few days later Bea, gently but firmly, made it quite clear that going to Daddy's office had not been the *best* idea I'd ever had, and it would be just as well not to do it again.

* * *

Even with all the stresses of the war, Gus somehow managed to spend some time with the family, and while he may have been an easy mark for a child's ice cream cone, such was not the case if bad behaviour were involved. The example that always sticks in my mind is the tennis incident.

One day while being badly outplayed by my opponent on the tennis court, I put on a disgraceful display of temper. Gus, who until then had never seen me play, unfortunately chose that exact moment to see how I was progressing. Retribution was swift. In seconds I was off the court, and not permitted to play again for a week. This disastrous piece of news was accompanied by a stern lecture on sportsmanship and winning and losing with grace, ending with the dictum that if I couldn't abide by those rules then I was not to play at all. I believe I was paroled after two or three days, but by that time the lesson had been well and truly learned.

There are much more pleasant memories of his participation in a miniature version of the game, i.e. table tennis. This took place in the "trunk room," which was located on the top floor of the house, and, as its name implied, was the storage place for all shapes and sizes of trunks, some filled with those famous curtains "to fit any window in Canada." These were arrayed down both sides of the attic with the sloping roof providing only minimal overhead clearance in the middle where the table was set up. The whole family often participated in sets of doubles, which were invariably interrupted at some point by a curse and a cry of pain from Gus as he hit his head on one of the exposed beams.

The other favourites were backgammon, poker dice, twenty questions, charades (at which Billy was particularly adept), and most loved of all, table hockey. There are a number of versions of this game but ours featured a board whose high point was at centre ice and then sloped gently down on either side towards each net. A little silver ball represented the puck and because of the design of the goalie "stick," it was maddeningly difficult to keep the ball out of the net. These were spirited, high-scoring games when shouts of joy from one player were greeted by groans from the other as the score seesawed back and forth—and naturally we played for the Stanley Cup.

* * *

After accompanying the Duke of Kent on his cross-country tour in the summer of 1941, at the end of October Gus flew once more to Washington. A flurry of activity followed as he prepared to take up his appointment in

9 - THE SECOND WORLD WAR - PART I: 1939–1941

Arrival of HRH The Duke of Kent in Canada. Summer 1941
The Evening Citizen, Ottawa

London as Air Officer Commanding, RCAF Overseas. The house was full of people coming and going, suitcases everywhere, the telephone constantly ringing as plans were changed and then changed again—a chaotic time, to be sure. Billy came home from boarding school for the weekend of 2 November, and on Sunday there was a surprise "special treat" for us: lunch in what was then the main dining room of the Château Laurier Hotel. Gus's farewell letter to his mother reveals what he thinks awaits him:

> I go to command all the Canadian airmen in England. From the little back room in No1 Hub to that post is a very long way.
>
> But although my station is high & my spirit & courage higher I am not unmindful of the task that faces me. There will be danger but I am not unaccustomed to that. . . . There will be problems to face that I have seldom faced before: there will be battles to fight the like of which I have never heretofore contemplated. There

will be matching of wits and a front to put on. The cost in money will tax my meagre resources for governments seldom compensate their servants. There will be great jealousy & a measure of hate from among my enemies of whom, I am thankful, I have many: for most men are made by their enemies. But as I told you when I took on my present appointment "such are the penalties on them that rise." I may fail (may God grant that I don't!) & if I do it will not be in consequence of a faltering effort or a baseless conscience. It will not be for want of heart or courage or any of the human things I have striven so hard throughout my life to understand and achieve, but rather, defeat if it comes shall be laid across the threshold of the door which opens and discloses the frailties of human beings.

The future is uncertain: the past is clear. Whatever success may follow my path, whatever achievements may be possible, whatever good may rise out of the welter of uncertainty, there is one single answer: your help & guidance now bears fruit. . . .[80]

Fearing bad weather over the North Atlantic would delay his departure, Gus booked passage on the Pan-American Airways flying boat or "clipper" service from New York to Lisbon, but this was cancelled as "circumstances beyond my control necessitate travel Ferry Command." On the evening of 3 November he gave a fifteen-minute broadcast over the CBC and the next day boarded the aircraft—giving us the "thumbs-up" sign from his seat by the window as it turned to taxi down the runway. His fear that weather would delay the trip proved prophetic. The events of the next two months can best be described by a series of signals, the first of which was sent on 10 November from Gander to Ottawa:

ATTENTION W/C MACKELL. PLEASE TRANSMIT FOLLOWING MESSAGE SIGNED GUS TO THE MINISTER DEPUTY MINISTER CHIEF OF AIR STAFF AIR MEMBERS OF COUNCIL AND MRS EDWARDS QUOTE SITTING UNQUOTE.

After languishing in Gander, he considered returning to Montreal and

---

[80] Handwritten letter dated 27 October 1941.

9 - THE SECOND WORLD WAR - PART I: 1939–1941

taking the clipper, but finally the weather broke, and on Friday, 21 November, to the CAS:

> NOW INFORMED THAT FERRY AIRCRAFT WILL ARRIVE ON SUNDAY CONSEQUENTLY CONSIDER IT WISER TO REMAIN HERE AND PROCEED WITH IT. IN CASE MISCARRIAGE OF PLANS HOLD RESERVATIONS ON CLIPPER IF MADE. ALSO PLEASE ENSURE THAT FERRY AIRCRAFT COMING ON SUNDAY IS EMPTY AS THIS PLACE IS JAMMED FULL OF PEOPLE AWAITING TRANS/ATLANTIC TRANSPORTATION.

On 9 December, having arrived in England on 22 November:

> SECRET. TO MINISTER OF NATIONAL DEFENCE FOR AIR REPEAT TO DEPUTY MINISTER CHIEF OF THE AIR STAFF AND MRS. EDWARDS. I HAVE BEEN DOWN FOR THE COUNT FOR THE PAST WEEK WITH THE FLU BUT WITH THE HELP OF MILD STIMULANT I AM NOW BUBBLING TO THE SURFACE. EVERYTHING IS SHAPING UP. WE HAVE ACQUIRED A NEW BUILDING. WE HAVE ALL BEEN RECEIVED WITH OPEN ARMS AND ALTHOUGH THE JOURNEY ACROSS REMINDED ME MORE OF PAUL REVERE THE RIDE FROM NOW ON SHOULD WELL BEFIT THE OLD COWHAND.[81]

On 15 December:

> SECRET. BREADNER FROM CURTIS. ALTHOUGH THERE IS NO CAUSE FOR ALARM I DO THINK YOU SHOULD KNOW THE FULL PARTICULARS OF THE CONDITION OF AIR VICE MARSHAL EDWARDS. HE ARRIVED IN THIS COUNTRY COMPLETELY EXHAUSTED NO DOUBT REACTION FROM THE EFFECTS OF THE LAST TWO TO THREE YEARS PLUS A SLIGHT ILLNESS AT GANDER AND FINALLY THE DIFFICULTIES OF THE TRANS-ATLANTIC CROSSING. ON ADVISE HE WENT TO

---

[81] The RCAF offices moved from the Sun Life Building on Cockspur Street (Canadian Military HQ) to 20 Lincoln's Inn Fields.

QZ—secret evacuation point from London:
Foxley Mansion, Mansell Lacy, Herefordshire.
RCAF photo courtesy John Smith

Q.Z. ARRIVING THERE ON THE NIGHT OF DECEMBER FIRST AND THAT NIGHT WAS STRICKEN WITH A BAD CASE OF 'FLU AND INTERCOSTAL NEURALGIA THERE WAS EVIDENCE OF INCIPIENT PNEUMONIA WHICH FORTUNATELY DID NOT DEVELOP. LOCAL AIR FORCE MEDICAL PERSONNEL INCLUDING DAY AND NIGHT NURSES PHYSIOTHERAPISTS AND SPECIALIST OFFICERS WERE CALLED AND IN ATTENDANCE WITH ALL MEDICAL EQUIPMENT. HOSPITALIZATION WAS DISCUSSED BUT WAS CONSIDERED AN UNWISE RISK TO MOVE HIM ALSO HIS PERSONAL ACCOMMODATION AT Q.Z. WAS BETTER THAN COULD BE PROVIDED IN HOSPITAL. SQUADRON LEADER OSBORNE WAS DESPATCHED FROM HEADQUARTERS. RECOVERY WAS FAIRLY RAPID BUT UNFORTUNATELY A RELAPSE TOOK PLACE ON THE SIXTH. IMPROVEMENT THEREAFTER CONTINUED UNTIL THE NIGHT OF THE THIRTEENTH WHEN A FURTHER SLIGHT SET-BACK TOOK PLACE. IT IS ANTICIPATED THAT WITHIN ANOTHER TEN DAYS

9 - THE SECOND WORLD WAR - PART I: 1939–1941

TO TWO WEEKS HE WILL RETURN TO DUTY. GROUP CAPTAIN HUNTER IS ALSO IN ATTENDANCE. HE HAS BEEN PUT ON A STRICT DIET OF MILK EGGS AND FRESH VEGETABLES OF WHICH THERE IS A SUPPLY ON THE HOME FARM OF Q.Z.[82]

On 28 December in a letter to his mother:

I wrote you from London. Since then I have been ill: not so ill as to cause any alarm, but feeling awfully miserable. I have been in bed for three weeks. In my letter I told you I could not describe the place in which I lived but since then I have managed to write a bit about it which I hope you will like. I am attaching it to this letter. I have given a copy to the people who own the place and they love it.[83]

We had a lovely Christmas. Nine officers came down. We got a turkey and a Christmas tree & we decorated it with the tinsil [sic] out of cigarette packets. Drink is scarce but we managed to get enough to go round. Among the officers who came down was Carlton Coffey—Bea's brother. It was nice to see him. . . .

* * *

As he recuperated at QZ, little was going well in the execution of the war, with British forces suffering defeat after disastrous defeat. The capture of Hong Kong, where Canadian troops of the Winnipeg Grenadiers and the Quebec Royal Rifles had been sent in a hopeless attempt to shore up its defences, was a snapshot of Japanese military successes in the Pacific. After occupying a good part of China in the late 1930s, they had experienced victory after victory in quick succession as they invaded and overran Burma, Thailand, and Malaya. With Western Europe occupied by the Germans and the Luftwaffe continuing its bombing offensive in England, the one military bright spot for the British was in North Africa where its Eighth Army relieved the garrison at Tobruk, which had been under siege

---

[82] Q.Z. was the code name for a secret location in Herefordshire that had been requisitioned to serve as the evacuation point for the Canadian forces stationed in London. The RCAF was assigned a section of the area that included a large house located at Mansell Lacy, about seven miles northwest of the city of Hereford.

[83] He is referring here to an essay he wrote entitled "The Old Crooked Ceiling."

by Rommel's Afrika Corps.

But December proved to be a pivotal month in the war. In Eastern Europe, Soviet forces, which were unprepared for, and initially overwhelmed by, the ferocity of the German attack begun the previous June, finally halted the advance on the outskirts of Moscow, and the Japanese attack on Pearl Harbour on 7 December brought the United States into the war.[84] With the US and the USSR now partners in the Allied cause, the tide began to turn, but at the end of 1941 victory was still nearly four agonizing years in the future.

RCAF Overseas Headquarters, 20 Lincoln's Inn Fields, London.
Strength, All Ranks: 166 (not all present). January 1942
RCAF photo courtesy Glenn Curtis

---

[84] The son of the Japanese Ambassador to Canada was a Grade 6 classmate of the author's. He was last seen at school on Friday, 5 December. He returned to Japan with his parents the following Monday, the day after the attack.

10

THE SECOND WORLD WAR - PART II
CANADIANIZATION

Under Article XV of the original British Commonwealth Air Training Plan, of which the United Kingdom and Canada were signatories in 1939, twenty-five overseas squadrons were to be formed with RCAF aircrews. Often referred to as "the Article XV squadrons," in June 1942 their number was increased to thirty-five, with a further provision to gradually replace RAF ground personnel in these squadrons with RCAF personnel. The term "Canadianization" came into being to describe the government's administrative policy to create these RCAF squadrons, post Canadians to them, and, in Bomber Command at least, see to it that as far as possible they served under a Canadian command structure—No.6 (Bomber) Group. It also embraced the notion that Canadian rules and regulations regarding promotion, for example, would be enforced no matter where individuals were serving.

Several years into the war, only forty percent of RCAF personnel serving overseas were required for the Article XV squadrons. Considering the thousands of RCAF personnel who served overseas in RAF squadrons, it is difficult to understand why these goals could not be met without acrimony, but such was not the case, and Gus's attempts to do so became a *cause célèbre* in Canada. What follows is an overview of the opposing views held, and hotly debated, on this subject. These differing opinions provide background for the chronicle of events in succeeding chapters. The first is from *The Official History of the RCAF*.[85]

---

[85] This section summarizes the account of Canadianization in Chapters 2 & 3 of *The Official History of the Royal Canadian Air Force Volume III, The Crucible of War 1939–1945* by Brereton Greenhous, Stephen J. Harris, William C. Johnston, and William G. P. Rawling (Toronto: University of Toronto Press in cooperation with the Department of National Defence and the Canadian Government Publishing Centre, Supply and Services Canada, 1994). The full story of Gus's struggles with the British Air Min-

Gus, with his wide range of experience in administration, his concern for the welfare of both officers and other ranks, and certainly his forceful personality, was the best choice to command the RCAF overseas and to see that the terms of the BCATP were carried out. Before leaving for London, he and his deputy, A/C W.A. Curtis, were told by the Minister of National Defence for Air, the Hon. C.G. Power, in no uncertain terms to "put the RCAF on the map" and "to get as many squadrons as possible complete with Canadian aircrew and Canadian officers."

When Gus arrived in England at the end of November 1941, the first thing he did was to meet with all the officers and let them know how HQ was to be run under his command. He informed Ottawa:

> I found the place, to be quite honest with you, as dead as a doornail, everyone complaining that they had nothing to do, but nobody doing anything about it. In fact, I am pretty disgusted with the whole thing . . .
>
> The discipline of the place is lousy. The men are turned out in a frightful manner. Nobody seems to give a goddam whether the ship sinks or swims, but above all, I found that everyone was diametrically opposed to all the policies emanating from Canada.
>
> I got all the officers together the moment I appeared in the office, and for the first time in my life I felt I was in a hostile atmosphere, but I do think that when I had finished with them, they were more friendly disposed, and could see the light as I wished them to see it.
>
> As far as our troops in the RAF are concerned, I find that they are being dispersed all over Hell's half acre, without restraint. The officers that we have put in the posting departments have apparently, due to poor direction, just let the thing slide, and have done little towards concentrating our troops into Canadian squadrons . . .

The reality in England was in stark contrast to the apparent simple orders issued by the Minister. Soon after their arrival, the British Air Ministry was

---

istry and the RAF in England, the Chief of the Air Staff of the RCAF, Air Marshal Lloyd S. Breadner, and the Minister of National Defence for Air, Hon. Charles G. Power in Ottawa, is told in that volume. All quotations in this section are from chapters 2 and 3 of the above-referenced work and are reprinted with permission of the Department of National Defence.

made aware of the importance of the Canadianization issue by Curtis:

> Definite instructions have been received at this Headquarters from RCAF Headquarters, Ottawa, to the effect that action is to be taken to ensure that the personnel comprising aircrews of all RCAF squadrons, is to be made completely Canadian as rapidly as possible.

It was difficult to pinpoint exactly who was responsible for the lack of progress. By June of 1941, despite the fact that 10,000 Canadian aircrew had arrived in the United Kingdom, the Air Ministry maintained it was impossible to do more than form twenty-one nominally RCAF squadrons while, at the same time, posting Canadians to thirty-nine new RAF squadrons. The Air Ministry had certainly made RAF command aware of the requirement to form RCAF squadrons, but aircrew had first to be posted to RAF Advanced Flying Units (AFUs) and then to Operational Training Units (OTUs), where crews were formed and posted to squadrons. One would think, then, those in command of the OTUs were the culprits; but things could go awry anywhere in the system, prompting Gus to send one of his more colourful signals to Ottawa: "I find myself in a state that I want to get at somebody's liver, fry it and jam it down his neck, but for the moment I cannot get my hands on the proper person."

Power, however, thought the fault lay with the Air Ministry, and was prepared to embarrass it by bringing the matter up in the House of Commons and publicize it in the press, but Gus was not convinced the Air Ministry alone was at fault. He was certainly not in favour of breaking up established crews, but finding the cause continued to elude him, and he proposed two solutions, the latter a radical one:

> I am putting officers in each command to watch postings . . .
>
> I cannot get to the root of the trouble. The Air Ministry is most co-operative but people in the field do not or will not realise the importance of the matter. The Air Ministry has sent and continues to send strong letters to commands. If I cannot make a more satisfactory report by March 1st I shall be prepared to recommend that the RCAF be withdrawn from Air Ministry control and that we organize our own air force, the Joint Air Training Plan notwithstanding.

Gus's attempts to convince senior RAF officers of the justice of his case often fell on deaf ears and, in some cases, were met with indifference or even disdain. He felt this was particularly true after a heated argument with A/M Sholto Douglas, C-in-C Fighter Command and A/M Trafford Leigh-Mallory of No.11 Group.

While acutely aware that he was powerless to effect change to a system totally controlled by the RAF, he was not going to give up the fight. He even suggested he be given a seat on the British Air Council, but this suggestion was met with shock by the British, and quickly quashed by Ottawa, presumably in case the British would want a reciprocal arrangement in Ottawa.

At the end of March, he vented his frustration in a signal to the CAS, A/M Breadner:

> As far as my own position is concerned, in spots it is ludicrous, for although we are breaking in everywhere we can and taking control wherever we can, I have no command whatsoever except the handful of men at Headquarters. It just means this, that I, or the man who may replace me, will get tired of breaking his way in, with the consequent nuisance and unpopularity.

His determination to soldier on is evident when he tells Power: ". . . [but] whatever difficulties may be presented, or whatever opposition, personal or otherwise, I shall inevitably meet with, you may rest assured that I will go ahead even if it brings about my social, if not my official, utter damnation."

Although there was some improvement in the percentages of Canadians in the Article XV squadrons by the end of March, his frustration with the status quo led him to elaborate on a previous suggestion:

> Whether we get Article 15 squadrons Canadianized or not is not, to my mind, the proper answer. Under the existing conditions we shall never be able to have a truly Canadian Air Force Overseas. I think that in time the only way to do it is to follow roughly the processes that the Americans are proposing. They admit that there must be unified direction, and, as far as Fighter Command is concerned, Chaney, the American chief here, is recommending . . . that their Fighter units and formations should take their instructions from Fighter Command. As far as Bomber Command is concerned, they are all out to have a Bomber Command of their own which

will operate independently but get direction as to objectives from the Air Ministry, where they would have representation, in order not to have the RAF and themselves doing the same job.

Whether the British Authorities would agree to such a change or not, bearing in mind the Joint Air Training Plan Agreement, I do not know, but I do think that sometime in the future the people of Canada will make the discovery that they have not got an Air Force at all, with consequent complaint. It would of course, run into more money. Whether Canada would be prepared to meet it or not, or whether we could do it through Lease Lend or not, I do not know, but I do feel that more and more developments will be unsatisfactory . . .

To have a unified Canadian Air Force Overseas, with Canadian control and, of course, complete co-operation, is, to my mind, our only and final objective, if for no other reason than to meet the demand of national pride.

While some senior RCAF officers were strongly opposed to Canadianization, and were joined by many RAF officers who actively promoted the view with RCAF personnel that mixed crews within the RAF were preferable to separate RCAF squadrons, the Canadian government was equally strong in its desire to exercise more control over RCAF personnel overseas. In May, the Cabinet, while not going so far as to approve of an independent force, did advocate gaining as much control as possible over Canadian personnel, including postings of Canadians to the Article XV squadrons.

While negotiations at the Ottawa Air Training Conference held in May–June were conducted in a friendly atmosphere, the British conceded only minor points, and little of substance. One bone of contention was removed when they agreed to the RCAF's right to grant commissions to those it saw fit. Agreement was also reached on the formation of ten more Article XV squadrons, the establishment in England of a Canadian Personnel Reception Centre (PRC), and to the formation of a Canadian Bomber group, the principle of which had been agreed to the previous year. Even with these concessions, the RAF would, a year and half later, still maintain control over

---

[86] In a curious footnote to the conference, Power showed Gus's memo to Harold Balfour (Parliamentary Undersecretary of State for Air and head of the British delegation) but cautioned him to keep it confidential, as he had not shown it to Prime Minister Mackenzie King.

some 6,000 RCAF aircrew in RAF squadrons.[86]

When Gus returned to London at the end of June 1942, having been promoted to Air Marshal with the new title of Air Officer Commanding-in-Chief, he was optimistic that a new spirit of co-operation would be evident and Canadianization would proceed quickly. At first this optimism seemed justified when he joined the Minister and the CAS at a meeting with A/M Sir Arthur Harris AOC-in-C RAF Bomber Command, on 19 August at High Wycombe. As he travelled to the meeting with Balfour, Power was in no mood to give in, as he wrote in his own words:

> To Bomber Command . . . with Balfour. He made some reference to Canadianization. I told him I was fed up going around asking favours and would ask no more. I realized that there was so much antagonism that from now on I would run my own show.
>
> He talked of Bomber Group and intimated that Harris was sticky on it. I said that if Harris mentions it to me I would most impolitely tell him to go to hell and that it was none of his business but a matter of Government policy. Balfour agreed.

Harris had made his position quite clear that he found the idea of an RCAF group "quite unacceptable" to have "almost the entire expansion going into Canadians for the rest of the year." "What with Canadians, Poles, Rhodesians and Australians we shall . . . very soon arrive at the stage where most of the operational squadrons are manned by coloured troops." That would be unfortunate because, from his perspective, "the British, being in general better educated and more amenable to discipline, are apt to be quicker in the uptake during the complicated training which has to be given."

Strangely, at the meeting, he completely reversed his stated views and promised complete co-operation, even to the extent of withdrawing complete RCAF crews to be transferred to RCAF squadrons. Similarly, Fighter Command promised to be equally co-operative.

But Gus's optimism was short-lived as he began to despair that a true change of attitude would ever come about. He was not informed by the Air Ministry in advance of the Dieppe raid, nor was it helpful in establishing the agreed-upon Personnel Reception Centre, with which he went ahead on his own. His attempt to establish a War Room was also met with resistance and was not fully functional until early in the new year, aided immeasurably by Power, who more properly referred to it as "an RCAF Intelligence Room." This facilitated the issuance by the RCAF of its own communiqués,

10 - THE SECOND WORLD WAR - PART II: CANADIANIZATION

which, prior to then, had been the sole prerogative of the RAF. With these new communiqués, public awareness of the RCAF's role in the war was substantially increased, both in England and Canada.

It was on 5 September that the debate on Canadianization became an even more public one in Canada. On that day, Gus had held a press conference in London, following which he spoke "off the record." During these remarks, he most unwisely criticized the editorial policy of *The Globe and Mail* and the Montreal *Gazette*, saying, ". . . some people are talking a lot of bloody nonsense about splitting the Empire. If Canadians who see it from that point of view want to be mugs all their lives, that's their business. I can see no reason against Canadianization."

The reaction from the newspapers in Canada was swift and severe:

> [And] the leaked comments provided those papers opposed to Canadianization with fresh ammunition. Breadner quickly cabled Edwards to inform him that "your statement to Canadian editors as reported on this side . . . is causing very considerable furore [sic] here." Bassett talked half an hour with Minister and dealt at length on your lack of diplomacy. *Gazette* in editorial headed "Air Marshal Edwards is Wrong" categorically denied your charge and stated you must have been misinformed. This morning's (Ottawa) *Journal* carries full column editorial generally upbraiding you. Have not yet seen *Globe and Mail* reaction. Minister feels however that whole of Press in Canada will take up cudgels and that members during next session will make strong attacks on the Government. Discussed this question at length with Minister this morning who requests I wire you and ask that you give serious consideration to an immediate statement notifying all concerned that you had been misinformed as to the attitude of the papers concerned. I feel certain that only by such action can you save the government, this department and yourself any unnecessary headache and that present snowball of criticism levelled at yourself will become an avalanche directed at you for the sole purpose of causing your removal.

Gus did issue a retraction, which saved his appointment, and Power need not have feared that all the newspapers would attack the Government's policy. In the event, only the Ottawa *Journal*, the *Toronto Telegram*, and *The Globe and*

Mail were dead set against Canadianization. The vast majority supported it, including papers in the larger cities: the *Winnipeg Free Press* (which called *The Globe and Mail's* stance an "absurd hullabuloo"); the *Vancouver Daily Province* (declaring "the storm was largely synthetic with the air marshal an innocent victim"); the *Toronto Star*, the *Edmonton Journal*, and the *Ottawa Citizen*. Support was also expressed by some smaller newspapers such as the *London Free Press*, the *Financial Post*, the *Kitchener Daily Record*, and Québec's *L'Action Catholique*. As far as the airmen overseas were concerned, a survey showed "Canadianization is being welcomed by most of the officers and practically all the airmen with whom we discussed it."

In January 1943, Gus was convinced that anti-Canadianization was on the rise rather than on the wane. Statistics bore him out: only 68.1 percent of aircrew in RCAF squadrons were Canadians, and this despite the arrival of 5,000 RCAF aircrew, two or three times the required number for Article XV squadrons. He was convinced that RCAF personnel, particularly those in small groups, were being pressured to remain attached to the RAF. The idea that mixed crews were superior to all Canadian crews was stressed, without discussing the benefits of membership in the Article XV squadrons.

The solution was simple enough: that Canada control RCAF postings; but the Air Ministry was adamant in denying this request. In view of the Air Ministry's intransigence, and on the other side, the constant prodding from Ottawa to improve the situation, Gus decided the time had come to take off the diplomatic gloves, force the issue, and meet the problem head on. Not to be dissuaded in this approach by Curtis, he sent a signal to Ottawa at five o'clock in the morning, venting his frustration in typical direct fashion:

> I could not agree more with your query. The answer is simply for reasons that I have given you many times during the past year. The question of manning RCAF squadrons with one hundred per cent Canadian aircrew has been continually referred to Air Ministry authorities ever since my arrival overseas. We all appreciate that certain difficulties were apparent but as over a year has now elapsed since the problems were realized I can see no reason why our objective should not have been reached by now and can only conclude that for some reason unknown to us an attempt is being made to frustrate the implementation of the policy. I have today sent an official letter to the Air Ministry pointing out that sufficient time has now elapsed to put into effect any necessary corrective measures and bearing in mind the large number of RCAF Aircrew

10 - THE SECOND WORLD WAR - PART II: CANADIANIZATION

arriving in this country and the small proportion required by our Canadian units, there is no reason why the Canadianization of our squadrons should not have been completed long ago. I have requested that instructions be issued that no RCAF aircrew are to be posted from the United Kingdom except to Canadian units until the RCAF squadrons have one hundred per cent RCAF aircrew and that I am recommending to you that this Headquarters take over the postings and records of all RCAF personnel. This I do hereby recommend most strongly. The numbers required to completely Canadianize our squadrons are so small as compared with the numbers arriving in this country that this whole question is ridiculous . . . The fault lies with the provisions of the JATP Agreement whereby our personnel are turned over to the RAF for disposal and while we can recall any officer or airman it is subject to operational expediency, the final decision on which rests with the RAF. The expression "operational expediency" is used greatly, almost to the same extent that many shortcomings are hidden behind the expression "there is a war on." . . . To give you some idea of the atmosphere, one member of the Air Council advised me that if my Headquarters had never been formed it would have made no difference to the war. It is easy to be wise after the event but we should never have participated in the JATP but should instead have built up an Air Force of our own. I have sent a copy of this signal to the Air Ministry. Only 585 aircrew required to complete Canadianization [of] our squadrons and yet there are approximately 8518 RCAF aircrew in the UK excluding Bournemouth where there are 4000 aircrew, the majority being RCAF.

In his equally direct letter to the Air Ministry, he wrote:

I am at a loss to know why the implementation of the Canadianization policy is proceeding so slowly and can only assume that it is being unfavourably received in certain quarters of the RAF to such an extent that progress is being retarded.

Canadian aircrew have been proceeding, in very large numbers, to the United Kingdom for almost three years and it is difficult to understand why the small proportion required to fill Canadian squadrons could not be provided. This is particularly disturbing as it could so easily have been arranged, without disrupting other units, if it had been implemented through initial postings . . .

I regret very much that it is necessary to write a letter of this nature, but I do think that the co-operation which we anticipated has not been given. We, on our part, have done everything possible to carry out the provisions of the JATP Agreement. You will note . . . that thousands of groundcrew personnel are being posted overseas. This, as you know, is not part of the agreement and is being done in order that the RCAF may provide greater assistance. It seems rather futile, however, to send such large numbers of groundcrew, which involves the taking up of valuable shipping space, when the simple matter of posting aircrew, in small numbers from the thousands available, cannot be arranged without ill feeling.

As he expected, reaction came on two fronts: from the British director-general of postings "using a carefully woven combination of irrelevant, misleading, and false information, . . . prepared a memorandum concluding that posting Canadian aircrew to RCAF squadrons was too difficult an undertaking ever to prove successful"; and from Breadner in Ottawa, "our signals were not intended to start you on the warpath." But Gus was steadfast in his belief that "this matter had to come to a head sooner or later. It is either that my interpretation of what we want and what we are entitled to is wrong or else the Air Ministry is wrong. The only way to find out is to come out into the open. An understanding must be reached if I and my successors are to live a life that more nearly approaches one that is fit to live."

Now Gus could feel the support slipping away when Breadner, having discussed the situation with Power, replied,

> Strongly urge you do not take up an uncompromising position. You did go off the deep end and apparently have stirred up much more hard feeling than subject warranted. Minister feels you should have made sure of his backing before going to bat. Possible therefore he may not be in a position to support your action. You should do all in your power to pour oil on troubled waters and not under any circumstances go gunning. Would it help your position any to return here immediately to get things straight this end? If so let us know and come ahead. Nothing reported here yet and if you can stop it you should do so. Good luck.

Good luck, indeed. His reply:

> Your cable strikes strange notes. You demand vigorous action and protest the slothful inactivity in pursuit of your declared policy. I fight for this and now must struggle both ways without aid. To compromise now would determine the end of the RCAF as an entity overseas. To pour oil on troubled waters would avail nothing. Coming home would bespeak weakness which I cannot accept. I have done all with firmness, candour and truth conscientiously believing that I was right. I stand or fall on that come what may.

The Air Ministry's misrepresentation of the facts prompted an emergency meeting of the Empire Air Training Scheme "to have Sir Charles Portal [CAS of the RAF] invite his Canadian opposite number to 'satisfy himself as to the steps taken by the Air Ministry to implement the policy of Canadianization.'" Power, wanting to sweep the controversy under the carpet and thus keep it from the prime minister and his Cabinet colleagues, now abandoned his previous call to arms of "telling the RAF to go to hell" and rushed Breadner to London in February to appease Portal. "According to Vincent Massey the Canadian CAS 'very nearly had to disown' Edwards in making his peace and, drawing the appropriate conclusions, the Air Ministry would continue to make little progress in Canadianizing the RCAF Overseas until 1944."

Power's and Breadner's lack of support had the predictable two-pronged effect of undermining Gus's position and encouraging Air Ministry intransigence. However, the formation of the RCAF Bomber Group created the structure that did help the process along. In July, Gus appointed G/C Denton Massey "to investigate and report on the present state of Canadianization." In November, Massey reported "*Postings* of aircrew from No.3 (RCAF) PRC right through to HCUs for Bomber Command, or Squadrons for Coastal and Fighter Commands, *are completely in the hands of the RAF*, . . . The solution therefore was to establish a wholly Canadian training chain in the United Kingdom . . ."

Presumably Gus would have supported Massey's conclusions but Breadner replaced Gus as AOC-in-C Overseas on 1 January 1944 and "he dismissed [the recommendations] off-handedly, telling Ottawa on 5 February that the proposal was 'uneconomical due to the fact that they are already being done by the Air Ministry.'"

[T]he Canadianization process received its biggest boost—and the British attitude towards the Canadian service its greatest shock—as discussion turned to the RCAF's role in the war's "second phase," following the defeat of Germany, when a few Canadian squadrons would be part of the occupying force in Europe, but most would be formed into "a fully integrated Canadian Air Force available for service wherever the Canadian government may decide." To carry out that policy, "RCAF personnel, who are presently attached to the RAF, will at once become effectively and unconditionally at the disposal of the Canadian government." With that statement, presented to Harold Balfour in an aide-memoire dated 10 February [1944], Ottawa made it clear that the lingering effects of Article XIV of the original 1939 BCATP agreement, which had placed Canadian aircrew "at the disposal of the Government of the United Kingdom" would end with the defeat of Germany and that the RCAF would once again become an autonomous air force.

A Differing British View

A British view, differing from that of the Canadian one expressed above, is outlined in a biography of MRAF Sir Arthur "Bomber" Harris. Here the author documents the views expressed by some senior RAF officers of the concept of Canadianization, the formation of a Canadian Bomber Group and of Gus's character and ability to command.

We must bear in mind in these discussions the international nature of the force that Harris led. As his Despatch tells us, no less than 37% of his pilots in January 1943 were Canadians, Australians or New Zealanders, and two years later the percentage had risen to 45%. While many served in RAF units an increasing proportion were in RCAF, RAAF and RNZAF squadrons reflecting the Dominions' desires to have their contributions properly recognized. It needs to be said that not all Dominion airmen were enthusiastic about having separate squadrons; they realised the operational value of integrated units within which their men could profit from the wider experience of their RAF colleagues and advance to command decisions on individual merit, and this became a subject of continuing controversy—particularly in Canada, which provided well over half the Dominion pilots in Bomber Command. In 1943, however, Air Vice-Marshal Edwards, Air Officer-in-Chief RCAF Overseas was under firm remit from Ottawa to push forward the "Canadianisation" policy under which all RCAF squadrons, hitherto mixed-manned, were eventually to become entirely Canadian, and to arrange for a separate Canadian Bomber Group to be formed.

Given the major and growing Dominion contributions to his force these were matters of considerable importance to Harris, who shared the doubts of the Canadian critics and of men such as Carr, 4 Group's NZ AOC, about the wisdom of forming separate squadrons. On this matter he bowed to the inevitable, but in August 1942 he raised with Freeman [RAF Vice-Chief of Air Staff] a wider issue arising from a decision that Bomber Command's immediate expansion should be based almost completely on new Canadian squadrons. "Canadians make good crews," he wrote, "but I for one would be most perturbed to see almost the entire expansion going into Canadians for the rest of the year. We are always being accused, as a nation, of fighting with the bodies of Colonial and Dominion personnel in preference to British—so far unjustly. But why lend colour to it?" The consequence, he went on, would be a Canadian Group out of all proportion to the others, and with other "national" squadrons being added Bomber Command would end up with most of its operational squadrons manned by what he called "coloured troops." This was a plea for more balanced expansion, but while Freeman readily took Harris's point he could hold out little hope of altering the situation.

A few days later Harris told Portal that Edwards and his staff were going round some of his bomber stations in connection with plans for the future Canadian Group without having made any attempt to seek his authority, and were also upsetting some of the existing Canadian crews. They had never met, Harris said (though he had heard Trenchard [a former RAF CAS] describe Edwards as an appalling fellow quite unsuited for any sort of command), and hopefully Portal could do something to put matters right. They did in fact meet soon afterwards, when Edwards accompanied Power, the Canadian Air Minister, to High Wycombe. Power, warned to expect the worst, found his host most co-operative and expressing willingness to help in every way; "Of all the senior officers we have met overseas on our two trips," he wrote in his diary, "Harris has put himself out more than anyone else thus belying the reputation that has been built up for him both by our people and by the UK authorities." He had turned on the charm, presented himself as one of the RCAF's greatest supporters—which indeed he was—and come to terms with the fact the Canadians were going to be allotted their own Group and must be given every assistance.

It would not, however, be plain sailing. Harris remained unenamoured of Edwards, as indicated when he wrote again to Portal complaining of the Canadian's "ignorant and voluble chatter" in asserting that "no crew stands a hope of completing a second tour"; this false assertion was gaining widespread currency, was having serious effects on morale, and reflecting badly on Edwards' discretion.[87]

Other Canadian Views

A second Canadian view is put forward by the authors of *Reap the Whirlwind*. While generally in agreement that 6 Group was rushed into operation prematurely, they differ substantially from Harris in their assessment of Gus's character and abilities.

> The outbreak of World War II found Edwards in charge of the RCAF's Personnel Division, a highly intelligent, well read and capable individual in his mid-forties, intensely proud of the RCAF and his adopted country, Canada, a practical man who enjoyed French-polishing furniture and working on a blacksmith's anvil, yet one also devoted to poetry and the opera. A tough talking, outwardly severe man, Edwards exuded self-confidence but was rarely seen without his cap, being sensitive about the baldness that had afflicted him since his twenties. . . .
>
> [I]n England in 1942, he was the RCAF's chief negotiator,

---

[87] Henry Probert, *Bomber Harris, His Life and Times* (London: Greenhill Books, 2003), pp. 213–14. Reproduced here with permission of the publisher. NB 1. The author incorrectly lists Gus's rank and title in 1943 as A/V/M and AO-in-C, which, from July 1942, was A/M and AOC-in-C. 2. Probert omitted some of Harris's more derogatory remarks about Canadians and their leadership abilities vs. the superiority of the British—see earlier in this chapter for a more complete account of his remarks. 3. Under the terms of the amended version of BCATP, Appendix IV Paragraph 2, Gus [would] ". . . at all times have access to Commanders of Stations and Groups."

10 - THE SECOND WORLD WAR - PART II: CANADIANIZATION

responsible for many of the final arrangements for the creation of 6 Group. He proved to be a formidable adversary at the conference table, able to hold his own with the likes of Portal and Harris. Some of the old colonial attitudes still lingered, and Edwards had to keep reminding the senior RAF officers that Canada, in spite of strong emotional ties to the Old Country, was independent. No longer was it merely a supplier of manpower, obliged to do whatever London demanded. Evidently, he made the point effectively. Harris was later quoted in a message deliberately "leaked" to the RCAF: "I will get that so and so Edwards out of this country if it is the last thing I do."[88]

C.P. Stacey, the Canadian historian, gives his account of the policy objectives and the impossibility of the task that Gus faced.

The aim was, of course, to get as many Canadians as possible into the Article 15 squadrons. Major Power at first set his sights on making all R.C.A.F. squadrons 100 per cent Canadian. This objective had to be modified as the problems involved became better understood. But from the closing months of 1941 until the end of the war the country's administrative policy concerning its overseas air force could be summed up in one rather unlovely but expressive word—"Canadianization." Increasingly, as time passed, there was unity of mind and purpose on this question between the political and professional chiefs of the Royal Canadian Air Force. The professionals, notwithstanding their well-founded conviction that Canadianization must be gradual, could not reconcile the obvious lack of method in obtaining the posting of R.C.A.F. personnel with their conception of the future shape of the R.C.A.F. Overseas. Power, while also concerned about the future of the force, continued to be troubled about the growing number of Canadians posted to R.A.F. units, who could be sent anywhere in the world at the discretion of British authorities and over whom their own government had no control. He knew, moreover, that these matters had a close relationship to recruiting and public morale.

---

[88] Spencer Dunmore and William Carter, Ph.D., *Reap The Whirlwind, The Untold Story of 6 Group, Canada's Bomber Force of World War II* (Toronto: McClelland & Stewart Inc., 1991), pp. 17–18. Reprinted with permission. As to Gus's being sensitive about his baldness, perhaps he was, but I do not remember this being the case.

On 25 November 1941 Air Vice-Marshal Harold Edwards succeeded Air Commodore Stevenson as the senior R.C.A.F. officer overseas with the task of inaugurating the new phase in Canadian policy. . . . It would be an error to assume that Edwards' opinions, close as they were to the Air Minister and the Chief of the Air Staff, were the only reason for selecting him. As Air Member for Personnel he was well acquainted with the overseas situation and had assisted in overcoming some of the problems that had arisen. It is worth noting too that as A.M.P. he had played an important part in R.C.A.F. development, having been responsible for the introduction of Medical, Accounts and Provost and Security branches. . . .

The importance attached to Edwards' task is reflected in the Air Minister's decision to set "no specific limitations" on his authority. The mission, however, was not an enviable one. To move too fast was certain to arouse misgivings and opposition at the Air Ministry; to go too slowly was just as certain to meet with reproof from Ottawa. It is small wonder that before Edwards' two years of overseas service ended he had, at different times, incurred the displeasure of both sides and become known as the most controversial officer in the Royal Canadian Air Force.[89]

The final words on the subject go to C.P. Stacey, who highlights the financial issue that may have been the underlying cause of all the acrimony.

In the course of the crisis there had been a development which doubtless helped to resolve it and changed the whole atmosphere of the Canadianization discussion. We have pointed out above the contradiction between the manly policy of independence which Canada was trying to follow in respect of the R.C.A.F. Overseas and the idea of allowing Great Britain to pay most of the bill for the force. The new B.C.A.T.P. made in June 1942 saw Canada assume a larger proportion than formerly of the cost of the Training Plan, but the opportunity to take on also the cost of the overseas R.C.A.F. squadrons and personnel was not embraced.

[89] C.P. Stacey, *Arms, Men and Governments, The War Policies of Canada, 1939–1945* (Published by Authority of the Minister of National Defence, 1970) pp. 270–71. Reproduced with the permission of the Minister of Public Works and Government Services, 2006.

That autumn the Air Member for Finance in the Canadian Air Council, Air Commodore K.G. Nairn, returning from a visit overseas, voiced a conclusion which he certainly was not the first to reach: as a matter of "broad equity," and also from the point of view of efficient administration and the welfare of Canadian personnel, it was desirable that Canada should assume the whole cost of her overseas air effort. The Chief of the Air Staff and the Air Minister accepted the recommendation. On 13 January 1943 the Cabinet War Committee, as part of a general reorganization of financial arrangements with the United Kingdom, approved in principle the assumption from 1 April of the responsibility of equipping and maintaining "the thirty-five R.C.A.F. squadrons now forming or to be formed in the United Kingdom" at a total cost of $287 million for the year, plus possibly certain miscellaneous establishments costing $60 million more; as well as the assumption from the same date of responsibility for "pay and allowances, clothing and other personal necessities, of all Canadian aircrew now serving in the R.A.F., at an estimated cost of $35 million, and possibly capitation charges of about $15 million, in addition." On 22 January (the day Edwards boiled over in London) these proposals were approved by the full Cabinet. The decision was announced in the Governor-General's Speech at the opening of Parliament on 28 January in general terms, and in more detail by the Prime Minister in the House of Commons on 1 February. The whole Canadian position on Canadianization—both moral and practical—was thus vastly strengthened.

Had an early intimation of the proposed change been sent to Air Marshal Edwards, who had evidently himself recommended it, much trouble might have been avoided. As it was, he was not told until the decision was made final on 23 January. Breadner cabled him, with reference to his recommendation that his headquarters take over postings and records. "It is our assumption that in effecting an operative basis for pay and personnel, R.C.A.F. maintenance of records must automatically follow. There is no point therefore in raising this issue at present with Air Ministry. We feel that Air Ministry may mistrust our reasons for suddenly wanting to pay our share and therefore consider that any pressure for control other than is necessary for effective working of pay arrangements may be viewed with suspicion and for that reason be ill-timed." Edwards replied, "I certainly would have avoided this angle if I had known that you were pursuing the suggestion I put forward months ago."[90]

Lastly, a word about Gus's view of the behaviour of the newly trained RCAF personnel. As airmen began arriving in England in ever-increasing numbers, criticism was levelled at the Canadians for their lack of discipline and leadership skills. Gus, a well known disciplinarian, found the criticisms to be entirely justified and, appalled by what he saw, lost no time in making Ottawa aware of the problems and in submitting his recommendation to correct them.

> The discipline of our troops in England is tragic. How I regret my weak-kneed efforts to get our training department to spend more time on discipline training! They come over here with little idea of discipline, no idea as to how an officer or an N.C.O. should behave. . . . What makes it worse, the R.A.F. authorities are diffident about dealing with the R.C.A.F. airmen. They treat them (and I must say that it is kind of them) more like guests than culprits. . . . No thought has been given at all, despite my most vigorous protests, to teach[ing] these men leadership and time must be made to do it because in the end without it (and this is proven by present actual experience) the product of the Joint Air Training Plan leaves a Hell of lot to be desired.[91]

---

[89] C.P. Stacey, *Arms, Men and Governments, The War Policies of Canada*, 1939-1945, pp. 287–88.

[90] Ibid., p. 271. This is also part of the same letter quoted at the beginning of this chapter.

11

THE SECOND WORLD WAR - PART III
1942

Following the frantic activity prior to Gus's departure, the house Bea and I returned to after seeing him off on that grey November day in 1941 seemed drained of life, as if the oxygen had been sucked from it. With Billy away at boarding school, we were now on our own—except we were blessed to have our wonderful and much-loved housekeeper, Aldea, who happily was with us throughout the war; and, of course, Sandy still ruled the roost when not patrolling the streets of Sandy Hill.

It was a lonely time for Bea, as it was for other wives and mothers across the country. And just as they were doing, she knitted socks, gloves, and scarves, packed them into parcels with food and cigarettes, and sent them overseas. She sold raffle tickets to raise money for cause after cause, bought War Savings Bonds, wrote hundreds of letters to Gus, and prayed every day for his safe return. But she was more fortunate than most, for he was gone for only two years, and came home three times to attend meetings.

Early in the war, she had joined the Red Cross and devoted a day a week to various works undertaken by the organization. One of these was to provide sandwiches to factory workers engaged in war production. Because of rationing, dietitians were trying to find protein substitutes to replace meat and needed volunteers to test their new concoctions before giving them to the workers. Bea also chose to become proficient in advanced first aid, which was required to treat casualties in case of enemy attack. Aldea and I were the natural ones to be seconded to assist in both these ventures. There was much laughter as we tasted countless sandwiches made of the most unappetizing combination of ingredients, rejecting some as unfit for human consumption and a sure way to sabotage rather than increase production. To practise first aid, we spent many an hour with our limbs in strange positions while one of us read the manual aloud and Bea tried to master the art of applying splints and bandages to various body parts. But master it she did, after a fashion, and thankfully for any potential wounded, no enemy attack ever took place.

While all these activities were important, her greatest contribution was the time she took to visit the next of kin of RCAF personnel reported missing or killed in action overseas. These were heartbreaking visits that in the beginning required an afternoon a month, but, as casualties increased with the bombing offensive, were made more and more frequently. She dreaded these days, feeling her words were inadequate in the face of such crushing grief, so courageously borne by these wives or mothers who had lost their husbands or sons. One particularly poignant visit was to a mother she had seen *twice* before and this concerned her *third* son who was missing over Germany. When she left the house after witnessing this women's overwhelming grief she could only sit in the car and weep. Eventually she started for home but was still so upset and distracted that a few blocks later, she drove the car into a stop sign. Despite how difficult these visits were, she realized they gave some measure of comfort to those women with whom she talked, and she continued them for close to three years.

Bea Edwards. c. 1939

While Bea was visiting next of kin in Ottawa, in England Gus made a point of writing to every mother or wife who had lost a son or husband in the air force overseas. One such letter was to the mother of Sgt. Donald George Barnie, who was killed when his Hampden aircraft crashed during the night of 9–10 November 1942 at Turnberry, Scotland. His brother's letter tells the story.

> My late mother's first husband was killed in action in France during the First World War, leaving her with one son, who was later killed in action during air operations overseas with the RCAF close to Christmas 1942.

11 - THE SECOND WORLD WAR - PART III: 1942

HEADQUARTERS OF THE
AIR OFFICER COMMANDING-IN-CHIEF
R.C.A.F. OVERSEAS

CHRISTMAS, 1943.

Dear Mrs. Belcher:

On this great day, in the lives of all good people, I would like you to know that I have not forgotten.

Sincerely,

(H. Edwards)
Air Marshal.

Letter courtesy Micheal Belcher

My brother was the "bread winner" before he joined the RCAF as a WAG, he had just turned 24 years old, and his death left our family devastated.

During those grim days of the war most of the casualties were Air Force, and very young lads to say the least.

> My mother, who passed away many years ago, was so pleasantly surprised to receive the attached note from Air Marshal Edwards, a year after my brother was killed.
>
> This thoughtfulness of A/M Edwards, who must have been extremely busy at that time of the war, was very much appreciated by my family. It shows what a wonderful and compassionate man A/M Edwards was.
>
> We are very proud of this note, and it was framed and after 60 years still hangs in the entrance hall to our home in Collingwood Ont., for everyone to see.[92]

Another heart-wrenching example of the terrible toll the war was taking on those who fought it and on those who were left to mourn their lost sons was a letter Gus received from Agnes Rawson of New Liskeard, written on 4 July 1943:

> I have received a letter from you about my son, Flight Sergeant Douglas Rawson, late 403 Squadron, and I want to tell you how much your kindness meant to me.
>
> It was grand of you, with all your heavy responsibilities, to take the time and trouble to write to me.
>
> Your letter was especially welcome as it arrived the day after we got word that our second son, P/O James Rawson, 20373, was missing after a night raid on Dusseldorf. We are still hoping for better news of him. Douglas was just 21 years old, James not yet 20, and I've one other boy of fourteen, just crazy about the Air Force too.
>
> It's hard to lose two such grand boys but I'm proud to have had them to send to fight for my Homeland, and I'd send more if I had them; in full confidence that their lives will not be needlessly thrown away.

---

[92] Letter of 24 January 2003 from Michael Belcher, Sgt. Barnie's half-brother. Before he left for overseas, his mother had taken off her wedding ring, put it on his finger, and told him to return it to her when he came back from the war. It was returned to her with his other personal effects. Gus's letter to Mrs. Belcher was one of the last he wrote as AOC-in-C. He left for Canada on 22 December 1943.

11 - THE SECOND WORLD WAR - PART III: 1942

We have read all about you and admired you as a leader of our flying men, now I feel that you are their friend too, and it's a great comfort to a mother.

I am proud to have your letter and I pray that God will bless and protect you always, and give you strength for your tremendous task. . . .

* * *

In wartime Ottawa, milk and bread were delivered by horse and wagon, or by sleigh in winter. In our particular case, the milkman and horse were named Gerry and Peter—although I was never absolutely certain which was which. Peter—if indeed it was he—knew his route perfectly and would stop without command only at the houses that bought milk, passing by the ones that weren't his customers.

Public transportation was provided by those wondrous vehicles, the dark red streetcars of the Ottawa Electric Railway, with the initials "OER" painted in gold on the front of each car. As a child, what an adventure it was to "take the tram" by myself; with a ticket clutched securely inside my mitten, to watch the doors fold open, to climb aboard the lacework metal steps that had magically dropped down from their hiding place, then sink into what appeared, at least to my child's eyes, to be a luxurious leather seat—by the window.

The double tracks formed a huge rectangle around the streets of Sandy Hill; down Rideau Street from Sparks, right on Charlotte, right on Laurier, right on Nicholas to Rideau, then on up past the War Memorial and beyond. In the dead of winter, if heading "into town" and one missed the car going up Rideau, the alternative was to take the one going in the opposite direction (around Laurier), thus avoiding certain death from hypothermia while waiting for the next car.

Because of gas rationing, automobile traffic was severely restricted, with many families saving their allotment for the summer by putting their cars up on blocks for the winter. Almost everyone either cycled, walked, or took the streetcar to get where they were going.

There was one drawback to this mode of transportation. As anyone who has ridden a bicycle will understand, getting the front wheel caught in the tracks is a distinctly unpleasant experience. Unfortunately, I did not have the wit to impart this crucial piece of information to Canada's great air ace, A/M "Billy" Bishop. As if he were not doing enough to win the war, he bought a bicycle to conserve gas. One day I followed on my bike as he rode from his house to ours to test his riding skills. It had been years since he had ridden a bike. Setting off from his house he was a little shaky, but managed reasonably well rounding the corner of Laurier Avenue and Charlotte Street by the Soviet Embassy. As he gained confidence and speed, I realized too late that he was well past Besserer Street, where he should have turned right to avoid the traffic on busy Rideau. And then to my horror, ignoring the stop sign, he was turning *the wrong way* onto Rideau.

"*Right*, Uncle Billy,[93] you should've turned *right!*" I shouted.

"*I know*, dammit, I *tried*, but I'm stuck in the tracks and can't get out!" he called back nervously over his shoulder. When last seen, the dauntless World War One air ace was frantically trying to extricate the front wheel from the track, which was propelling him inexorably downtown.

On another occasion, my friends and I held a bazaar in our garage to raise money for the Red Cross. Items for the white elephant table had been scrounged from friends and relations; a more unappealing array of baubles, trinkets, and plain junk would have been hard to imagine, but we thought it a dazzling display. It was surrounded by smaller tables with homemade cookies, cakes, fudge, soft drinks, etc.—quite a feat by our long-suffering mothers, considering butter and sugar were rationed. Bea's contribution to this gala event was a large quantity of her renowned lemon drink, a far superior refreshment to mere lemonade. Food and drink sold for five cents, as did most of the other items, with a few extraordinarily valuable pieces going for ten cents.

Just after we opened for business, who should appear in the driveway filled with children, dogs, and bicycles but Uncle Billy, on *his* bicycle. By now he had mastered the beast and had pedalled over to join the fun. It is impossible to forget how he entered into the spirit of that children's effort to raise money, taking time to look at each table and then, as if choosing a ring at Birks, carefully selecting something he pretended was just what he needed. He handed me a five-dollar bill in payment, but so early in the day we had no change for such a huge amount. I asked if he could just give me the required ten cents. He replied he would certainly like to but was sorry to say he had not brought any change, and obviously the only way out of this impasse was for me to keep the five dollars.

Our total take that day was $33.15, so his donation represented fifteen

---

[93] As children we were permitted to address a few of Gus's friends and colleagues in the air force as "Uncle." Although not related, this was to avoid having to use their rank each time we spoke to them: hence "Uncle Billy" instead of Air Marshal Bishop, "Uncle Bread" instead of Air Marshal Breadner, etc.

11 - THE SECOND WORLD WAR - PART III: 1942

percent of the total—what a dear man.

The description of this event would not, however, be complete without mentioning the near-disaster caused by Bea's famous lemon drink. It seems the drink was contaminated in some way, causing half the neighbourhood children to become ill. Bea spent a great deal of time on the telephone apologizing to other mothers for poisoning their children, but we never did discover the cause of the problem.

* * *

When Gus arrived in England, one of his first visits was to a troopship that had brought the largest contingent of airmen ever sent overseas. The account of his welcome to the troops is described in *The Globe and Mail* of 21 January 1942:

> The air division, composed of every kind of expert from greasers to fighter pilots, was sent immediately to a dispersal centre with an inspiring message from Air Vice Marshal Harold Edwards.
>
> Air Vice Marshal Edwards received prolonged and spontaneous cheers as he mounted the gangplank to extend a personal welcome to lads crowded at the rails of each deck of the big liner which brought them to Britain.
>
> He wasted no time over formalities, making his way immediately to the quarters of the men on the lower decks of the vessel.
>
> There he strode briskly among them, offering cheery words to shirt-sleeved youngsters, many of them recovering from seasickness.
>
> After his quick inspection he mounted the bench of a mess table at which the men had just been given afternoon tea.
>
> In a few words he told them Britain needed as many of them as could be trained in Canada and accommodated in Britain.
>
> He added a note of caution, reminding his hearers that Britain had been at war for more than two years and that new arrivals were bound to find conditions different from those in their homeland. This, he warned, would necessitate an adjustment of their way of life.

> "The adjustments you must make," he said, "will extend to every phase of your daily living, your food, your living quarters, the customs of those around you, the price you pay for what you need."
>
> The air vice marshal told them bluntly they would miss the food to which they had been accustomed, that they would find their quarters cold and that there were dozens of other things that would cause them temporary difficulties. . . .

Just as he was settling into his new appointment, Gus was again admitted to hospital with another respiratory infection and his old nemesis, auricular fibrillation. After two weeks at No. 5 Canadian General Hospital at Taplow, Bucks., he was transferred to the RAF Officers' Hospital at Torquay in Devon and remained there until 26 March. It was at Torquay that doctors decided to replace quinidine with digitalis in an effort to correct his fibrillating heart. The new medication produced immediate results, controlling this nagging, debilitating condition, and he appeared to be free from any major health crisis for the next year and half.

When not laid low by illness, Gus spent the early months of 1942 bringing order to the chaos of personnel records. Astounded that he, as an A/V/M, was unable to trace the whereabouts of his own nephew, he set up a Records and Statistics Directorate to establish the whereabouts of RCAF personnel, increased RCAF medical staff at RAF hospitals, improved the postal system, and introduced the newsletter *Wings Abroad*. He recognized the importance of the postal service, as the needs of Canadians far from home were totally different from those of their British counterparts in the RAF:

> If an English boy does not get his mail it is unimportant, in that within a short space of time he can get leave to go and see his family or he can send a telegram for nothing. To a Canadian boy, who has no similar privilege, a letter or a parcel is of much greater significance and importance. It boils down to this, that to a Canadian lad, a letter is as equal in importance as four days leave. . . .[94]

While all this was going on, he was also participating in what was to

---

[94] *The Official History of the Royal Canadian Air Force, Vol III*, p. 62. NB During the war, the only way relatives could communicate with those overseas was by mail; e-mail did not exist, nor was transatlantic telephone service available to the average citizen.

11 - THE SECOND WORLD WAR - PART III: 1942

Visit to Chorley, Lancs. Speaking to Air Cadets. 19 April 1942
RCAF photo courtesy John Smith

become the never-ending series of discussions with the Air Ministry and RAF commands to implement the policy of Canadianization. But, in April, he was able to take a brief break to visit Chorley, the birthplace from which he immigrated to Canada as a boy of ten. He received a warm welcome from the townspeople and the mayor, met relatives and friends of his mother, visited the graveyard where his grandparents were buried, and reviewed the detachment of the Air Training Corps.

* * *

In mid-May, Gus returned to Canada for the BCATP conference. On this and future trips, we were always notified just hours before his actual time of arrival. Much to Bea's irritation, this never left time to have her hair done before meeting him at Rockcliffe—but clearly we were overjoyed to see him again, except for Sandy, who, with typical canine anger at his long absence, greeted his arrival with studied indifference. It was not until Gus sat in his accustomed chair at the dining room table that night that Sandy deigned to give him an effusive welcome.

After the conference ended, we set off by car to pick up Billy at his school in Port Hope, where Gus was to present the prizes at the closing on 13 June.[95] Kingston was on the way, and this was an ideal opportunity for Bea and Gus to see their old friends, the Hertzbergs, at the Royal Military College, where the general was commandant. One of his daughters recalls the visit:

Front row left: Gus's uncle, Major Bill Warburton of the Selsdon, Surrey Home Guard (a retired captain in the British Army who had fought at Gallipoli in World War I); when, as a spotter of enemy aircraft during the Blitz, he was asked to give an *accurate* count of the number he saw, is purported to have exclaimed excitedly, "Dunno, there are *thousands* of the buggers!" 2nd row right: W/C W.J. Brodribb.
RCAF photo courtesy John Smith

---

[95] Trinity College School where Bea and I, sitting in the audience, watched as Gus gave out the prizes, including the one for "Form IIIB— English" to Billy.

11 - THE SECOND WORLD WAR - PART III: 1942

Arrival at Rockliffe Air Station on 16 May 1942.
Bea, Gus, and the author with
A/M W.A. Bishop descending from the aircraft...
DND PL 8809

...and with a purposely disinterested Sandy.
DND PL 8808

The close friendship between my father and Gus Edwards began when they served together in Halifax in the mid 30s. It continued until the latter's death in 1952.

They saw each other as often as possible during those 20 years. The Edwards came as frequently as wartime circumstances permitted to stay with us at R.M.C. where we lived during the war and where I got to know him. It was a lovely relationship for me—a young teenager—and I was dazzled by this so attractive man who seemed interested in all my pursuits. I remember his telling me about Shakespeare—mostly the Sonnets—and about music—mostly Chopin. It was all very informative & very serious.

But he was also very funny. I remember them on one of their visits sitting with us, having tea or drinks (probably drinks!) on our lawn. Across the bay from R.M.C. was Fort Henry which had been converted into a detention camp for German P.O.W.s. We could see them from our garden sometimes, working in the fields or playing soccer. On this occasion Gus, who had been a P.O.W. in the First War looked up at them and suddenly said with a grin, "I think I'll go over there and show those fellows how to escape." His wife, ever fearful, almost took him seriously and was shocked. We didn't and were enchanted!⁹⁶

Towards the end of his time in Canada, in a speech broadcast over the national network of the CBC on 19 June, Gus spoke of RCAF activities overseas. Excerpts from the speech were reported the next day in *The Hamilton Spectator*: "Many of the men, flying over the Continent (of Europe), over the war theatre of the Middle East, over India, over the Far East, over Malta and Ceylon, over Britain, are Canadian boys. . . . We have bred them and trained them and sent them to far places to fight for us here at home."

He went on to describe a visit to a bomber squadron where "The crews who started on the raid 'fresh and young' returned 'dark-eyed and tired . . .'" and concluded with, "Air war—any war—is a terrible thing, and the sooner we finish it, the sooner this evil that has come upon the world is stamped out: then the sooner the fruits of progress will be available for shaping for good by all these young men who now must pause to deal in death."

---

[96] Thea Hertzberg Gray, *Reminiscences* (September 2002).

11 - THE SECOND WORLD WAR - PART III: 1942

"The Mad Tea Party." L to R: Dagmar and Dorothy Hertzberg, Gus Edwards, Dane and Thea Hertzberg, Bea Edwards. RMC, June 1942

Photo courtesy Thea Hertzberg Gray

* * *

He returned to London on the Pan Am clipper from New York to Ireland, and his letter of 4 July 1942 to his mother tells of the trip and what he was up to next.

> I arrived back in London just a week ago. This time, instead of travelling by bomber I made the journey by commercial clipper and it was much better. It took considerably longer but for comfort there is no comparison and I arrived feeling quite fresh after the long journey.
>
> As a result of my Canadian visit, new vistas have opened up over here, all of which means a good deal more work. However, it is the sort of work that I love and as you know me better than anyone else, you know that I am in my glory.
>
> I have marked July 1st, 1942, Dominion Day, as one of the greatest

days of my life. I returned from Westminster Abbey where I had witnessed one of the most stirring ceremonies that I have ever seen to find a cable from Bea congratulating me on what I believed to be my promotion to Air Marshal; 20 minutes later an official cablegram confirmed the good news.

The Abbey ceremony was to mark 75 years of Confederation and culminated a parade of Canadian Army, Navy, Air Force, and Firefighters which proceeded along a route past the Palace to Westminster Abbey.

The Abbey beggars description and I will not attempt it but it is a fit setting for the great history that has been made within its walls. It is filled with the holiness of age and the beauty of great craftsmanship.

When all were in their places the great organ which had been playing all along, suddenly stopped and seven trumpeters of His Majesty's Royal Horse Guards (The Blues) announced the entry of the clerical procession and, what few people knew as the information cannot be passed around in advance, the entry of the King and Queen.

The Queen was dressed in her usual powder blue with powder blue gloves. Her radiance touched us all and more than one person caught their breath at the sight of her. The King looked everything a king should be. The rest of the procession was composed of various members of the clergy dressed in their various robes of office and included the Archbishop of Canterbury.

The choir was magnificent. It rivalled the organ itself in depth of tone and colour. They made "Oh Canada" for once sound like something other than a funeral dirge.

After the ceremony I attended a luncheon in the Jerusalem Chambers of the Abbey as the guest of Mr. Massey, the Canadian High Commissioner. No one knows how old this part of the Abbey is but at least 600 years ago it was part of the great Benedictine Monastery and was used by the abbots as their "withdrawing room." . . .

The Middle East news hasn't been very good for quite a few days

11 - THE SECOND WORLD WAR - PART III: 1942

now but this is one of the setbacks that Churchill prepared us for and must be taken as one of the breaks of the game. The future will see fewer disappointments for us I am sure.

As you know, with all the things I had to do, my six weeks in Canada were pretty hectic but I thrived on it and am now feeling better than ever.

I am leaving on a tour, next week, of some of our squadrons and I expect it will take me to Scotland. I hope to be able to take a little time out for a spot of fishing as the break in the middle of the trip will be restful and should do me a lot of good.

I was so glad that I had the chance to see you. It made a particularly bright spot in weeks of conferences, discussions and debates. . . .[97]

* * *

Always concerned for the welfare of his troops, Gus was troubled that ground crew were not receiving the same public recognition as their more glamorous aircrew comrades-in-arms, and he set about to correct the situation by a live broadcast to Canada on the CBC on 20 July. Delivering it from London at 2:00 a.m. to be heard at 8:00 p.m. in Ottawa, he praised the contribution of those in overseas postings as well as those serving in Canada.[98]

In his continuing attempt to help the work of those in the field, he established seven district headquarters "'to facilitate the work of his field personnel'—including chaplains, public relations officers, doctors, and supervisors of auxiliary services—and to provide a 'channel of communication for RCAF personnel on matters concerning their RCAF career, pay, allowances, promotion, remusterings, etc.' . . . Similarly, the ever-increasing number of Canadian aircrew serving in the Mediterranean and the Far East led to the opening of a District Headquarters, Middle East, in Cairo on 25 September 1942 and another in Delhi, India the following summer."[99]

---

[97] He did manage some fishing, as his next letter indicates: " I did find time to relax for a Sunday and do a little fishing in the famous Brora River. I was lucky enough to hook a salmon, which buoyed my spirits a great deal."

[98] See Appendix B, "They Toil Without Glory," for complete text.

[99] *The Official History of the Royal Canadian Air Force, Vol. III*, p. 80.

* * *

Operation Jubilee was the code name for the controversial and calamitous raid on Dieppe on 19 August 1942—a date seared in the souls of Canadians. Gus had not been consulted about the raid, but the question of whether he had even been informed prior to its taking place is put to rest by a memo that came to light long after the war ended.

<u>Most Secret</u>   8-3-5/Ops
HQ First Cdn Army
9 Aug 42

Memo for File

1. GOC-in-C, First Cdn Army, informed me today what he had spoken to Air Marshall Edwards, RCAF, yesterday, 8 Aug 42, and had informed him that 400 and 414 Sqns, RCAF, had been detailed to participate in operation "JUBILEE".

2. This information had been given to Air Marshall Edwards confidentially, as an act of courtesy, in the belief that he, as the responsible head of the RCAF in England, should be informed, and with the knowledge that in all probability this information would not be forthcoming from any other source. Air Marshall Edwards confirmed that he had not been consulted concerning the employment of these units.

3. Gen McNaughton stressed that it conveyed no description or details of the plans, and had emphasized the need for extreme secrecy being observed.

Brig GS[100]

While the Army was making final preparations for the ill-fated raid, the Minister of National Defence for Air, Hon. C.G. Power and the CAS, A/M Breadner, were visiting London HQ. "We had a dinner for them the other night. . . . It was a great success and the Duke of Kent stayed with us until the farewells were said—something unusual for him." Less than two weeks later,

---

[100] Brigadier Penhale, BGS, of First Canadian Army. A copy of this memo was sent by the Army Historical Section to the Office of the Air Historian on 18 October 1961. See also Chapter 10.

11 - THE SECOND WORLD WAR - PART III: 1942

the Duke was killed when his plane crashed in Scotland, and Gus "had the honour of being chosen as one of the pallbearers" at his funeral at Windsor on 29 August.[101]

* * *

> "some people are talking a lot of bloody nonsense about splitting the Empire. If Canadians who see it from that point of view want to be mugs all their lives, that's their business. I can see no reason against Canadianization." Gus Edwards, 5 September 1942.

Strong words—some thought too strong—but nevertheless the opening salvo in "The Battle of the Bloody Nonsense," which brought down a barrage of criticism on Gus's head from *The Globe and Mail*, the *Toronto Telegram*, the Montreal *Gazette*, and the Ottawa *Journal*. Many of the skirmishes in the battle are covered in Chapter 10, but there are some additional facts not mentioned there that shed more light on the subject.

The cause is described in a signal of 10 September 1942:

<u>BREADNER FROM EDWARDS</u>

FOLLOWING IS A BRIEF RECORD OF WHAT ENSUED DURING SATURDAY'S PRESS CONFERENCE. AT OUTSET I SAID THAT I DISLIKED OFF THE RECORD DISCUSSIONS BUT THE NEWSPAPERMEN PRESENT SEEMED SO INTERESTED AND SO ANXIOUS TO OBTAIN ENTIRE BACKGROUND THAT I AGREED TO TALK OFF THE RECORD INDICATING WHICH REFERENCE MIGHT BE USED AND QUOTED. CANADIAN PRESS MAN WHO SAT AT FAR END OF THE TABLE APPARENTLY WAS UNABLE TO HEAR CLEARLY FROM HIS POSITION AND THEREFORE HE BECAME MIXED UP AS TO WHAT

---

[101] Letters to his mother of 18 August and 2 September 1942. Among the forty-three guests attending the dinner held at Claridges on 14 August were the CAS of the RAF and members of the RAF Air Council and the Canadian and New Zealand High Commissioners, as well as senior officers of the Canadian Army and Navy, the RAAF, the RNZAF, the USAAF, and officials of the Ministries of Aircraft Production and Information.

SHOULD AND SHOULD NOT BE PRINTED I FEEL IT IS UNWISE TO USE THIS EXCUSE AND PASS THIS ALONG FOR YOUR OWN INFORMATION ONLY.

Gus's spirited defence was published in daily newspapers across the country on 11 and 12 September and overseas in *Wings Abroad* on 23 September 1942:

> London, Sept. 11—(CP Cable)—Air Marshal Harold (Gus) Edwards, commanding officer of the Royal Canadian Air Force in Britain, tonight said that he champions the policy called "Canadianization" of the R.C.A.F. in the interests of the airmen themselves.
>
> **His Statement**
>
> He issued this statement:
>
> I am told that what I said at a press conference here the other day has provoked quite violent criticism in Canada.
>
> I am told by cable only that and cannot at this distance gauge the weight of the attacks which seem to be directed at me, nor can I say whether they are just or unjust. I simply do not know. All I know is that I championed the policy called "Canadianization" which means bringing our R.C.A.F. boys together into Canadian formations.
>
> I have fought for that cause because I believe it is the best possible policy for the men I represent. When I talk in favor of it, I am not speaking as Air Marshal Gus Edwards.
>
> I am talking as a spokesman for Sergeant-Pilot John Morrison who was over Germany last night—and got back safely, thank God, but lost his best friend in that other raid two nights ago.
>
> So far as that boy goes, what is called "Canadianization" is good policy. It means that all his personal troubles can be lifted from him, and he be left only with those which he has been sent over here to meet: which are success over his target, escape from flak, victory over night fighters, loyalty to his crewmates and fidelity to that love of freedom and of Canada which led him to stake his life for the principles in which he believes.

11 - THE SECOND WORLD WAR - PART III: 1942

Perhaps from a range longer than even a Halifax bomber can tackle, our Canadian critics cannot perceive this. The things that may distract that boy when he goes into combat and cannot foresee the outcome are things that can be readily adjusted only by Canadians.

What is Involved

They involve dollars and cents instead of pounds and shillings—dollars and cents going home to his wife or mother or saved for his marriage; they involve Canadian methods of promotion and discipline, on neither of which points we see eye to eye with others; they involve spiritual solace which he wishes to receive in the homely tongue of his fathers; they involve even the difficulty of finding baseball equipment in a country devoted to cricket.

All these problems we can solve for Sgt.-Pilot Morrison; all these worries large and small we can lift from his mind as he goes into that combat from which we hope he will emerge unscathed. We can solve them if we know where he is, if he is among enough of his countrymen to make his presence as a Canadian known to Canadian headquarters.

I think the all-Canadian squadron is best for these material and spiritual purposes. I think the all-Canadian wing or group is even better—and we should understand their problems after interviews we have with these boys, day after day, here in London and out on their stations. We see something else that may not be fully appreciated by either papers or public at home. We know these lads are very young by all our standards. If they were older they could not be aircrew.

Not Professional Warriors

This is the first absence away from home for many of them—I would go so far as to say for most of them. They are not professional warriors. Any homesickness they have ever encountered in their young lives—that visit maybe to relatives not so far away or to school or job from which they could still phone home—is multiplied a thousandfold here.

Such vast distances lie between them and their homes, and their return can be dictated only by the exigencies of war.

Understand me again, I am not talking so much now as commander of these boys but as one who has tried to understand their problems as individual Canadians—and has tried to see too how their people at home must feel. I believe they will be happier if they can talk to other boys from Yarmouth or Mont Joli or Aurora or Portage or Chilliwack. Not only happier but far more efficient in the performance of their high task and that can happen only if we bring our overseas Canadians more and more together in ever-expanding battle formations. If we bring them "home" from 700-odd R.A.F. units among which they are scattered today.

This is what I was saying in behalf of Sgt.-Pilot John Morrison. I take time off to answer a press attack only because such an attack might undermine the Canadian people's faith in the direction of their lads in battle overseas, and faith is vital to us all. These lads cannot, thank God, fight the enemy from the soil of Canada; but fighting where they are, let us do our utmost to bring a bit of Canada to them.

* * *

If criticism in some newspapers had been strong, so, too, was the support by other Canadians after his statement was published. From across the country, mothers and fathers of boys serving overseas sent letters of encouragement. From an emotional father, himself a veteran of WW I, struggling with the English language:

Good God Air Marshal you will never know what a relief you gave us when you restated your stand re Canadianization of the R.C.A.F. . . . we knelt down and prayed and thanked God to have such a man as you to command and understand our boys overseas. . . . The greatest compliment I can make you is you spoke as a real father and we now know how you want them treated by others also. . . .

His views were echoed by the mother of a sergeant pilot:

As the mother of one of the very young boys in the R.C.A.F. overseas, I have nothing but praise for your attitude, and everything

11 - THE SECOND WORLD WAR - PART III: 1942

you mention is absolutely right and true. . . .

The head of the Gazette is the old Imperialist type who still thinks of Canadians as Colonials. Well, that day has long passed. Canada is a nation in her own right and making a magnificent contribution to the present conflict.

I hope you have every success. It is wonderful to think we have a high ranking officer with such understanding, the courage of his own convictions and who can so completely forget his own career to fight for the rights of young Canadians under his command. It is a tragedy for Canada there are not more men like you.

Many RCAF personnel agreed, as demonstrated by a letter from a leading aircraftman posted to an RAF squadron: "I read your statement. . . . I think it was damn good and all the boys here feel the same way."

As for Bea, it was a difficult time as she watched helplessly from the sidelines as her favourite newspaper attacked her husband. She was upset and angered by the Ottawa *Journal's* two virulent editorials on 9 and 11 September and was particularly incensed by these statements in the latter:

It looks very much as though the Royal Canadian Air Force has in one case got the wrong sort of man in authority overseas in the person of Air Officer-in-Chief H.E. Edwards.

and

Any "Canadianization" which may mean any divisibility of air command, or merely multiple jobs, or increase the personal importance of officers like A.O.C. Edwards seems to us, if we may be pardoned for quoting the gentleman's own phrase, to be "bloody nonsense."

Coming close to calling for Gus's removal and accusing him of self-aggrandizement was simply more than Bea could bear and she responded in the only way she could think of—she went to the telephone and, in the iciest of tones, identified herself and then cancelled her subscription. As she had been a long-time subscriber to the *Journal* and reading it was part of her daily routine, her gesture of defiance cost her dearly in the days to come. Withdrawal symptoms appeared immediately, growing in intensity with each passing day until, on day five, she could stand it no longer and rather sheepishly asked if I would go to the drugstore to buy the paper. I started to remind her why I shouldn't do that but never got past "But Mum, you—" when she quickly intervened with, "I know, but I can't stand it any longer, so please, just go!" So I went—that afternoon and every other afternoon for over a month—until she decided enough was enough and renewed the subscription for home delivery.

The whole sorry affair mercifully came to an end on 14 September when, at the urging of the minister and the chief of the air staff, Gus issued a second statement:

> The touring Canadian newspaper party visited headquarters and I explained to them that I disliked talking off the record but since they were so interested in getting the complete background of Canada's fighting forces overseas I would make an exception in this case. Consequently I talked freely man to man.
>
> Unfortunately, one member of the party did not understand that my rather outspoken references were not for publication. It was a case of sheer misunderstanding, for which no one was to blame. I have always placed such faith in the press that I have never deemed it necessary to see their stories before release. I accept full responsibility for all I said. I was not misquoted, but I think it my duty to point out the foregoing facts.
>
> I am very pleased to learn the information I received that the Montreal *Gazette* and *The Globe and Mail* of Toronto were opposed to concentration of Canadian fliers in Canadian organizations is not true.
>
> I am sure that all who were concerned in the report, including myself, regret its publicity and any embarrassment or annoyance which its circulation may have brought to the publishers of these papers.
>
> It might be a good thing if it were made clear once again to the people of Canada that so-called Canadianization of the R.C.A.F. has nothing to do with combat control, which must obviously be exercised by a single operational agency, but is designed solely to advance the efficiency and well-being of our lads for the benefit of the common cause.

11 - THE SECOND WORLD WAR - PART III: 1942

* * *

Shortly after the infamous press conference was held, Gus welcomed the first contingent of thirty members of the RCAF Women's Division (WD) to take up duties at Headquarters. The photo below shows everyone enjoying the reception in his office and was accompanied by the rather wry comment, "I can't recall him ever having one to welcome the guys, but that's life."

RCAF photo courtesy Norman Jeffries

Apart from flying combat missions, WDs overseas were exposed to the same dangers as their male counterparts: the voyage to England aboard crowded troopships, which took as long as two weeks, in a convoy exposed to attacks by German submarines; the air raids on London; or perhaps an equally dangerous posting to an operational station. At HQ one WD, LAW Jean Inglis, had another assignment in addition to her normal duties. It was not something she could have anticipated when she enlisted and it came about in a strange way.

For a period of a year and half after he assumed command in London, a two-room suite served as Gus's private quarters, next to his office on the second floor of the Headquarters building at 20 Lincoln's Inn Fields. One day a guest remarked that it needed something to liven it up and give it some semblance of a home rather than a hotel. He suggested a dog would be just the thing, and a few days later, what should arrive but a six-month-old English cocker spaniel from the famous Ware Kennels, breeders of many a world champion.

A general duties airman was assigned to take him for walks. For reasons known only to the airman, one day instead of walking the dog, he took him up to the roof of the building and left him there. The dog, left unattended and seemingly devoid of the gene that gave him a fear of heights, panicked and jumped off the roof to his death. To say Gus was upset would be an understatement. For several days he also wondered how to explain the incident to the man who had been kind enough to give him the dog. Somehow the news reached the donor and soon thereafter a second spaniel, "Whirlpool of Ware," aka Peter, arrived at HQ.

"Whirlpool of Ware"
—Peter's pedigree name—
in his "Lion in Trafalgar Square" pose. 1952

With his shining coat, long ears, and flowing "feathers," Peter was a beautiful example of his breed. Like many another highly bred animal he was not overly endowed in the brain department, but did have a gentle, affectionate nature and was a welcome addition to both quarters and office. This time more care was exercised in choosing who would look after the dog, and LAW Inglis, a true dog lover, was selected. She turned out to be the perfect choice, taking him for walks and generally seeing to his well being until early in 1944.[102] He then sailed aboard a troopship for Canada, where he was smuggled into the country to avoid the six months' mandatory quarantine.

As for the unfortunate airman who left the first dog on the roof, his punishment was an immediate posting—some said to the Outer Orkneys, never to be heard from again.

* * *

---

[102] Telephone interviews with WD FS Jill Wigg Kennedy on 9 February 2003 and 29 May 2005.

11 - THE SECOND WORLD WAR - PART III: 1942

First anniversary of the arrival of the original contingent of WDs S/O Nancy McArthur (née Smith) third from left, LAW (later S/O) Norah Botterill third from right.[103]
RCAF photo courtesy Norman Jeffries

The WDs were an invaluable addition to the air force, replacing men in such diverse fields as accounting, secretarial, administration, and flight control. Fifteen hundred served overseas, one of whom was S/O Nancy Smith, who was assigned to Gus's office as his PA; another, LAW Norah Botterill, accompanied him to Buckingham Palace when he received his CB.

* * *

Norman (Jeff) Jeffries was just twenty-one years old when the anniversary party was held and had already been in England for over two years. Much of the reorganizing of the Records section had fallen to him and he remembers

---

[103] It is not surprising that the arrival of the WDs at HQ spawned many a romance, at least three of which ended in marriage. In 1943, Gus "gave away" Nancy Smith at her wedding to Canadian Army Captain McArthur, and at least two other WDs married RCAF officers: FS Jill Wigg to F/L William T. Blakeney; and S/O Norah Botterill to F/O Norman Jeffries.

Gus as "a tough old 'B' but [he] had the human touch" and for this reason was "appreciated by we other ranks."[104] On 23 September Gus wrote to him:

> Dear Jeffries:
>
> I am very pleased that you have been appointed to the commissioned rank of Pilot Officer in the Special Reserve of the Royal Canadian Air Force.
>
> I congratulate you most heartily and in commending you for the work you have already accomplished in the Service I wish you every success in the future.

Jeff was one of thousands of boys barely out of high school who, eager to fly, had joined the air force at the age of eighteen. His story, told in his own words, provides a vivid picture of one young man's war. Like all the others, it is unique and compelling.

> I enlisted on 28 October 40 as an AC2—having been rejected for aircrew because of defective colour vision, I was mustered as a Clerk Admin at No. 1 Manning Depot in Toronto. At the end of Nov of that year I was posted to 6 Repair Depot at Trenton as a clerk. In Jan 41, having heard that remustering to aircrew was much easier in the UK, I applied for an overseas posting and was fortunate enough to get it, much to the envy of a lot of my contemporaries at the time. I left Trenton in April, got held back in Halifax for nearly six weeks and finally arrived in the UK in mid June—I celebrated my nineteenth birthday in Halifax. We subsequently were given to understand that things had piled up in Halifax because the Bismarck had been loose in the Atlantic. After she was sunk things finally got moving and, as I have said, I arrived at the Personnel Reception Centre in Bournemouth in mid June. We were the first draft into Bournemouth. From there I was posted to Overseas HQs—then housed on the fifth floor of Cdn Mil HQs in Cockspur Street.
>
> Needless to say, it was most exciting to be nineteen and in the great city of London. Somewhere along the line I had become an AC1

---

[104] E-mail of 13 August 2004 from Norman Jeffries.

11 - THE SECOND WORLD WAR - PART III: 1942

and in July 41 I was reclassified to LAC. My job was Records Clerk. In the Fall the word got around that we were to expand and were to move to larger quarters namely, 20 Lincoln's Inn Fields and the Land Registry Bldg on the south side of the Square. In Dec 41 I was promoted to Cpl—I can remember some weeks earlier my Sgt taking me aside and telling me that if I were to spend less time chasing "that English girl" . . . that I could anticipate promotion. In March 42 I was again promoted, this time to Sgt, and was 2 i/c HQ Orderly Room. By this time your father was in control and the HQs was growing apace—very busy. In Jan 43 I was promoted to Flight Sgt and placed in charge of the HQ OR.

We were paid a subsistence allowance and found our own accommodation. As I recall the allowance was 10 shillings per day for other ranks and one pound for officers. When I arrived in London in 1941 as an AC1 the subsistence allowance was more than my pay—the Pound in those days was valued at $4.40 Cdn. Initially most of us on arrival stayed at one of the hotels run by Auxiliary Svcs—in my case a hotel operated by the Sally Ann on Southampton Row. Once oriented, however, most found room and board or got together with others to rent flats or apartments. If meals were not included in one's accommodation arrangements we paid for them in restaurants. Sometime in 1942 a canteen was established in the Land Registry Bldg.

Throughout, I had not lost sight of the reason I had applied for overseas and had been before an Aircrew Selection Board in Nov 41 but was rejected again for defective colour vision. Sometime in the following months, because so many otherwise suitable aircrew material had been rejected for colour failure the category was split into colour vision defective safe and colour vision defective unsafe. Emboldened by this I got another board in the Spring of 1943 only to find that I fell into the unsafe category and was rejected once more.

My CO, the Camp Commandant of the HQ, was very aware that I had no wish to spend the war as a clerk in London so when the last attempt at aircrew failed he decided to recommend me for a commission in the Admin Branch. This occurred in August [43] and after completing the course at the RAF School of Admin,

I was posted to the Tactical Air Force, firstly to Biggin Hill to double bank the Adjutant of 411 Sqn and then to Kenley as Adj of 403 Sqn. At the end of Dec 43 I was alerted for posting to 143 Wing which was forming at Ayr in Scotland arriving there at the beginning of Jan to take the position of Adjutant of the Tech Sqn—Technical Adjutant. I remained with 143 for the remainder of the war. The Wing was comprised of three squadrons and we operated Typhoon Fighter Bombers. The squadrons had arrived in the UK as formed units, two having operated in the Aleutians and one from the East Coast. Off the top of my head I cannot remember their sqn numbers in Canada but in the UK they became 438, 439 and 440. Three other formed sqns arrived around the same time and these were equipped with Spitfires and became 441, 442 and 443 under 144 Wing.

We brought the Wing south in March 44 and the squadrons went operational. In mid June we went into Normandy, followed the Army through the Falaise Gap at the end of Aug, occupying airfields at Amiens [and] Brussels. In mid Sep we moved up to Eindhoven in Holland to provide close support for the battle at Arnhem. Following the withdrawal from Arnhem the front stalemated—we dug in for the winter at Eindhoven and did not move again until March 45 when we followed British 2nd Army into Germany. Airfields enroute were at Goch, Osnabruck, Celle—we ended the war there (seven miles from Belsen) and then in early May moved up to our final location at Flensburg on the German Danish border.

[A]bout bombing. I arrived at the tail end of the Blitz and experienced one that I thought was a big raid but was assured by the "veterans" that it was nothing like what had occurred in the previous months. After that the bombing seemed to tail off and apart from the odd surprise or sneak raid was really of no great concern through 1942 and early 1943. However, it did intensify in the Fall as I recall—the mini Blitz. From about June of 1944 until the end London and those stationed there had to contend with the V1 and V2 attacks. I was safely in the Beachhead, relatively speaking, but had reports from Norah who was in London throughout. When we were sitting at Eindhoven in the winter of 44/45 the V1s would pass over at about 300 ft enroute to Ostend

11 - THE SECOND WORLD WAR - PART III: 1942

and to the UK—nothing we could do about them which was frustrating.

I finished the war in the rank of F/O. Norah by this time was an S/O and, being at HQs, managed to arrange for us to be repatriated in the same draft. We returned to Canada in Aug 45 on the Duchess of Richmond.[105]

During his two years overseas, Gus was determined to see as many RCAF personnel as possible, no matter how remote or far-flung the area to which they were posted. In the UK this meant inspection trips to stations throughout England, Northern Ireland, and Scotland, including the Orkney and Shetland Islands. At the end of October 1942, he went much farther afield to see those who were stationed in the Middle and Far East.

BREADNER FROM EDWARDS I AM PROCEEDING IMMEDIATELY TO THE EAST TO INSPECT SQUADRONS AND AS MANY OTHER RCAF PERSONNEL AS POSSIBLE AND CLEAR UP PROBLEMS IN THAT THEATRE.

The journey was a dangerous one. Most of Western Europe and North Africa was either occupied or controlled by the Germans. In Europe only Switzerland, Sweden, Portugal, and Spain were neutral. In North Africa, Field Marshal Rommel's Afrika Korps was still a potent force even though the British Eighth Army, under its new commander, General Montgomery, was about to break out from El Alamein, where fierce fighting had been in progress since July. It was not until 8 November that the Allies landed in Morocco and Algeria, and it would not be until the following May that the last Axis troops were forced from North Africa.

In these circumstances, the shortest route over Europe and the Mediterranean to Egypt was clearly not an option, but rather a long, circuitous one to avoid potential encounters with enemy fighter aircraft. Consequently, the journey was started south, well off the coast of France, over the Bay of Biscay to Lisbon; then hundreds of miles off the African Coast to Senegal on board

---

[105] E-mails from Norman Jeffries of 23–25 November 2005. Jeff left the Air Force in 1945, but the lure of the Service was too great, and after articling for three years with a CA firm rejoined in 1948. He had a distinguished career over the next twenty-eight years, holding such important posts as Director of Budget and retiring with the rank of colonel (group captain) in the integrated CF.

Arrival in UK from Far East. L to R: G/C F. Wait, A/V/M W.A. Curtis, W/C W. Brodribb, Gus Edwards. 30 December 1942
RCAF photo courtesy John Smith

the Royal Mail aircraft *Berwick*.[106] He continued east to Nigeria and across Central Africa, north through Sudan, and eventually reaching Cairo, less than 200 miles from the fighting at El Alamein; then on through Jordan, Iraq, Pakistan, across India to Ceylon, and finally north up the eastern coast of India, ending at Chittagong. The entire trip out took 108 flying hours and, with stopovers, 19 days to complete.

A signal of 8 November explains a delay in Lisbon.

> MOST SECRET—BREADNER FROM CURTIS
> C IN C HAS ARRIVED FREETOWN AND SHOULD ARRIVE LAGOS LATER IN DAY WAS DELAYED FIVE DAYS IN LISBON DUE TO HEAD WINDS AND SERIOUSLY CONSIDERED STUDYING PORTUGUESE. PLEASE KEEP BEA INFORMED. WILL CONTINUE TO ADVISE.

[106] This was one of three Boeing 314 flying boats (the same type of aircraft used in Pan-American "clipper" services) that had been acquired for special wartime flights. The other two were named *Bristol* and *Bangor*. Gus's letter to his mother of 6 November 1942 written on board describes the flight: "we are whizzing along at the rate of knots. I am writing this in a nice room which Churchill occupied a trip or two ago. There is even a writing desk."

11 - THE SECOND WORLD WAR - PART III: 1942

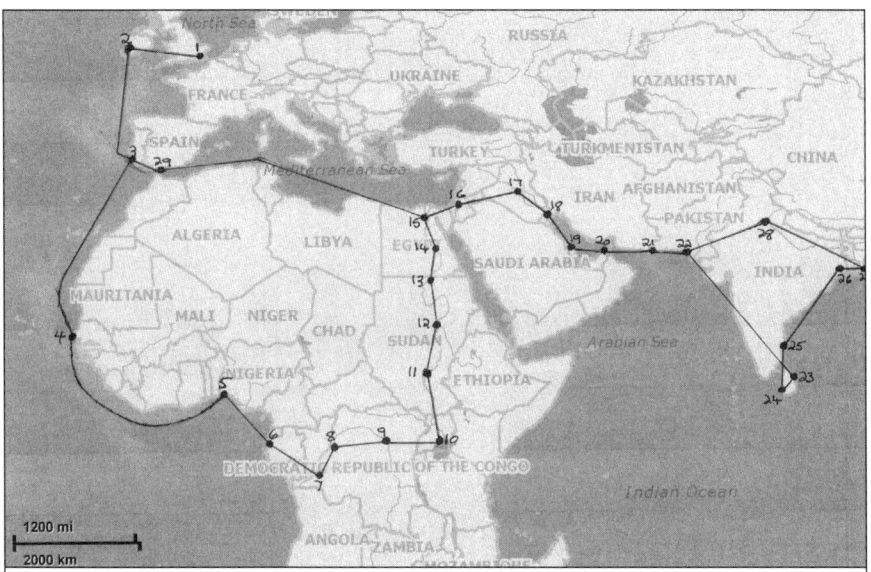

LEGEND:

1. London
2. Foynes, Ireland
3. Lisbon, Portugal
4. Bathhurst, Senegal
5. Lagos, Nigeria
6. Libreville, Gabon
7. Leopoldville (Kinshasa), Zaire
8. Coquilhatville (Mbandaka), Zaire
9. Stanleyville (Kinsangani), Zaire
10. Laropi (Kampala), Uganda
11. Malakâl, Sudan
12. Khartoum, Sudan
13. Wadi Halfa, Sudan
14. Luxor (El Uqsur), Egypt
15. Cairo, Egypt
16. Kallia, Israel
17. Al Habbaniya, Iraq
18. Basra, Iraq
19. Bahrain
20. Sharjah, United Arab Emirates
21. Jiwani, Pakistan
22. Karachi, Pakistan
23. Trincomalee, Sri Lanka
24. Colombo, Sri Lanka
25. Madras, India
26. Calcutta, India
27. Chittagong, Bangladesh
28. Delhi, India
29. Gibraltar

TRIP TO THE MIDDLE AND FAR EAST
31 October–30 December 1942
London–Chittagong, 108 Flying Hours
Calcutta–London, 54 Flying Hours

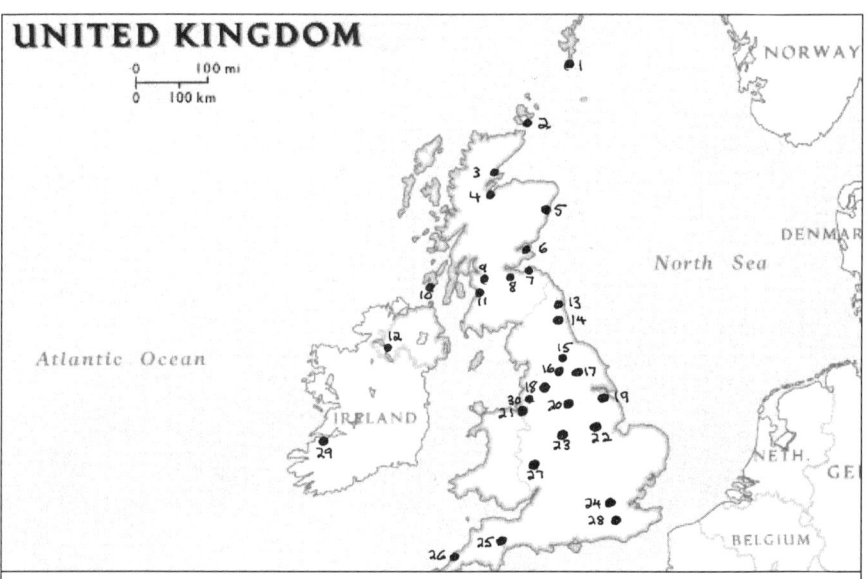

LEGEND:

Some of the Stations visited by air in 1942–1943

<u>Scotland</u>
1. Sumburgh
2. Hatson
3. Tain
4. Inverness
5. Dyce
6. Leuchars
7. Drem
8. Turnhouse
9. Glasgow
10. Port Ellen
11. Prestwick

<u>Northern Ireland</u>
12. St. Angelo

<u>England</u>
13. Acklington
14. Ouston
15. Tholthorpe
16. Linton-on-Ouse
17. Pocklington
18. Leeming
19. North Coates
20. Bawtray
21. Speke
22. Digby
23. Taten Hill
24. Hendon
25. Exeter
26. St. Eval

<u>Other Locations</u>
27. QZ
28. East Grinstead
29. Foynes
30. Chorley

11 - THE SECOND WORLD WAR - PART III: 1942

It was open season for spies from both Allied and Axis countries to operate in neutral countries, and Gus had a first-hand experience in Lisbon. One night during the enforced stopover, he returned to his hotel room after dinner to find both it and his luggage had been thoroughly searched by the Germans; but as his suitcases contained only his personal belongings, they found nothing of interest—except perhaps for what was referred to as the "hat box": a leather case with combination lock to carry the travelling bar that accompanied him on all his trips.

Another signal on 12 December gives an account of two inspections near Chittagong, showing just how close he came to the enemy:

> BREADNER FROM CURTIS
> . . . EDWARDS TOURED FORWARD AERODROME INDIA TODAY, TRAVELLED ARMED HUDSON AIRCRAFT ESCORTED BY FIGHTERS TOUCHED MOST ADVANCED LANDING GROUNDS IN COUNTRY[.] AT ONE AERODROME WHICH CLOSEST TO BURMA FRONTIER AND CONSEQUENTLY JAPANESE OCCUPIED TERRITORY MET FOUR CANADIAN RADIO MECHANICS WHO COULD BE CONSIDERED TO BE CLOSEST CANADIANS TO JAP FORCES[.] . . . TODAY'S TOUR WAS SECOND SINCE EDWARDS ARRIVAL INDIA[.] EARLIER IN THE WEEK HE HAD VISITED BOMBER AERODROMES OPERATING FROM ROUGH BUT ADEQUATE BASES FAR INTO INDIA'S "BLUE."

On the return trip he was a guest of the viceroy in New Delhi, then on to Cairo. Rather than returning by the outward route through central Africa, they flew back across the Mediterranean, stopping at Gibraltar and Lisbon. He sums it all up:

> All I will say about the Far East trip at the moment is that it took me two months and during that time I was two hundred hours in the air and had travelled thirty thousand miles before I returned to London. It was a wonderful and unique experience meeting Canadians so far from their home land and talking to them of their aspirations. The spirits of the boys were high everywhere I went but there were many things that could be done for them and I have been trying since my return to introduce every measure that

will relieve their lot abroad.

Of course I saw Bob in India and he looked very fit having had a happy convalescence in colourful Cashmere. I saw him three times so we had some good talks and I had arranged to meet him a fourth time before my departure from that part of India but the Japs came over to bomb and he was up after them and away before I could see him again. He is reputed to be one of the finest pilots in India.[107]

RCAF Overseas Headquarters, 20 Lincoln's Inn Fields, London.
Strength—all ranks, including 39 airwomen: 755; (not all present)
December 1942
RCAF photo courtesy Glenn Curtis

---

[107] Letter to his mother of 6 February 1943. "Bob" is his nephew, Robert B. Edwards, a F/L with 136 RAF Fighter Squadron. During the trip he also met his old friend Seton Broughall (he of the six-week spree in 1919), who was then a group captain in the RAF serving in India. In the meantime in Ottawa, Bea and I poured over the atlas, plotting his progress as details were received.

12

THE SECOND WORLD WAR - PART IV
1943–1944

Following Gus's return to London, it took an inordinate amount of everyone's time to file the requisite reports and expense accounts, with the latter taking months to finalize with Treasury. He was also well occupied with finding solutions to the problems he had encountered on the trip, to say nothing of the ever-present, gnawing difficulties of implementing Canadianization. His decision to force that issue to a head so that "an understanding . . . be reached if I and my successors are to live a life that more nearly approaches one that is fit to live" caused quite a stir in Ottawa, prompting the CAS to suggest he return to Canada to "get things straight this end." But he would have none of it. His reply bears repeating, as it illustrates how difficult the situation had become and how strongly he felt about the action he had taken:

> Your cable strikes strange notes. You demand vigorous action and protest the slothful inactivity in pursuit of your declared policy. I fight for this and now must struggle both ways without aid. To compromise now would determine the end of the RCAF as an entity overseas. To pour oil on troubled waters would avail nothing. Coming home would bespeak weakness which I cannot accept. I have done all with firmness, candour and truth conscientiously believing that I was right. I stand or fall on that come what may.[108]

But all was not controversy and battle. On 2 February, he was invested by

---

[108] Excerpts from *The Official History of the Royal Canadian Air Force Volume III, The Crucible of War 1939-1945*, pp. 89–90.

the King as a Companion of The Most Honourable Order of the Bath at Buckingham Palace. He describes the ceremony in a letter to his mother:

> The King was gracious and resplendent in naval uniform as we all filed before him to receive our various medals. There were Peers, Knights, D.S.Os and D.F.Cs in profusion and it was really a wonderful sight. I took with me Kath Warburton, who looked very sweet in her smart W.A.A.F. uniform, and also the youngest airwoman in my Headquarters, a young girl called L.A.W. Norah Botterill. I thought they would enjoy it more than anyone else and I believe they did.
>
> The King said a word or two to me but I noticed that he kept most of his words for the more junior people there. You remember Bill Brodribb my P.A. who received the M.B.E. The King spoke to him for quite a long time asking him how long he had been over here and other questions. The Queen was unfortunately not present as it is not customary for her to be there on occasions of this nature. You would have been very interested in the Beefeaters, who had come all the way from the Tower of London and they certainly added a dash of colour to the proceedings; even their faces were red, most of them have little white goatee beards. I was amazed that with their many years they could stand throughout it all without turning a hair. . . .
>
> I have had flocks of letters of congratulations and good wishes this last month. They just came pouring in and are still arriving from all parts of the world. . . .[109]

* * *

One of the characteristics of a sense of humour is the ability to laugh at oneself, and Gus was certainly able to do that. Having seen him roar with laughter at a cartoon of himself which appeared in the RCAF *Roundel*, I am sure he would have been equally amused by one that was drawn during his time in London. It concerns an encounter he had with FS Ernest Hibberd, whose daughter describes the incident:

---

[109] Letter dated 6 February 1943. Bill Brodribb was Gus's invaluable executive assistant and accompanied him everywhere. He can be seen in several of the photos.

12 - THE SECOND WORLD WAR - PART IV: 1943–1944

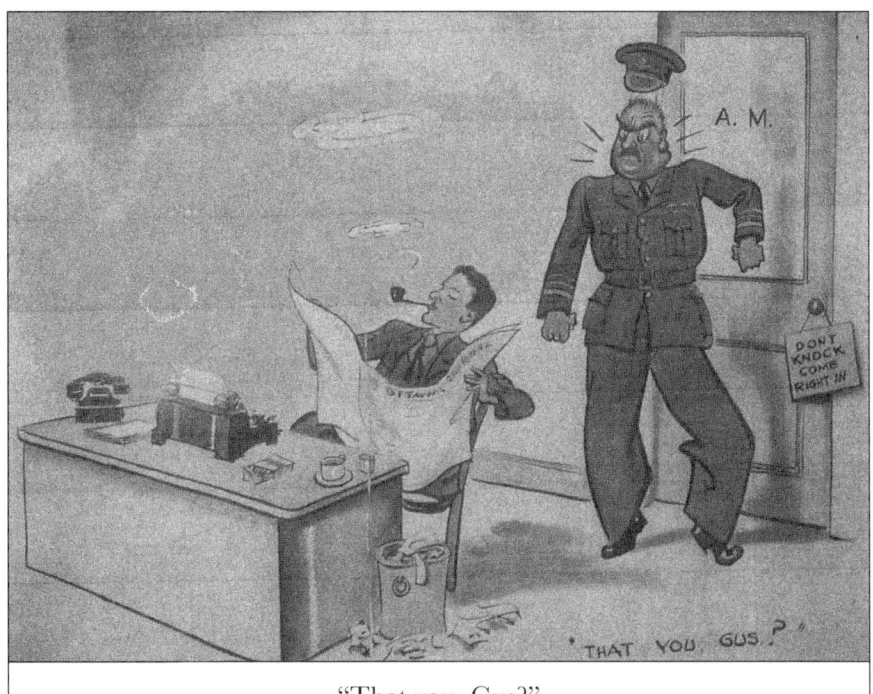

"That you, Gus?"
Cartoon courtesy Julia Hibberd

Dad served under "Gus" Edwards in London during the war. Apparently . . . Gus had the habit of roaming the corridors at night—this particular night my Dad was on duty but "Gus" came up behind him, catching him reading the newspaper with his feet on the desk. My Dad (please note he was in his early 20s) was terrified he would be court-martialled.

He told the story to a cartoonist friend (someone he stayed with while recuperating from devastating injuries suffered during a bombing raid on his living quarters in London)—Mr. Ternent, whose cartoon "Mr. Potter" appeared in the *Glasgow Bulletin*. After getting a full description of the event and of "Gus" he came up with the cartoon.[110]

Happily for the flight sergeant, he was not court-martialled—the fact that he thought such action might be taken was punishment enough.

[110] E-mail from Julia Hibberd, 23 January 2003. Sadly, her father died in December of that year.

* * *

Even during the war, London was a wonderful place to be for someone like Gus, a lover of classical music and opera, for it was there that Dame Myra Hess, the renowned pianist, so endeared herself to the British people.

> Amidst the extraordinary circumstances of wartime Britain, there arose a musical heroine, the pianist Myra Hess, whose leadership in bringing music to her countrymen from London's National Gallery was ofttimes an act of considerable bravery. In defiance of the Nazi raids, Myra Hess, along with hundreds of other musicians, performed Classical music concerts as bombs fell on the city. . . . In these remarkable times, Myra Hess became a symbol of British resolve to withstand the attacks, and she earned a special place in the hearts of the people and in the history of music. . . .
>
> In the first months of the Second World War, all live music performances ceased in Britain. Dame Myra cut short a tour of America that was in progress, and on returning to London, she inaugurated what was to become a remarkable and popular series of lunch-time concerts at the National Gallery, a building then emptied of its treasures for safekeeping during the Blitz. This was exactly what people needed since the black-outs made it difficult for London's suburban residents to travel up to town after dark. And so Classical music symbolically and physically replaced the paintings and sculptures of the National Gallery, and an audience which included not only regular devotees, but also many who had never heard such music before came about as a result of Hess's brainchild to replace one kind of art with another, enabling the National Gallery to continue functioning as Great Britain's chief center of art.[111]

I do not know whether Gus ever attended any of these concerts, but I do know he had been privileged to meet Dame Myra several times when they were guests at the same dinner parties. On these occasions, to everyone's great delight, she would sometimes play for them after dinner. One of his most cherished possessions—and one that we were only permitted to listen to at

---

[111] www.carolinaclassical.com.

12 - THE SECOND WORLD WAR - PART IV: 1943–1944

Christmas or some other special time—was her famous recording of Bach's *Jesu, Joy of Man's Desiring*, a copy of which she had autographed for him.

* * *

Gus was back in Ottawa again for meetings in May and returned to England in mid-June. His time of departure coincided with a violent thunderstorm, and Bea pleaded with him to delay taking off until it abated. But he wouldn't hear of it, and so we watched for the ritual "thumbs-up" as the aircraft started to taxi down the runway. And then it lumbered off, gained altitude, and quickly disappeared into the low-lying clouds. Several weeks later, in London on 17 July, he refers to the storm at the end of his letter to his mother.

> There is one thing that I would like to do though, at some time, and that is to inspect the Cadet Squadron in Glace Bay. The Commanding Officer wrote me and asked if they could call it after me, and I said that I had no objection. Since then I have had no word from them and I don't know whether they have adopted that name or not. . . .[112]

> Outside of getting out to play a little golf, I seldom seem to leave my Headquarters these days. Things get busier and busier. But with these long evenings it seems such a pity to be indoors all the time and particularly so when the blackout will be on us again at something like four o'clock in the afternoon, before many months have passed.

> The country just now is at its best. There has been a bit of a drought but the rains of the last few days have made everything green again. All the gardens are filled with flowers, in fact London outside of the areas that have been blown down but have been cleaned up to such an extent that they look no more than vacant lots, hardly represents a city that has gone through the things it has in the past four years. . . .

> There is nothing much to tell you except that my trip back was as pleasant as the one going over. It took me exactly twenty-four hours to get from Ottawa to my front door in London, with stops

---

[112] The cadet squadron was, in fact, named "45 AM Edwards Squadron" and flourishes to this day. Details of its history, etc. may be found on its Web site, www.cadets.net/atl/45air.

in the state of Maine, Newfoundland and Scotland. The weather was good to us generally speaking, although for about an hour around Montreal we were tossed about in a violent thunderstorm. I am sending you a copy of a little sketch I wrote during this thunderstorm which I hope you will like. . . .

Departing Ottawa for England In Flight
in bad weather   10:00 A.M.
                               June 15th, 1943

I LEAVE MY TREASURES BEHIND

Heaven's gales worry our frail ship; the blast of thunder is unheard here in its noisy belly. Lightning's flash no more than changes the misty light on this stormy and tear-drenched morning. The craft trembles as a vessel at sea; straining itself to conquer Nature's violence. Earth is eclipsed, the pale sky greys to a smouldering black, rain, hail and thin watery shadows.

Thus do I leave my treasures.

Forward I see, mile by mile, my path bespoken and matched by this tumult. A changing course, uncharted and narrow, fraught with peculiar vagaries. A tempest that abates at the end, with scant interval. A path that can but end, inevitably, in storm and shadow.

A star in its highest ascendency falters, dips, then sets. The changing moon, thin and listless, grows to full face and blooms; wanes and then is extinguished. So, too, is the fate of man. Forward again I see hope high and tidy; few doubts assail me; the light of battle stirs the blood, brightens the eye; warms the heart. Calm follows the tempest.

The peril of yesterday is a joy tomorrow.

Behind I leave my treasures of family swept away in the return again towards the war. Hearts are heavy with the sting of parting. A separation that comes to brood, hurts and seldom loses its meaning. There is a clutch that holds in joy and sorrow; the clutch of love that ever springs from full hearts, no matter what turn life's changes take. The firm hold of family ties; the rapture of each other's presence;

the slow forgiveness for a thought unkind: for we hurt the most the ones we love the best! Fatherly succour—maternal conquest—lives bred new to bless and cherish: first helpless and weak, then growth to strong fine stature; the process reverses, wherein filial care commands. Age languishing and tolerant—youth intolerant and provocative. The scheme melting down to a serious, wistful whole. Burdens carried together; joy shared equally; life's mystery partially unravelled, partly understood; but above all an emotion transcending all others, that few, who have not felt it, could ever see or understand. Such treasures I leave!

I leave the Treasure of Friendship.

No greater test confronts mankind. Characters vary and change. One bares his heart to another. Who but a friend can bear this enlightening of his weakness and his faults? Who, but a friend, could brook his faults, laud his achievements, though seeing him so often, suffer his habits? Who, but a friend, would praise his fame and stand his domination, forgive his suspected haughtiness or subordination. Who would recognize his greatness but a friend; though greatness is imaginary and ephemeral until supported by history.

They stood calmly but bravely in the pelting rain, sad but brave.

There are treasures in parchment, in metal and stone, but in the heart of man the greatest treasures lie.

The Treasures I leave behind.

* * *

In the same letter, he attached a copy of a letter he had received from Lord Brownlow following a speech he had made at American Air Force Headquarters. I believe it refers to remarks concerning cooperation between the RAF and the USAAF, which, due to differing views held by members of both services, was sometimes difficult to achieve. A good working relationship between the two was essential to the conduct of the war, and Gus, British born but North American in outlook, understood both cultures and made every effort to bridge the gap that prevented their understanding one another.

> COPY OF LETTER.
>
>   Headquarters,
>   EIGHTH AIR FORCE.
>   Etousa
>
>   Office of the Commanding General.
>
> Dear Air Marshal,
>
>   As the R.A.F. Staff Officer attached to General Eaker's office, may I tell you how enormously I enjoyed your admirable talk in the War Room - it was quite excellent and most valuable to British and Americans alike - much of it had not been said before but needed saying badly.
>
>   I have never before seen applause after any speech in the War Room, in five months' experience - either for U.S. or British officers - which, you may feel, is a pleasant reward and high compliment.
>
> With sincere good wishes,
>
>   Yours sincerely,
>
>   BROWNLOW,
>   S/L.

* * *

Throughout his career, Gus received a constant flow of visitors; several family members were included in this parade. As a child in Ottawa, I had led the field, looking for five cents for an ice cream cone. A couple of years later, at HQ in London, a young cousin from Glace Bay was equally insistent that he have a chat with Gus.

My dad, Roy Edwards, used to tell the story of his visit with the Air Marshal. Dad would have been about twenty years old and

12 - THE SECOND WORLD WAR - PART IV: 1943–1944

Parade to the Town Hall.
RCAF photo courtesy John Smith

Bearing the flag into the Council Chamber.
RCAF photo courtesy John Smith

Presentation of RCAF Ensign to His Worship the Mayor of Holborn. On left: Vincent Massey, Canadian High Commissioner to the United Kingdom; far right: Gus Edwards and W/C Bill Brodribb. 26 July 1943

stationed somewhere in England. I believe the year was 1943. My grandfather, Frank Edwards [Gus's cousin], had suggested that Dad should go to visit the Air Marshal. So, on one of his leaves, Dad decided to do just that.

At the time, I believe Dad would still have been a private. He walked into the headquarters where he was met by a particularly officious orderly. The orderly brusquely asked Dad what he wanted. Dad was no shrinking violet. "I'm here to see the Air Marshal," he announced. Apparently this amused the orderly who mockingly called out to a nearby colleague, "Hey, Joe, this fellow's here to see the Air Marshal!" At that moment the Air Marshal appeared at the doorway of an adjacent office. Whether he had heard the commotion or appeared by accident I cannot say. The two orderlies stood to attention. The Air Marshal immediately recognized my father. "Roy," he said, "Come in." The Air Marshal put his hand on Dad's shoulder as he ushered him inside. I can see the gleam in my father's eye as he looked back and made eye contact with the chastened orderly.

Dad would always end his account with a chuckle; "I've never seen two guys snap to attention like that in my life!"[113]

* * *

During his trip to Canada, the Minister had approved his request to replace the small two-room suite at headquarters, which had served as his living quarters for a year and half, with more adequate accommodation "for the purpose of contacting and, on necessary occasions, entertaining officers and officials of Allied Government Forces." He had been authorized to rent a furnished private home similar to those which had been allotted to General McNaughton and senior officers of the American Forces. His memo of 19 July to the Air Member for Accounting and Finance tells how it could be handled:

NON SECRET, NAIRN FROM EDWARDS -PERSONAL-

I HAVE DISCUSSED WITH AIR MINISTRY THE

---

[113] Letter of 10 December 2006 from Hon. Justice Frank C. Edwards.

12 - THE SECOND WORLD WAR - PART IV: 1943–1944

QUESTION OF AN OFFICIAL QUARTER. AS OUTLINED IN MY MEMORANDUM TO THE CAS DATED MAY 29, THEY SUGGEST AND I WOULD BE GLAD TO TREAT THIS SUBJECT ON THE SAME LINES AS THOUGH IT WERE A PURELY RAF PROBLEM THAT IS TO REQUISITION A HOUSE ACCORDING TO THEIR SPECIFICATIONS PRESCRIBED AND FIXED FOR AN OFFICER OF EQUAL RANK AND POSITION AND HAND IT OVER TO US ON A STRAIGHT REPAYMENT BASIS IN LIKE MANNER TO THE ARRANGEMENTS MADE FOR THE AMERICANS BUT ON A MUCH LOWER SCALE. THEY WILL TAKE RESPONSIBILITY FOR UPKEEP CONTRACT INVENTORY AND SUCH THINGS PREVAILING IN ENGLAND THAT WE HAVE LITTLE KNOWLEDGE OF. I RECOMMEND THE ABOVE FOR YOUR APPROVAL. THE APPROXIMATE COST SHOULD NOT EXCEED SIX HUNDRED POUNDS PER ANNUM. I SHOULD BE GRATEFUL FOR EARLY APPROVAL TO TAKE ADVANTAGE OF SUMMER WEATHER AND IN CONSIDERATION OF HEALTH WHICH PRESENT QUARTERS IMPAIR. IT WILL BE NECESSARY TO KEEP SOME OF PRESENT TWO ROOM QUARTERS AT HEADQTRS IN CASE OF BLITZ IN ANY OF ITS FORMS AND CONSEQUENT LACK OF TRANSPORT . . .[114]

Thus, "Highdale" was leased, and Bea received a description of it from S/O Nancy McArthur in a handwritten note dated 27 August.

Dear Mrs. Edwards,

The Air Marshal departed in a cloud of dust for Scotland and Ireland and I _did_ want to get these pictures of his new abode off to you. I do hope you won't mind my writing to you but the pictures bear a little explanation.

The pictures glamorize "Highdale" considerably as it hasn't looked this way in three yrs. The owner I believe became a little

---

[114] Memo to the CAS 29 May 1943. Other than that "Highdale" was "just outside" or "just south" of London, its exact location remains a mystery.

"Highdale," the official residence of the
AOC-in-C RCAF Overseas from September 1943.
Photo courtesy John Smith

timid about the war and vanished to America leaving his home (complete with furniture) and garden to fall into a horrible state of disrepair. The furniture has since been removed, but there are many rennovations [sic] to be made within the house itself. We hope these will be completed within a fortnight or so.

The garden is intended to be an uncultivated garden, as the owner had a mania for wild flowers. However there are 40,000 bulbs scattered helter-skelter throughout. They will appear in rotation come the early spring, and we understand, make a dazzling show. The Air Marshal has hired a very good gardener, who has done a considerable amt. of landscaping in his day, so that we expect over the next few months to have restored some of its former beauty.

Unfortunately, Gus enjoyed the benefits of the garden a scant four months,

12 - THE SECOND WORLD WAR - PART IV: 1943–1944

for he would be in hospital, thousands of miles away, when the bulbs burst into bloom the following spring.

In mid-October, the Minister was "considering changes in appointments affecting a number of senior officers [and] would appreciate opportunity to discuss this with you. To this end can you arrange to be in Ottawa on or about 1 Nov."[115] Gus returned to Canada for two weeks to learn the die had been cast and he was to be replaced by A/M Breadner as AOC-in-C Overseas at the end of the year. His last letter from London to his mother:

November 23rd, 1943.

My dear Mother,

It was a great pleasure to me to get the telegram that you sent while I was in Ottawa. The trend of life has taken a very steep turn but, although it was unexpected and came strangely, it was not, indeed, one of those things that could not, in the course of a long and colourful life, be unanticipated.

It appears, after this long period of time associated with a great and noble Service, that my connections will be at last severed, but, in so separating myself from this Service which I adore, I am not unmindful of a feeling of great pride. For twenty-eight years I have passed through a period of great human understanding. I have seen men rise and fall; others never rise at all. I have felt the pride of things well done. I have been thrilled by great achievement, for no man, no matter his emotions, could be more surprised and more pleased with having achieved the height of his profession.

I am thankful that you, my wife and my children may point their finger at me and say, with due acclaim, "There is a man," but in this pride I am humbled by the thought of your great endeavour and great efforts on my behalf. I do not forget the trunk from which I was hewn. In the fullness of time history will speak and when it has spoken I shall be happy with its word. But whatever may have been done in the past; whatever great things may have fallen parallel to my path, I look forward wistfully and with great

---

[115] Signal from Minister of National Defence for Air, 16 October 1943.

courage to the future. Great things need to be done; great things are possible; whether it will fall to my lot to achieve these in like manner to the ones I have heretofore achieved is a matter of only bold speculation. Should I again be faced with the problems that heretofore have faced me, I do hope that with your blessing I shall see them clearly, honestly, and with great heart; but, if I do not, once again you may chalk failure down not to the lack of great purpose but to something through which humanity might normally err.

In you I place my lasting trust; from you there came my best and greatest impulses; to you, now, I repeat my great thanks.

Ever your loving son
Harold

The sketch he wrote in the summer included the prophetic comment that his path could ". . . but end, inevitably, in storm and shadow." But from this letter, and the phrase, "although it was unexpected and came strangely," he apparently had not foreseen the end would come so swiftly, nor the manner in which it was handled. The only post senior to the one he held was Chief of the Air Staff and, rather than accept a lesser position, he chose to retire. In a very short time, that choice proved to be the correct one, for soon after he returned to London his health took another turn for the worse, this time requiring surgery.

But before he left England for the last time, there was one more ceremony to attend, one he had eagerly anticipated and worked towards for months: the laying of the cornerstone on 11 December for the new Canadian Wing at the Queen Victoria Hospital in East Grinstead.

At the beginning of the war, Sir Archibald McIndoe, a plastic surgeon, took over the small thirty-six-bed hospital at East Grinstead to treat the anticipated burn and facial injuries that would be suffered by RAF fighter pilots. In 1942 he was joined by W/C Ross Tilley MD, a plastic surgeon from Toronto who had been the chief medical officer at RCAF Headquarters in London since 1941. By 1943, as the air war intensified, the hospital expanded with a further 120 beds to accommodate casualties amongst bomber crews, not only from the RAF but from other Allied Air Forces as well. To meet the need for still more capacity as the casualties continued to rise, the Canadian Wing was completed in 1944, adding fifty more beds.

12 - THE SECOND WORLD WAR - PART IV: 1943-1944

During the early stages of WW II, W/C Ross Tilley, (left) and Dr Archibald McIndoe (later Sir Archibald) were pioneers in applying ground-breaking plastic surgery techniques to air combat casualties which included severe burns, trauma injuries and frostbite.

This was a hospital like no other. McIndoe and Tilley, with their teams of doctors, dentists, and nurses, performed extraordinary feats in treating the horrific injuries their patients had received as they escaped their burning or crashed aircraft. These were the early days of plastic surgery, and they used innovative techniques to grapple with the intricacies of multiple skin grafts as they reconstructed ears, noses, faces, and fingers, while at the same time making these young men realize they were not destined to retreat from the world, but would recover to go on to live happy, productive lives.

But recovery took time—usually months, but in some cases years—and their emotional needs were met in a number of different ways. Unlike in military hospitals, they were permitted and indeed encouraged to wear their uniforms; there was a piano on the ward and a constant supply of beer; they walked or were wheeled to the pub in town, sometimes returning to the ward a bit the worse for wear; they were taken on trips to London, and WDs came from London to visit; and the townspeople, those remarkable residents of East Grinstead, entertained them in their homes. All of these things aided their recovery, but they knew only too well they were guinea pigs for this experimental surgery—and thus The Guinea Pig Club was formed, complete with anthem.

The Guinea Pig Anthem

We are McIndoe's army,
We are his Guinea Pigs.
With dermatomes and pedicles,
Glass eyes, false teeth and wigs.
And when we get our discharge
We'll shout with all our might:
"Per ardua ad astra"
We'd rather drink than fight.

John Hunter runs the gas works,
Ross Tilley wields the knife.
And if they are not careful
They'll have your flaming life.
So, Guinea Pigs stand steady
For all your surgeons' calls:
And if their hands aren't steady
They'll whip off both your ears.

We've had some mad Australians,
Some French, some Czechs, some Poles.
We've even had some Yankees
God bless their precious souls.
While, as for the Canadians—
Ah! That's a different thing.
They couldn't stand our accent
And built a separate wing.

We are McIndoe's army . . .
(As first verse)[116]

Gus's health continued to deteriorate, but this time he was confronted by a new challenge: X-rays indicated surgery was required to remove the right

---

[116] www.queenvic.demon.co.uk/plastic.htm. Reproduced with permission of The Guinea Pig Club. After the war the wing was turned over to the hospital by the Canadian Government "as a memorial to the large number of Canadian Servicemen who were treated during the war." For the stories of these gallant young men who made up twenty-seven percent of the membership of The Guinea Pig Club, see Rita Donovan's *As For The Canadians—The Remarkable Story of the RCAF's "Guinea Pigs" of World War II* (Ottawa: BuschekBooks, 2000).

kidney. The operation had been planned for mid-December in London but was postponed until he returned to Canada. Just over two years after first arriving in England, he prepared to turn over command to his successor. Two signals from London to Ottawa on 20 and 21 December describe the transfer:

LECKIE FROM EDWARDS
EXPECT DEPART VIA U.S.A.T.C. DEC 23RD. TRAVELLING BY THE SOUTHERN ROUTE AND THE JOURNEY NORMALLY TAKES SEVEN OR EIGHT DAYS. WILL YOU PLEASE HAVE A SERVICE AIRCRAFT MEET ME IN NEW YORK. WOULD ALSO APPRECIATE IT IF YOU WOULD ADVISE HOMER SMITH OF MY PLANS. WILL BE ACCOMPANIED BY BRODRIBB.

SECRET POWER FROM BREADNER
EDWARDS LEAVES DECEMBER 23. STRUCK OFF

> 27th January, 1944.
>
> Dear Sir,
>
> I am enclosing the Toast List of the annual dinner of the Guinea Pig Club held at East Grinstead last Saturday evening, as I am sure you would be much interested in having it.
>
> I have had it autographed by several members whom you knew well, including, as you will see at the bottom, Miss Frances Day. All those who have signed the Toast List wish to be remembered to you and all were very sincere in their regrets that you were not present.
>
> There were 22 Canadians there, many of whom you were acquainted with, including your old friend and champion, F/Lt. Henry Mann. You will be interested to hear that he is now at an O.T.U. and expects to return to operations before long.
>
> The wing is progressing favourably and the walls are now up some 8 or 10 feet. From now on it is expected that the progress will be much more rapid but it is not expected that the building will be occupied before the end of May. A signal from Ottawa indicates that the barrack furniture, including the Gatch beds in which you were particularly interested, is water-borne.
>
> I have had the profile photograph, taken in the garden at "Highdale", re-photographed and enlarged to bring the bust up to about 18" in diameter. Mr. McIndoe says it is splendid and is proceeding with the bronze plaque.
>
> That is about all I can say in regard to East Grinstead, other than that Stanford Cade asked if I had heard anything about you since you returned to Canada and would I please let him know what was the decision of the surgeons in Canada, if any. I also would be very interested to have news in this regard.
>
> Respectfully,
>
> (J.E. Hunter)
>
> JEH:IK.

Photo of the bronze plaque referred to in the letter. It can be seen in the background of the photo of McIndoe and Tilley. The inscription reads:

AIR MARSHAL H. EDWARDS CB
AOC-IN-C RCAF OVERSEAS
1942-1944
A MAN OF HOPE & FORWARD
LOOKING MIND

STRENGTH 31ST AND RELINQUISHES APPOINTMENT AOC IN C 31ST. BREADNER TAKEN ON STRENGTH JANUARY FIRST AND ASSUMES APPOINTMENT AOC IN C JANUARY FIRST. . . . BRODRIBB LEAVES WITH EDWARDS.

12 - THE SECOND WORLD WAR - PART IV: 1943–1944

RCAF photo courtesy Glenn Curtis

RCAF photo courtesy Glenn Curtis

Departure from London for Prestwick. 22 December 1943

It was a very happy New Year's Day for us when Gus arrived home safely, and this time to stay. Once again the house buzzed with activity, a far cry from the quiet days of the last couple of years. But that environment soon changed to what can best be described as semi-controlled chaos when Peter arrived from England.

Gus and I went to Union Station to meet the train that was to bring home a contingent of airmen, one of whom was smuggling Peter into the country. Finally the train arrived, troops poured out of the cars, and suddenly out of the throng there was Peter, straining on his lead, bounding up the platform. He seemed none the worse for wear for an animal whose daily routine had been radically altered by a lengthy time on board ship, sleeping in a hammock, followed by a long train trip. He climbed all over Gus in his enthusiasm at seeing him again, and then off we went to show him to Bea and introduce him to his new home, all of us blissfully unaware of what lay ahead.

In the excitement of Gus's return, no one had given any thought to how Sandy might react to Peter's arrival. Sandy by now was well on in years, but was still an extraordinary dog, far and away the smartest we had ever owned. He seemed to be able to accomplish things few other dogs could. For example, one day his penchant for roaming far and wide got him into serious trouble. He had been picked up by someone and, despite his tag with our telephone number, had been kept and tied up. Gone for three days, he reappeared on the fourth, bedraggled and dirty, with a piece of rope dangling from his neck, which he had evidently chewed in order to escape. Another time, at three o'clock one morning, he experienced an urgent call of nature. This posed a considerable problem for him; not only was it the middle of the night, but at the time he was in Bea's bedroom with the door closed. Undaunted, he jumped down through the small opening in the double window onto the snow-covered garage roof, attended to business, then barked impatiently to be let back in. In the midst of this drama, I awoke to shrieks of laughter from the bathroom, where I found the double window had been removed and placed in the bathtub,

Gus's 82-year-old mother, Kate Edwards, with Mr. Hopkins, the postman who delivered Gus's letters to her during the Second World War. Glace Bay, 1944

Photo courtesy of Marion Edwards

and Aldea, held at the ankles by Bea, dangling precariously out the window after retrieving Sandy, who was now running down her back. This was no ordinary dog.

Enter Peter—to the canine manor born. It was simply no contest. Peter, whose previous world had been his oyster, now found himself playing second fiddle to Sandy, who outwitted and dominated him at every turn. Take, for instance, when Aldea served dinner. Sandy had always stuck close to her heels, ensuring he entered the dining room through the swinging door at exactly the same moment she did. This forced Peter to follow behind and invariably be hit in the nose by the door as it swung back into place. It took three nights for him to realize this was a losing battle and he had better use the other door into the dining room. Or the fireplace: as soon as it was lit, Sandy placed himself strategically in front of it, forcing Peter to the side.

Then one day Peter committed the cardinal sin: trying to curl up at Billy's feet.[117] That did it. Sandy flew at him, snarled, bared his teeth, and bit Peter's ear. Throughout the attack, Peter simply shut his eyes in horror and gave a tiny yelp of pain. For several days, Sandy continued to bite his ears if he perceived Peter was in any way getting out of line. During these episodes, long-suffering Peter never fought back but merely shut his eyes waiting for the torture to end. Then one day he'd had enough and, to everyone's amazement, retaliated by biting Sandy's paw. Sandy was stunned. He lifted his paw in astonishment and looked at everyone as if to say, "Did you see what he *did*?" From then on, hostilities came to an end and each seemed to accept the other's presence, albeit reluctantly.

* * *

News of Gus's impending retirement was announced in January, and past differences, so hotly debated at the time, were set aside by *The Globe and Mail* in favour of an open-handed editorial on 15 January:

Air Marshal Edwards Retires

The retirement on pension of Air Marshal Harold Edwards, C.B., marks the end of a long and distinguished career from which Canada and the cause of freedom have both benefited. His last

---

[117] Billy, now an Ordinary Seaman in the RCNVR, was home on leave and also took great delight in making room for his seaman's cap amongst the brass hats belonging to air force officers who came to call.

appointment, that of Air Officer Commanding-in-Chief the Royal Canadian Air Force Overseas, which he has just relinquished after two years of successful occupancy, was the crown of a creditable record of accomplishment during his 28 years' service in the air force.

In his periods of high command, both at Ottawa and in Britain, Air Marshal Edwards had the happy gift of being able to impress his standards of efficiency, skill and general conduct upon all the units which came under his supervision, and he deserves a large measure of credit for the fine record which the R.C.A.F. has achieved during the last four years. But, firm disciplinarian that he was, he also won for himself the esteem and affection of all who served under him, while he has a wide circle of admiring friends outside the ranks of his own service. He could wish for no better testimony of the regard in which he is held by the personnel of the R.C.A.F. overseas than the editorial which their special organ, "Wings Abroad," published after the announcement of his retirement:

> It is doubtful whether any other officer has left such a lasting imprint on the everyday life of the service. The salute we use on state occasions is an Edwards salute; the boots and buttons and greatcoats we wear are Edwards-designed kit. A fair part of "Kings Regulations, Air" is a formulization of Edwards' rulings. He knew "the book from back to front," and vice versa, and he never let himself become hidebound within its blueboard covers. He let a roving imagination range across each major problem, alight at last at a frequently daring position, and stand out there, come hell or high water, Ottawa or Whitehall.

It is true that he had some of the defects as well as the qualities of a vigorous, masterful personality. But, if he sometimes revealed a strain of flamboyant exuberance in his utterances, it almost invariably derived from his zeal for the interests of the force, in whose high quality he took such pride. At one stage of his career he came under the lash of severe criticism for the policy of the Canadianization of the R.C.A.F. overseas, but if he championed this policy it should be remembered that it was in obedience to his political chief, the Minister of National Defence for Air, who originated it.

But respectful compliance with the wishes of politicians did not earn him their permanent gratitude, and demotion came to him suddenly without any explanation being given. It is, moreover, an open secret that by way of consolation he was offered a high post with inspectorial duties attached, but it was consistent with his record and high principles that he refused a position which in his eyes would have been a sinecure. By this refusal he rejected a chance of emoluments substantially larger than the pension he will now receive, and by thus saving the taxpayers several thousands of dollars per annum he has made an uncommon personal sacrifice.

He has left the service in which he has earned such well-deserved laurels with the consciousness that he did his duty faithfully and efficiently in very responsible posts and maintained its fine traditions. When the history of this war is written he will have an assured place as one of the architects of the coming victory of freedom, and the Canadian people will learn to appreciate the value of his contribution.

* * *

It appears Gus had well and truly learned his lesson about off-the-record comments with the press, for he remained silent about his plans for the future. While he said nothing about the rumours that were circulating, a newspaper article reveals what was occupying his time and what options he was considering:

While Air Vice-Marshal [sic] Edwards has given no hint of what he plans to do in the future, many rumors are circulating in the capital.

The slim, handsome airman who directed R.C.A.F. operations overseas is known to have accepted his recall to Canada philosophically, although it must have been a great disappointment to him not to be in on the invasion fighting when it comes. . . .

[He] now is cleaning up his desk in a special office in the big air force headquarters building here. He is also answering scores of letters from the parents and next of kin of the lads who served under him. . . .

It is known that he has told Air Minister Power he does not want the post originally intended for him—that of inspector general of the air force.

It also is known that he has a deep interest in the rehabilitation and postwar welfare of the men who fought under him and one report has it that he will accept a Government offer to direct a demobilization program for the R.C.A.F. or perhaps all three services.

Another rumor says his keen interest in his men's welfare on their return to Canada may also cause him to accept a nomination for a Parliamentary seat where he could become a servicemen's advocate. And a further report is that several companies have offered him directorates.

Air Vice-Marshal Edwards, himself, says nothing.[118]

* * *

Our joy at having Gus home soon changed to anxiety when he was admitted to the Ross Memorial, part of the Royal Victoria Hospital, in Montreal on 21 February. This was intended to have been a relatively short stay for surgery to remove the right kidney, but instead became a nightmare of complications, requiring him to remain in hospital for nearly four months.

At first Bea went down to Montreal for short, overnight stays, and then, as it became evident he would be there for an extended period, I was brought along for a two-week stay at the end of March. My hopes of a holiday from school were soon dashed—Bea had seen to that—when, on the last day before leaving, my teacher presented me with a huge pile of homework to be completed and handed in on my return. We spent the better part of each day at the hospital, arriving about eleven o'clock, usually to find his room crowded with what Bea referred to as his "harem"—the nurses and lab technicians who had fallen under his spell. The pattern was the same each day: Bea stayed with Gus while I worked on the wretched homework at the desk in the sun room until mid-afternoon. When it was finished, I joined

---

[118] Excerpts from a CP despatch dateline Ottawa, Jan. 23 and published in *The Globe and Mail* the following day.

12 - THE SECOND WORLD WAR - PART IV: 1943–1944

them, usually to play backgammon with Gus who, much to his frustration, invariably lost due to my incredible luck with the dice.

* * *

While all this was going on, at HQ in Ottawa there was much dotting of i's and crossing of t's leading up to the final approval by the Privy Council and Governor General that Gus be posted to leave on 30 March and his retirement date fixed at 29 September 1944, at an annual pension of $5,845.25. A/M Robert Leckie, the new CAS as of 1 January, in recommending these dates to Minister Power in his memo of 9 March, provides the official reason for retirement when he writes that he "be retired to pension under K.R. (Air) Para. 151 (1) (cc) . . . 'because he is not advantageously employable in his present rank.'"

* * *

It was early summer when he was finally discharged from hospital. Anxious to try playing golf again, he soon discovered that the clubs he had bought in England were not in the cases that had been sent to Canada by ship. For three weeks, staff appear to have been totally preoccupied with the search for the lost clubs. A bevy of signals flew back and forth across the Atlantic. In England, enquiries made of packers and shippers, and searches conducted at Highdale and Headquarters, were all to no avail. Then, on 1 August, to everyone's relief, someone in London put two and two together and found the solution:

> EVERY POSSIBLE ANGLE OF INVESTIGATION SEARCHED TO EXHAUSTION WITH NO TRACE OF MISSING GOLF CLUBS. IT DEVELOPS HOWEVER 2 COMPLETE SETS GOLF CLUBS WERE SHIPPED OUT FOR A M. CURTIS. IS IT POSSIBLE 1 SET OF THESE ARE A/M EDWARDS MISSING CLUBS. . . .

As Gus convalesced during the summer, he retained hope that his physical ailments were now behind him and he would be capable of undertaking one of the "great things [that] need to be done," as he had written in his last letter to his mother, and, at age fifty-one, it was reasonable for him to assume he had many more productive years ahead of him. At the time, several possibilities were being discussed, one of which was with the United Nations Relief and Rehabilitation Administration (UNRRA), the UN agency charged with the enormous task of providing aid and relief to the millions of victims of the war in countries that had been occupied by the Axis powers. A letter in response to a request from UNRRA for information of Gus's record and qualifications provides details of his prewar record and then goes on to say:

> With the outbreak of the present war Air Marshal Edwards quickly revealed extraordinary gifts for organization and leadership which led to his meteoric rise from the rank of Group Captain to the rank of Temporary Air Marshal, the highest rank in the Royal Canadian Air Force, in a period of less than three years.

The letter goes on to outline his duties prior to his appointment as AOC-in-C Overseas and then gives an assessment of his performance in that post:

> During his tenure of this appointment, he made a great contribution to the success of the Royal Canadian Air Force administration and operations in the United Kingdom, the Middle East and the Far East, and was recognized [as] an outstanding figure in the prosecution of aerial warfare against the enemy. His great success in this position was attributable not only to his training and experience but also to his wit, his wide knowledge of world affairs, his marked ability as an executive and as a speaker, and his warmth and charm of personality.[119]

* * *

The Second World War ended during the spring and summer of 1945, first in Europe in May, and later in the Pacific in August. It had raged for six agonizing years, causing a staggering 50,000,000 deaths and leaving untold millions of other casualties in its wake. And Gus was one of those casualties; but it took some months for him to realize his health would never again allow him to perform at a high level in a stressful position. Thus the great adventure, begun so many years earlier in the coal mines of Cape Breton, ended—as all things must in time.

---

[119] Letter to the UNRRA liaison officer in Ottawa from G/C H.B.Weed, on behalf of the Chief of the Air Staff, dated 23 September 1944. Canada was one of forty-four signatories to the *Agreement for UNRRA*, signed on 9 November 1943, which outlined the administrative structure necessary to facilitate the provision of this aid and relief.

13

RETIREMENT
1945–1951

In retirement, Gus may not have been able to make a full-time commitment to a new position but this did not mean he was idle. On the contrary, the next two years were taken up with such diverse activities as speaking to the Air Cadet Squadron in Glace Bay, to serving on the boards of the Ottawa Humane Society and the John Howard Society. The bulk of his time, however, was devoted to his primary concern: the RCAF Benevolent Fund, where he served as president and chairman of the executive committee of the board of directors.[120] Nor did he shrink from controversy when he advocated the unification of the armed services in June of 1946—twenty-two years before it actually took place—with the publication in *The Ottawa Citizen* of his article "Unite the Fighting Forces."[121]

* * *

My father was a firm believer in learning by doing, and in the summer of 1946, when I was fifteen, I was handed several road maps with the instruction, "Just tell me where to go and I'll drive there." This was the beginning of a two-week journey by car from Ottawa to British Columbia, where Bea and Gus were to spend the better part of a year in Victoria as a prelude to moving there permanently. I was given a general outline of the route to the West Coast—mostly through the United States, as the Trans-Canada Highway was but a dream in those days—and off we went.

---

[120] RCAF Benevolent Fund records indicate he served as a director from 5 June 1945 until his death in 1952. The records do not, however, show the length of his term in office as president—only that it began in June 1945.

[121] See Appendix C for the complete text of the article.

My navigational skills were unimpeachable, if finding our way through the city of Chicago is excluded. My fall from grace was caused by its infamous "Loop," but fortunately it was a Sunday with light traffic, otherwise we might still be there. It was Bea who realized something was amiss; she remarked it was strange that she had seen the same policeman a second time and that he had smiled and waved as we drove past. It seems we were going around in circles, and it was not until the third encounter with the policeman, who by this time was actually laughing, that I finally found the way to the street that would take us out of the city to the highway.

It was a long drive to the West, and, as Bea often remarked over the years, Gus never liked to be behind another car on the highway and would seize the first opportunity to pass a slower driver. He drove at a fast pace, often exceeding the speed limit by a wide margin, but managed to evade the long arm of the law. It was in Iowa, on a road as straight as an arrow dissecting endless fields of ripening corn, that his heavy foot on the accelerator produced the dreaded wail of the Highway Patrol siren. This time we were sure Gus was in for it and wouldn't escape without a fine. We watched as the formalities of producing his licence etc. were completed and then were stunned to see him join the trooper, leaning casually against the side of the patrol car. There they remained in animated conversation about, of all things, fishing in Ontario. Fifteen minutes later, when they had finally exhausted their fish stories, we were on our way, and Gus had again escaped without a ticket.

They loved Victoria and being with their old friends the Hertbergs, whose daughter, Thea, describes her time there:

> I also saw a good deal of them in 1946 in Victoria. My parents had retired there and bought a house. The Edwards came for a prolonged stay to be with them . . . I think they considered moving there for good but Gus's health was precarious by then and so they decided to return to the east. I was told that before my arrival at the new house for the first time from McGill, there was a great rush to get everything ready. The Edwards were commandeered (or more likely volunteered) to help. Gus polished the brass.
>
> At that time I was going out with a former bomber pilot—a pathfinder. Gus had a huge admiration for these young men (and this young man, needless to say, had a huge admiration for him). So we two used to go & see them often when we went out

13 - RETIREMENT: 1945–1951

together. They were good times with good talk which we all four enjoyed . . .[122]

In the meantime, at boarding school at the Convent of the Sacred Heart in Vancouver, I was evidently having a difficult time surviving on my $2.00 monthly allowance. I had written pleading for an increase, apparently reasoning that Bea would intercede with Gus on my behalf. How many fathers would send this reply?

> November 20th. 1946.
>
> My dear Sue,
>
> With considerable interest I have perused your recent epistle deposited, in the proper receptacle, by the courier early this ante meridian. While the salutation was in the singular (Dear Mum) I felt that the ominous foreboding I normally experience at this period of the month, *comme la coutume*, elevate itself to a graver suspicion that I was about to be pluralized, with deep significance (somewhere within the document) with the *destinateur*. A surreptitious, though casual, glance summoned a confirmation of my direst doubts. Careful digestion of its contents arouses in me a sense of mutual economic peril vis-a-vis one another. Anent my own financial status I cherish the desire to survive: an emotion which we apparently do not share. I would challenge a reciprocal charge. Let us analyse the fiscal position quite dispassionately.
>
> For myself, what do we see? A man worn and tattered, working his bleeding fingers to the bone in the struggle of life. Old, creaking and bent under his pitiful burden. With bowed head he stumbles in his path, too weak to stagger farther as he drips the last drop of his blood into the drained coffers of his family care; denying himself everything, begging for a morsel of bread and is accorded but a stone. Cold and weary he gives his all that his family might luxuriate in extravagant splendour. Even the dogs sniff and snap at his heels.
>
> Now the other side—that of the children. What do we see here? Light and sweetness; not a care, not a tithe of worry; a procession

---

[122] Thea Hertzberg Gray—Reminiscences, September 2002.

<u>EDWARDS, SKYNFLYNT, EDWARDS & EDWARDS CO.(VICTORIA) LIMITED.</u>

<u>BANKERS</u>

<u>Secretary</u>

A.Drehdful Skynflynt,
    O.B.E.,Esq.

Loans,payments and Debts made all over the World.

Loans without groans.

Victoria B.C.
January 27th. 1947.

Dear Madam,

    I am directed to forward herewith a cheque made out in the sum of $10.15 (Ten dollars and fifteen cents) drawn on Messrs The Royal Bank of Canada, payable in your favour to the Convent of the Sacred Heart. We trust this will meet with your concurrence.

    I am also directed (By our Manipulating Vice President, Madam L. Borgia) that the sum of $3.60 (Three dollars and sixty cents) having currently accumulated to your account must so remain pending a decision as to whether the same might be transmitted through the medium of His Majesty's Mails, having regard to the legality of the same and its source.

    Be assured Madam of our high regard and profound desire to serve you. We are;

    Yours faithfully,

    Edwards, Skyflynt, Edwards & Edwards.
    Per. Pro. *A.D. Skyflynt* ...Sect.
        (A.D.Skynflynt)

Miss Sue. Edwards,
Convent of the Sacred Heart.
Vancouver, B.C.

---

of lunches, taxis, silks and satins, velvet and gold. Diamond tiaras, glistening furs, pictures and paintings and all the fine arts. Heads held high in a just pride and capped by the coiffure of the House of Lucien de Paris. *Jours de Congé* by land, sea and air. Classical educations *d'hautes formes* in Greek and Latin and Sanskrit with liberal helpings of lavish and luscious sweetmeats. A sheltered and gilded life.

I have, therefore, reached a final and irrevocable decision.

Having regard to the economic, social, humane, academic, psychological, panegyrical, altruistic, paternal and indulgent considerations of the problem I shall (even though it provoke my ultimate and irremediable end) raise your monthly allowance by 100%, a token of which is herein enclosed.

Yours truly
(Signed) H. Edwards

There were also a number of the EDWARDS SKYNFLYNT series that accompanied anything to do with the transfer of funds. I was particularly pleased to see that A. Drehdful Skynflynt had been invested with the O.B.E.

In the summer of 1947 we returned to Ottawa to make arrangements to move permanently to Victoria, but another illness, this time emboli to his brain and other parts of his body, made that move impossible. His condition now required constant monitoring and his doctors in Montreal recommended that he be within a couple of hours' drive of the Royal Victoria Hospital. He attacked the problem of where to live by positioning one leg of a compass at the hospital, and, with the radius calculated to show an area extending about fifty miles from there, he drew a circle around Montreal. He and Bea then scouted the countryside within the circle, eventually settling on St. Sauveur des Monts in the Laurentians.[123]

Prior to the installation of a private line, the house they purchased was equipped with an antiquated telephone system where one spoke into a six-inch mouthpiece that protruded from a large wooden box mounted at eye level on the wall. Thus were we introduced to the joys of a party line—one line shared with seven other nearby residents. Each subscriber was assigned a combination of short and long rings—Bell's own version of the Morse code—with our particular call number being five short rings. Each time the phone rang activities would cease, and silence reign, as we all listened intently for our five rings; and then everyone, in unison, would call out,

---

[123] The Duke of Leuchtenberg, a Russian émigré, was also a resident of St. Sauveur. When he and Gus met, they discovered, to their astonishment, they had both been awaiting evacuation from the port of Novorossisk, Russia, in the same chaotic week in March 1920.

"THAT'S US!" and someone would rush to pick up the receiver before the operator disconnected the call. Despite Bea's half-hearted objections, Gus enthusiastically joined in the rural pastime of listening in on his neighbours' conversations, keeping us up to date on the latest local news and gossip.

As well as suffering from his heart problems, Gus was now in constant pain with phlebitis in both legs, a condition that was to rob Gus and Bea of so much enjoyment throughout the four years that followed. Nevertheless, without complaint they adjusted to quiet country life, a far cry from their lives of just a few years previously. Gus became a well-known figure in the village, where he spent time with the blacksmith at his forge, or chatting in the post office, bakery, or his favourite haunt: the old-fashioned general store. There were visits from *Monsieur le Curé* and the school tax assessor, whom he confounded by offering to be registered as either a Catholic or Protestant rate payer, whichever was cheaper. On one occasion, as we sat in the car waiting for Bea, he spotted a runaway horse. As it galloped down the road he manoeuvred the car in front of it and, watching its movements in the rear-view mirror, cut it off each time it tried to veer left or right, until gradually it slowed and came to a halt, allowing its owner to regain control of it.

Now back in the East, I returned for my last year of high school to the one I had previously attended, the *Pensionnat du Sacré Coeur* in Montreal. That year, *HMS Pinafore*, the Gilbert & Sullivan classic parody of the Royal Navy, was the planned gala school production. Mother McCaffrey, the Sacred Heart nun who directed this extravaganza, was quick to realize that Gus would be a valuable source of needed props. She asked me if he could provide "a few medals and a sword" to complete the uniform for that renowned ruler of the sea, Sir Joseph Porter, KCB. Without enquiring if he would be willing to do so, I promised to bring them back after the Christmas holidays. Fortunately for me, Gus readily agreed and, with great glee, produced the requested items. I was quite a sight, and given a wide berth, as I returned to Montreal on a crowded ski train, clutching the sword and trying to avoid stabbing anyone in the process.

A few months later, Bea and Gus attended the dazzling performance, but it wasn't until many years later that I made the connection between the KCB in *Pinafore* and Gus's CB. Reverend Mother Davis, whom Gus had known and admired at schools I had attended in both Halifax and Vancouver, obviously did make the connection, because she always referred to him, much to his amusement, as "The Lord High Admiral."

On a beautiful day the following May, my parents picked me up at school to attend the investiture aboard the French naval training ship *Jeanne*

13 - RETIREMENT: 1945–1951

Gus Edwards being invested with the *Croix de Guerre avec Palme* and *Officier de la Légion d'Honneur* by the Ambassador of France on board the French naval vessel *Jeanne d'Arc*. Montreal, May 1948

d'Arc, which was docked in the Port of Montreal. With Gus resplendent in uniform, and Bea and I appropriately attired in our Sunday best, we drove down to the dock area, arriving in what we thought was ample time for the ceremony scheduled for eleven o'clock. There was just one problem: we couldn't find the ship. We cruised up and down the docks without success and, as the appointed hour grew closer and closer, with the atmosphere in the car growing ever more tense, Bea suggested it might be helpful to ask directions.

"Nonsense," said Gus cheerily. "Stick with me and you'll wear diamonds"; to which I chirped up from the back seat, "We're stickin' and we ain't wearin' no diamonds." The tension broken, we all laughed, and suddenly, to everyone's relief, we spotted the ship—and not a moment too soon. We

Bea and Gus in retirement in
St. Sauveur des Monts, Québec.

climbed the gangplank a scant two minutes before the appointed hour, and Gus, completely composed as if he had planned the time of arrival to the second, was piped aboard. We were shown to our seats on the deck, and with a barely audible sigh, Bea sat down, turned to me, and raised her eyes heavenward.

In November 1948, while a freshman at McGill University, I invited a friend from college to spend the weekend at St. Sauveur. While driving around to show her the area, we were involved in a serious car accident. She suffered severe facial injuries which later required extensive plastic surgery, performed by Dr. Fred Woolhouse in Montreal.[124] She was also seen by Sir Archibald McIndoe, of East Grinstead fame who, as luck would have it, was in Canada for a reunion of The Guinea Pig Club. Little did I know when I first heard of his exploits in 1944 that four years later he would play such a direct role in our lives.

At the time of the accident, Gus was in Glace Bay visiting his mother, who had been hospitalized with a broken hip. To his great sorrow, she never recovered from the injury and died two months later at the age of eighty-five. He returned to Glace Bay for her funeral and at the wake, as he leaned over

---

[124] During the war, Dr. Woolhouse served in the RCNVR but was seconded for training in plastic surgery under various leaders in the field, including Sir Archibald McIndoe in the United Kingdom.

13 - RETIREMENT: 1945–1951

and kissed her, he was heard to whisper, "Goodbye, Comrade."[125]

* * *

Bea, who had never spent a great deal of her life in the kitchen, took up cooking with a vengeance and in no time began to produce delicious meals. There was, however, one exception that brought hoots of laughter from guests: instead of a casserole she had prepared for the occasion, she almost served a special concoction of crushed egg shells and tomatoes that had been prescribed by the vet for some ailment of Peter's. Fortunately we discovered the error in time.

Billy had embarked on his writing career as a reporter on the *Montreal Star*, and on weekends the house in St. Sauveur was often overrun by either his friends or mine from McGill, or both. Bea referred to this influx of our friends as the "hordes" and, bless her heart, somehow managed to feed us all by preparing vast quantities of spaghetti and her famous meat sauce. Other than during those hectic winter weekends, life was, thankfully, much quieter for them.

Nor was Gus forgotten by the air force. Officers and airmen often wrote him seeking advice about their problems. Groups of four to six of his former brother officers would drive up from Ottawa for the day. Participants in these visits varied, but the nucleus of A/C Dave Mackell and W/C Bill Brodribb never changed. And every so often one of the new jet aircraft would zoom in over the house, dip its wings in salute, then zoom off over the mountains.

Their friends were invited for lunch or dinner and the visit usually lasted no more than a few hours, which, as the years went on, was about the limit for Gus. While he enjoyed these times enormously, it was only after everyone left that one could see the strain it had been. Here are the recollections of two of those visits. The first is from Thea Gray:

> I also saw them from time to time after they retired in the Laurentians. I was married by then . . . and settled, with a new baby, in Montreal. We used to drive up for lunch to see them. For some reason I've forgotten, Gus had a reputation as a polisher of shoes, and it shocked my husband when I generally brought with me a couple of pairs for him to attend to on these occasions.

---

[125] Telephone interview with Marjorie Edwards MacLeod, 29 May 2004.

He was one of the first grownups that played a role in my life and took me seriously. I loved him and think of him often.[126]

Alan Mann, who had served as a sub-lieutenant in the RCNVR during the war, was Bea's nephew-in-law and recalls the first time he met Gus:[127]

> [A]s improbable as it seemed, I did get to meet the great "Gus" Edwards. Not by my own efforts, but merely that I had, in 1950, married Mary Evelyn Coffey, who was a niece of Gus's wife Beatrice Coffey.... I was very happy to take up her offer to come and visit them in their habitat in the Laurentians... with all kinds of built-ins that he himself had made and with a very huge and cozy, comfortable fireplace....
>
> It is fair to say, I think, for Canadians of my generation that 1939–1945 was the kind of defining era for us. Everybody we knew, just about, was in the army or navy or air force or doing something interesting in the war, and all of us lost good friends, schoolmates or just sometimes people we had just barely met but happened to be along side of when things blew up. This made talking to a famous Canadian war leader even more fascinating for me. In the course of our long talk, Gus recounted many experiences and in so doing many high ranking names were mentioned—not name dropping, definitely not, but stories concerning his adventures and sometimes misadventures with the high and mighty and some of the pretenders-to-be to the high and mighty. He was quite hilarious with some of his stories about the British and often turned the butt of the joke against himself....
>
> On the day that I met him, I was 26 and in the midst of my first year of post graduate training.... He was able within 2 or 3 minutes to know what I was interested in, where I had been, what I was doing, what we might have in common, who we might know in common, and he talked in a way that made me think that he was genuinely happy—really delighted—to make the acquaintance of such an interesting and intelligent fellow as myself.

---

[126] Thea Hertzberg Gray, Reminiscences, September 2002.

[127] Alan M. Mann MD went on to become associate dean of medicine at McGill University from 1969 to 1971 and psychiatrist-in-chief at the Montreal General Hospital from 1971 to 1990.

13 - RETIREMENT: 1945–1951

He did not talk down to me; he did not do any boasting about his exploits, which were many indeed; he simply chatted and I found myself totally taken in by this man's charm and wit and his sharp and quick mind with its keen and cutting sense of humour, with generous lashings of sarcasm thrown in.

Within a very short time, I became a Gus Edwards fan and he holds a special place in my memory as a man who has seen things, and done things, knows how to talk to men and to women and became one of the most interesting and charming people I have ever met—and I have met one very large number of people in my life. . . . [He talked] about how difficult it was for him to have to interview every airman who was being mustered out of the service on grounds of "Lack of Moral Fiber." This refers to airmen who just couldn't go on any longer and could not fly. Today we would say they were suffering from post-traumatic stress disorder. . . . Gus told me there was not one of these airmen he interviewed who did not cry in front of him when saying how badly they felt about what was happening, and noting while he interviewed them how brave they had been and how much they had given. He felt strongly that there could have been a better system, but this was another one of the Edwards wishes that did not get fulfilled.

After dinner we had a few little drinks here and there, and Gus showed no visible effect of a semi-Churchillian intake except perhaps to a slightly more ruddy glow to his features. We talked on and on into the evening and finally had to take off for the ride home.

Alan goes on to recount the hilarious details of buying a car from Gus which, the day after he bought it, refused to start and thereafter turned into a sinkhole for money. His narrative ends with his description of his attendance at Gus's funeral and the words,

> Yes, there were many tears and in many eyes, and I am not ashamed to say that I was among that group. A most unforgettable time, and a most unforgettable man. What charm! What courage![128]

* * *

---

[128] Alan M. Mann MD, Reminiscences, December 2002.

In the hope of providing some relief from the unremitting pain in his legs, Gus underwent more surgery in the spring of 1951. But it was of little benefit, and in the fall he was advised by his doctors to seek a warmer climate for the coming winter. Before leaving for the South, he wrote one last letter on 31 October 1951. It was to Billy, who had sought his advice about changing jobs. The letter ends:

> Whatever decision you reach will, of course, carry with it our complete accord. Whichever road you take we hope that it will be the one that you will most enjoy and the one that we shall most admire.
>
> Love
> Dad

14

THE LAST TRIP
1951–1952

In 1951, the Korean War was in its second year and "McCarthyism" was raging unchecked in the United States. The Senate Committee on Un-American Activities, chaired by Senator Joseph McCarthy, was holding hearings in an effort to identify communists and their sympathizers. It was an era of intense anti-communism when smear tactics, innuendo, and denunciation led to reputations being ruined, some on mere suspicion. A dark period in American history to be sure, and I witnessed first hand how far the government of the day was prepared to go to keep communists out of the country.

Since 1946, the United States government had sought an opportunity to invest Gus as a Commander of the Legion of Merit, but ill health had prevented him from attending a ceremony. As we planned to be in the States for an extended period of time and needed travel documents from the consulate in Montreal, arrangements were made in October for the official presentation to be made by the consul general at the same time.

On arrival at the consulate, we were ushered into the consul's office, the presentation was made, and then I was taken to be fingerprinted. Next the fateful question: "Are you now, or have you ever been, a member of the Communist Party?"

Instead of simply answering the question "No," I stupidly elaborated by saying "No, but I once went to a meeting when I was a student at McGill." Stunned silence. No one seemed to know what to do next. Even the official, who I now realize was probably either an FBI or CIA agent, was nonplussed. Were they going to refuse *me* entry? And then what of this air marshal they had just invested with one of their highest honours? It was, as they say, a sticky wicket. Then Gus broke the silence by asking what had gone on at the meeting. "I don't know," I replied, "I just watched for a minute from the doorway and then left." The sense of relief in that room was palpable.

In early November, I was the designated driver as we headed south to the U.S. To reach the warmer climate as soon as possible, we drove due south through Virginia, Tennessee, and Mississippi. Just north of New Orleans, in the little town of Pass Christian on the Gulf Coast, Gus's condition took a turn for the worse, and we stayed there for a month before he felt well enough to continue west to Arizona to join friends already there.[129] We rented an apartment in a large antebellum house that had been converted to a duplex and we soon discovered the young couple living upstairs. He had been a pilot in the USAAF during the war and after their first conversation became an instant fan of Gus's, thereafter referring to him in his slow Southern drawl as "The Maawshul." He told us the story of walking into the mess on his arrival in England where he was greeted with a friendly "Hi, Yank" from one of his fellow Americans. To him this was not a greeting but an insult, rubbing salt in the wound, and he replied, "Don't you *evah* call me a *Yankay*!" If the issue was ever in doubt, this was proof positive that the Confederacy still lived on in the minds of many Southerners.

Time passed pleasantly. Gus and I, both confirmed explorers, took daily trips into bayou country or along the coast, often purchasing seafood direct from the fishing boats and becoming experts in the preparation of such culinary delights as Oysters Rockefeller. These were the days of strict racial segregation in the South, and nowhere was it more evident than in public transportation. One day I boarded a bus and, in reply to my question about the amount of the fare, was told I could not ride on that bus because it was for blacks only. I turned and looked at the passengers and, sure enough, a sea of black faces stared back at me. Unlike Rosa Parks, who four years later ignited the civil rights movement by refusing to give up her seat to a white, I stepped meekly back onto the sidewalk to await a "white" bus.

The economic disparity between the races was also apparent, with blacks at a clear disadvantage. There was an unforgettable incident while Bea and I were shopping in New Orleans. The shops were decorated for Christmas, the windows full of enticing gifts. We had stopped at a shoe store, and beside us, with his nose pressed against the window, was a small black boy. He couldn't have been more than five and was holding his older brother's hand. Wearing battered sneakers that didn't look as if they would last the day, he stared

---

[129] In August 2005, Hurricane Katrina caused devastating damage to Pass Christian.

14 - THE LAST TRIP: 1951–1952

longingly at a pair of red shoes in the window. Suddenly he broke his silence and said, very slowly, "I's gonna git a paih o' red shoes fo' Crizzmuz." I hope he did; even now I still wonder.

In early December we headed west to Arizona, crossing Louisiana, Texas, and New Mexico, arriving in Phoenix just before Christmas. We were fortunate to rent two small guest houses on a ranch just outside Scottsdale and planned to stay until the end of April. There certainly wasn't any noticeable improvement in Gus's health, but the bright sunshine and clear desert air were definitely a welcome change from the rigours of a Québec winter. For nearly two months, he carried on as best he could, on one occasion even attending a luncheon in his honour.

In my youthful naïveté, I assumed Gus would win out over the diseases that wracked his body, just as he had always done. But of course Bea knew better, even though she hoped against hope that his indomitable spirit and the benign climate would be enough to prevent, or at least forestall, the inevitable. But recovery was not to be, and his long, painful struggle ended peacefully when he died in his sleep on 23 February 1952 at the age of fifty-nine.[130]

The call to Ottawa on Sunday morning set in motion a remarkable chain of events organized by the RCAF. By late that afternoon, an aircraft had been dispatched to Arizona to bring Gus's body back to Canada. B/Gen W. Don Stewart (Ret'd), then a flying officer, describes the flight:

> In Feb 1952 I was serving as a young navigator on 412 VIP Sqdn at RCAF Stn Rockliffe. Late in the afternoon of 24 Feb we received a tasking to proceed to Phoenix AZ. We departed Ottawa at 2000 hrs on the 24th flying Dakota 270 captained by F/L Hal Carling. As you may be aware the aircraft was very slow by comparison to today's jets and we flew 14hrs and 15 minutes air time plus stops at Selfridge USAF base near Detroit and Witchita KS arriving in Phoenix mid afternoon on the 25th Feb.[131]

---

[130] On 26 February 1952, Dr. Samuel H. Hale, 222 Scottsdale Road, Scottsdale, Arizona, wrote the following letter: "TO WHOM IT MAY CONCERN: I was called to see Air Marshall Harold Edwards, for the first time, at approximately Nine AM, Sunday, February 24, 1952. Upon examination of the above named patient, I found he had expired and estimated that he had been dead for approximately 8 hours. His apparent cause of death was Coronary Thrombosis, although a cerebral vascular accident could have led to his death."

[131] E-mail, 29 January 2003.

I met the aircraft at the Phoenix airport, and what a relief it was to see the familiar air force roundel on the fuselage as the aircraft taxied down the runway, then to watch the figure of Uncle Quiller (G/C C.C.P. Graham) step down onto the tarmac.

Those three days were a blur of telegrams and telephone calls: to Billy in Montreal, the air force in Ottawa, and friends and relations across Canada. But by late Tuesday afternoon, with an airman on his way back to Ottawa with the car, everything was at last in place and we were ready for the journey home.

With evening approaching as the aircraft climbed to cruising altitude, I watched as the angle of the sun bathed the mountains surrounding the valley in stunning hues of reddish blue until gradually it all disappeared from view. We headed northeast, with the flight plan the reverse of the one from Ottawa, each of us conscious of the casket concealed from view in the tail of the aircraft. The crew was thoughtful and considerate throughout, but there was little conversation above the noisy drone of the piston engines. The hours dragged slowly on through the night. Numbed by grief, we retreated into our own thoughts, trying to absorb the reality of Gus's death.

When we flew over Chicago, F/L Carling invited me up to the cockpit to see the city spread out below. It was a dazzling sight, with row upon row of street lights stretching mile upon mile in either direction, like a giant illuminated chessboard. Then I remembered the policeman years before waving at the car as we passed him on The Loop, and I couldn't help but smile. Eventually, at about six-thirty a.m., we landed for refuelling at the USAF base near Detroit, then took off again on the final leg to Ottawa.

At ten-thirty a.m. on Wednesday the 27th, we arrived at Rockliffe—the scene of those joyous arrivals during the war. Not so this time. Recent events had so preoccupied me that I had kept my composure throughout the previous three days, but the sight of Billy with other relatives and friends standing next to A/M Curtis so unnerved me it was as if a switch had been thrown, opening the floodgates, and I totally disgraced myself by bursting into tears. I fled out of sight to one of the waiting cars, where a kind aunt sat with me as I wept until eventually there were no more tears. Bea, on the other hand, as she always did in public, kept her emotions in check and carried on during that extraordinarily difficult homecoming.

While we were preparing to return to Ottawa, RCAF Headquarters was preparing to bury an air marshal for the first time in the history of the service. Copies of signals that crisscrossed the country during that period reveal the extraordinary lengths to which the air force went to ensure everyone who

14 - THE LAST TRIP: 1951–1952

Dominion Chalmers United Church.
Ottawa, 29 February 1952
DND PL 53715

wished to attend had access to the flights being arranged.[132] Their task was even more difficult because hotel accommodation, always scarce in Ottawa in the fifties, was almost impossible to obtain due to the opening of Parliament. In fact, the Château Laurier, our first choice, was booked and we were even fortunate to obtain reservations at the Lord Elgin.

Billy and I went to the funeral parlour several times and were moved by seeing so many who came to pay their respects. For us one was particularly touching. On Thursday evening we were astonished to see, amidst all the uniforms, the tiny, bent figure of Mrs. Cain, in her black coat and hat. It had been more than ten years since we had seen her when she had sometimes looked after me; such a dear soul who suffered terribly from arthritis and who said simply, "I just had to come."

---

[132] Despite repeated assurances he had been notified, inexplicably word never reached General Hertzberg in Victoria that Bea wished him to be a pallbearer and that air force transport was available to Ottawa. In view of the extraordinary effort expended by the air force to carry out Bea's wishes, and the support given to our family, this communication breakdown is mentioned here not as a criticism but rather to explain his absence—a bitter disappointment for both our families.

Friday, 29 February, was a memorable day; cold, bright, and windy, so typical of Ottawa near winter's end. The funeral took place from Dominion Chalmers United Church, and in true military fashion nothing was left to chance, with every detail planned.

His body lay at the front of the church. Four flight lieutenants stood guard, one at each corner of the casket, his decorations and medals on a stand nearby. Shortly before the service began, the casket was closed and brought to the back of the church.[133]

It took some time for those attending to fill the large church, and then, just before eleven o'clock, a young officer escorted Bea from a side entrance to the front pew, while I followed behind. Promptly at eleven the procession moved up the aisle. The casket, with the air force flag, his hat, and his sword, was flanked by the honorary pallbearers.[134] Next came the insignia bearer with his decorations, followed by Billy with our two cousins, S/Ls Harold and Robert Edwards on either side.

So many years later, one detail still stands out above the others: when the organ played Bach's *Jesu, Joy of Man's Desiring*, we stiffened in anguish, recalling happier times when we had all been together and listened to the cherished recording by Myra Hess.

After the service, Bea and I sat in the car for what seemed an eternity waiting for the parade to form up and then move off in slow time along O'Connor Street. The car followed the carriage to the corner of Laurier Avenue and Elgin Street and then returned to the hotel. Billy of course continued in the parade as it wound its way to Beechwood Cemetery and witnessed the final farewell on that sparkling winter day. With the volleys from the Firing Party, the Last Post and Reveille from the trumpeters, and the last salute from the last officer, in the snow and the cold and the wind Gus was gone from us.[135]

---

[133] One of the four was Ernest Hibberd, now a F/L, whom Gus had discovered reading the newspaper on duty in 1943.

[134] The three pallbearers on the right were: W/C William J. Brodribb, A/C David E. Mackell, and A/V/M C. Roy Slemon; and the three on the left were G/C C.C.P. Graham, A/V/M Frank G. Wait, and A/V/M Frank S. McGill. The Chief of the Air Staff, A/M W.A. Curtis, with A/M R. Leckie and A/C/M L.S. Breadner, marched in the parade directly behind the car in which Bea and I were seated.

[135] I am still baffled by the policy that women were not permitted at the cemetery. Billy and I exerted all the pressure we could on air force officials to change that policy so that I might attend. But our pleas fell on deaf ears, and so, crestfallen, I did not go. So many years later it is ironic that the current regulation surely allows women not only to attend as spectators, but probably has women members of the CF as active participants in both the firing and bearer parties. One person who marched in the cold and wind was Norman Jeffries, then a F/L at HQ in Ottawa. (See Chapter 11.)

14 - THE LAST TRIP: 1951–1952

D.ND PL 53729

D.ND PL 53740

DND PL 53738

DND PL 53739

Funeral Parade and Interment
Beechwood Cemetery, Ottawa[136]
Section 19—Grave 367 - 29 February 1952

---

[136] Even more difficult to accept than not attending the interment was the refusal of Bea's request that Gus be buried in the military section of Beechwood Cemetery. The request was denied on the grounds that only those who had died on active service could be buried in the section. In June of 2001, the section was expanded and formed the nucleus for the creation of the long-awaited National Military Cemetery (NMC). It is here that all current and former CF members who have been honourably discharged are now eligible to be buried. My request, in the fall of 2001, for DND to assume the financial burden of relocating Gus's remains to the NMC was denied.

AFTERWARDS

The letter Bea wrote to the CAS was the first of hundreds in reply to those she received over the course of the spring and into the summer; one was addressed simply, "Mrs. Edwards, Ottawa."[137]

> 398 Wilbrod St.
> Ottawa
> March 6th, 1952

Dear Air Marshal Curtis,

My gratitude to all members of the Royal Canadian Air Force for their sympathy and the assistance which was so freely and kindly given following the death of my husband cannot really be expressed in words. All I can say is that nothing which would help to ease our burden has been left undone.

The Air Force, as you know, was very close to my husband's heart and the R.C.A.F.'s tangible demonstration of their esteem and affection for him has been the greatest source of comfort to me and my children.

I would be most grateful if you would express my thanks to everyone.

Sincerely,
Beatrice Edwards

---

[137] Bea destroyed all the telegrams and letters save one, from A/M John Plant; see Appendix D.

After collecting Peter from the Graham's where he had spent the winter, Bea and I left Ottawa and drove home to St. Sauveur. Poor Peter, it was heartbreaking to watch as he went from room to room looking for Gus and, not finding him, to finally lie across the doorway of his room to wait. Each morning he returned to the same spot to take up his vigil until, days later, he finally gave up. He was getting old, his muzzle graying; he was slowing down, and ear infections were causing him considerable distress. The vet was unable to prevent the infections recurring, and in August we made the decision all owners dread and had that devoted, gentle animal put down.

In the fall of 1952, Bea sold the house in St. Sauveur and moved to Montreal, where she lived until her death on 24 July 1973 at the age of seventy-two. At the Funeral Mass in St. Joseph's Church in Ottawa, the organ played Bach's *Jesu, Joy of Man's Desiring* as Billy and I followed her casket up the aisle.

After several years in Montreal and New York, Billy moved to Toronto, where he lived until his death at the age of sixty-eight, as a result of a traffic accident on 17 October 1995.

In 1955, I received this letter from General Hertzberg.

Montreal, 20th Jan.'55

Dear Sue,

In the Autumn of 1943 I was in London with Pete who was awaiting orders to join his Regt. in Italy. We saw a good deal of your Father. He was very good to us; we wined and dined and did shows together and he placed at our disposal a big car with <u>two</u> Airmen in the front seat—one to drive and the other to open and close the door! And, then for our last week-end together, he took Pete and me to his place just outside London where he entertained V.I.Ps!

That was a very happy week-end and it was the last time I saw Pete, and when we were saying "Good-bye" he said to me "Dad, I think you should get some little thing for the A.M. as a token of our thanks for all his kindness to us"—I promised him I would—I never did—and, then, it became too late and the thing has hung over me like a cloud for nearly twelve long years. Then seeing you and your Mummie again, I thought perhaps I might redeem my promise to my son through your Father's Daughter—

AFTERWARDS

So, here it is—a little thing as Pete said—but it holds a great deal of love to you and your Dad from Pete and me and this, I think, you will understand.

HFH Hertzberg

The "little thing" was a silver cigarette case with the inscription:

To
Air Marshal H. Edwards, C.B., R.C.A.F.
From P.H.A.H.—*London*, 1943

...

To
"Sue"
From H.F.H.H.—*Montreal*, 1955

Captain P.H.A. (Pete) Hertzberg, Royal Canadian Regiment, was killed in the Lamone Crossing action near Ravenna, Italy, on the night of 4–5 December 1944. He was twenty-four years old.

Gus Edwards, Pete and Dane Hertzberg.
"Highdale," Autumn 1943
Photo courtesy Thea Hertzberg Gray

EPILOGUE

A number of factors contributed to the debilitating heart, respiratory, and circulatory problems that plagued the last fifteen years of Gus's life and resulted in his early death: the years in the mines; the prison camps; the remnants of malaria contracted in Russia; the ever-present cigarette; the strain of managing the relief project; and finally the overwhelming stress of the Second World War. Or perhaps Billy's explanation summed it up best when he said: "he simply died of overwork." No matter the cause, the wonder is that in spite of ill health he managed to achieve what he did, living life to the fullest, blessed with a happy marriage, abiding friendships, and a fiercely loyal staff. No one could ask for more.

The fact he was never appointed Chief of the Air Staff, a post one can only surmise he aspired to attain and was disappointed not doing so, should in no way detract from his extraordinary accomplishments. All his professional life, he fought passionately for what he believed was right for the air force and for the welfare of his troops; as his World War I commander commented: "[He] always realized the great importance of protecting his flight." A complex man of many parts, making it impossible to capture his spirit in a few words, but surely the inscription on the plaque in the Canadian Wing of the Queen Victoria Hospital at East Grinstead is a fitting epitaph:

A MAN OF HOPE & FORWARD LOOKING MIND

His story ends with Bea, she who knew him best and loved him most. Sometime during the 1960s I asked her if she had ever considered remarrying.

"No," she replied; and then, more firmly, "No, no . . . never."

"Why not?"

"Because . . . I had the best."

APPENDIX A

> The following undated article is reproduced
> with the permission of the Minister of Public Works
> and Government Services, 2006.

HALIFAX—DARTMOUTH AND
THE ROYAL CANADIAN AIR FORCE
1918–1939
Prepared by the Air Historian

Halifax's connection with the Air Forces of Canada dates back to the spring of 1918 when the Dominion Government, at the suggestion of the Admiralty, took steps to establish two air stations in Nova Scotia, one at Halifax and the other at Sydney. At Halifax a small site of about 26 acres was selected at Baker's Point on the eastern shore of Halifax harbour, about 3 1/2 miles south of Dartmouth, and the construction of slipways and hangars began. Some months later, in September 1918, a Royal Canadian Naval Air Service was formed to carry out anti-submarine operations from the two stations in Nova Scotia. While the personnel of the R.C.N.A.S. were being trained in the United States and the United Kingdom, the U.S. Naval Flying Corps took over the stations and carried out coastal and convoy patrols during the last 3 1/2 months of the war. The U.S.N. officer in charge at Halifax was Commander Richard E. Byrd, who later won great fame as a trans-Atlantic flyer and Antarctic explorer.

When the First World War ended the R.C.N.A.S. was disbanded and the flying equipment of the two Nova Scotia stations was donated to Canada by the U.S. Government. For the next 20 months Halifax station was left on a care and maintenance basis until, in the summer of 1920, it was transferred by the Department of Naval Service to the newly formed Air Board for use

APPENDIX A

as a base for the erection and repair of seaplanes.

One of the Air Board's first operations was a trans-Canada flight which started from Halifax on 7 October 1920 and ended at Vancouver ten days later. Relays of six aircraft were used on this historic flight which required 49 hours and 7 minutes' flying time. It is of interest to note that the first non-stop trans-Canada flight, which the R.C.A.F. completed in the reverse direction, Vancouver to Halifax, in January 1949, took only 8 hours and 32 minutes.

For some years after 1920 Halifax Air Station was used as a repair depot and a base for Canadian Air Force co-operation exercises with the Army and Royal Canadian Navy and for civil government operations of the Air Board. The latter consisted chiefly of photographic surveys to complete and correct the maps of Nova Scotia and the other Maritime provinces. In 1924, for example, some 3,000 miles of Nova Scotia were photographed from the air.

On 1 April of that year, when the Royal Canadian Air Force was born as a permanent component of Canada's defence forces, Halifax was one of the six air stations operated by the Force. It was the only air base east of Ottawa. The next year, as the R.C.A.F. completed its reorganization along military lines, the small establishment at Halifax-Dartmouth was designated No. 4 (Operations) Squadron. Its establishment was only three officers and nine airmen, and its aircraft consisted of two ancient HS2L flying-boats. The squadron operated, on civil government duties chiefly, only during the spring, summer and autumn months; during the winter the station was closed and the personnel moved to Ottawa.

In 1926 the Squadron was inoperative due to lack of funds and for the next eight years only a nucleus was maintained at the air station to serve detachments which came from Ottawa to work during the operational season. Photographic work was carried out from 1927 to 1933. In 1927 R.C.A.F. aircrews flew 157 hours to photograph 2215 square miles, chiefly in the Shelburne area. The next year a Photo Detachment from Ottawa, working from Dartmouth, carried out nine assignments in the Maritimes; and so it went year after year. In addition to photography there were other operations. In 1927, for instance, aircraft spent over 38 hours on an experiment in dusting forests in the Bras d'Or Lakes area in an effort to combat the spruce bud worm pest. In 1928 and 1929 the R.C.A.F. made many flights for the development of air routes and air mail services between Halifax and Ottawa.

A new activity began in 1932 when customs preventive patrols, which had been started on the west coast some years earlier, were extended to the Atlantic coast. Special RCMP detachments of the RCAF were sent from Ottawa to operate during the season from bases at Gaspé, Shediac, Sydney and Dartmouth; with their aircraft they patrolled a beat that extended from Rimouski, via Miscou Island and Cape North, to the Bay of Fundy. In 1933 almost 2100 hours were spent on this work.

A new chapter in the history of Dartmouth opened in 1934. For some years the station had been on a care and maintenance basis and was "operational" only during the summer season. Now it was re-opened as a permanent base to accommodate No. 5 (Flying Boat) Squadron which was formed from the four MP detachments previously sent out from Ottawa. A program of repair and new construction at the station was begun as an unemployment relief project. There was much to be done; the original light frame buildings erected in 1918 had deteriorated and new, more permanent structures were necessary. Expansion of the seaplane base was also necessary to provide a more sheltered area for the flying-boats. In the spring of 1935, by authority of P.C. 921 of 12 April, an additional area of about 25 acres was acquired to the south-east of the original site.

Through 1934, 1935 and 1936 No. 5 Squadron continued its preventive patrols along the east coast. It also did some photographic work and in 1936 assisted in the rescue operations for the men entombed in the Moose River gold mine.

By this time the European situation was becoming increasingly grave, and in 1937 the R.C.A.F., supported by much larger appropriations, began a rapid expansion. A survey was made of the east coast and new sites were selected at Yarmouth, Sydney and Truro. The development of Dartmouth station continued on a still greater scale to make it the main base for the air defence of the Atlantic seaboard. Hitherto Dartmouth had been only a seaplane base; now it was enlarged to accommodate landplanes as well. An area of approximately 614 acres was acquired at a cost of $24,681 (P.C. 2789 of 10 November 1937) to permit the construction of runways, hangars and other facilities. In the period between the two World Wars over $600,000 was expended on the development of Dartmouth. In the early years the expenditure was very limited, amounting to no more than $13,300 in the fiscal years 1921–1923. In 1934, when the Unemployment Relief Project began there, $5,000 was spent. This was followed, through further relief expenditures and special supplementary estimates, by $90,445 for 1935–36, $21,342 for 1936–37, approximately $94,940 for 1937–38, and an estimated $410,000 for the last pre-war year.

APPENDIX A

In 1938, while the development of east coast bases continued, several major developments occurred. On 1 April the formation of an auxiliary squadron, No. 116 (Coast Artillery Co-Operation) was authorized in Halifax. A Station Headquarters and No. 4 Repair Depot were formed at Dartmouth. Most significant was the creation, on 15 September of that year, of Eastern Air Command, with Headquarters at Halifax under G/C N.B. Anderson. Indicative too of increasing activity in the R.C.A.F. were long distance flights by aircraft of Nos. 2 and 3 Squadrons from Ottawa to Halifax and return.

1939 was highlighted by the visit of their Majesties, the King and Queen. On their departure from Halifax in June No. 5 Squadron provided an aerial guard of honour. Late in August, as the war clouds darkened over Poland, the R.C.A.F. began moving to war stations. From Trenton No. 2 Squadron flew eastward to Halifax and thence to Saint John, while No. 3 Squadron ferried its aging Wapitis from Calgary to Halifax Municipal Airport.

When Canada entered the conflict on 10 September the R.C.A.F. order of battle on the east coast was: E.A.C. at Halifax; Station Headquarters, No. 5 (GR) Squadron (Stranraers) and No. 4 Repair Depot at Dartmouth; and Nos. 2 (AC), 3 (B) and 8 (GP) Squadrons newly arrived at, or en route to Saint John, Halifax and Sydney respectively. In addition, two new units, No. 5 Equipment Depot and No. 22 Magazine Detachment, had just been formed at Moncton and Debert. The two east coast Auxiliary squadrons, Nos. 116 at Halifax and 117 at Saint John, were still in preliminary stages of organization and were disbanded shortly after the outbreak of war. From this small nucleus of air units Eastern Air Command grew, in the course of the next five years, into the powerful force which played so important a part in the Battle of the Atlantic.

APPENDIX B

> This talk was originally broadcast from London to Canada by the Canadian Broadcasting Corporation on 20 July 1942 and is reproduced with the permission of the CBC. It was also published in several Canadian newspapers.

"THEY TOIL WITHOUT GLORY"
By Air Marshal Harold Edwards

I would like to talk to you about those four simple little words—and all they imply in the Air Force here, in Canada, in the United States of America and everywhere. To us in the Air Force, they, perhaps, have a meaning that others do not see. To us, they are symbolic of men who have done much to make the Air Force what it is today.

Without them; we should fail. Without them; the Battle of Britain would have been lost. Without them (and I say this deliberately) this mighty island might, long since, have been battered to its knees.

But thank God we had them. They (no less than the men in the air) helped send the Luftwaffe back into Germany, to lick its wounds. They (no less than the men in the air) made it impossible for flames to roar over this island as they did over London more than fifteen months ago.

I pay tribute to the men of the ground crews—the riggers; the engine mechanics; the cooks; the radio operators; the armourers; the clerks; the equipment assistants; the transport drivers; the instrument makers; the parachute riggers—all that host of people in Air Force uniform who are among the fifty ground crew trades that we have today.

The air crew—the men who fly, the valiant young men before whose sheer, stark courage I always feel humble, when I see them off on a raid—they are a gallant company. I would take away from them no whit of the credit they

APPENDIX B

so rightly deserve. But I would ask you to remember that an air force is a team—a team in which each section is interdependent on the other. Those gallant young men in the air are the brilliant half-backs who carry the ball. The ground crews are the men who run interference for them and make their spectacular gains possible. Few of the ground crew are youngsters. Those who are, you can take my word for it, would be in the air if they could follow their own desire.

Many of the ground crew are long past the age when Air Force service means high adventure, travel, a chance to see new things.

You reach an age, you know, when you like to come home in the evening after your day's work is done; and, depending on your walk in life, take off your shoes and put on slippers, loosen your collar (so to speak) and spend a quiet evening with your wife and children. Many of those ground crew have reached that age. They held good jobs in peace time. There were many foremen mechanics among them. The majority were already skilled tradesmen.

But they had in them that love of fair play—that hatred of a bully—that characterizes our people wherever you find them. They tossed aside their good jobs. They accepted the lowest rate of pay in the Royal Canadian Air Force. They exchanged the comforts of home for a life in huts. They bade their wives and children goodbye and headed out for a future in which everything was uncertain.

But perhaps I am going too far when I say that everything was uncertain. There was one thing that was certain—that (as ground crew) their lot would be "toil without glory."

There are several definitions for the word "toil." But the one that I feel most properly describes it, as applied to the ground crew, is the one that says toil "is hard and unremitting work." That is true, very true!

I would like to add to that definition. In addition to being hard and unremitting work, the toil of ground crew, in the Air Force, is vital work. It is "win the war" work that means the difference between life and death to the men who fly the aircraft.

Let us look at these ground crew for a few minutes and I will try to let you see them as I see them. On one of our stations there's a man called "Paddy." Paddy is the sort of man you'd pass in the street and never notice him. Paddy is forty-seven years old and (if you could get him to talk about it) he would tell you of a dirty night, near Amiens; in another war, long years ago. He brought back a souvenir from that war—a jagged one that the surgeons dug out of his shoulder. When this war came along Paddy enlisted again. He knew he was too old for active service. But he also knew he was a first-rate cook.

Paddy is up there in the Midlands with one of our Canadian squadrons. Just about now (and it is just after two o'clock in the morning over here in London) Paddy is likely busy over his pots and pans for (on the nights our aircraft are on operations) Paddy knows what it means to keep the fire going all night long. He knows too, just what an important effect bacon and eggs, if he can get them, have on morale when he serves them to tousle-headed crews at all hours of the day and night.

Away to the north of this aerodrome is another. The wind never seems to die down there. In the winter it howls from the north and brings on its frozen breath that hard, stinging sleet that numbs the fingers and chills the marrow. There are fine Canadian boys flying the aircraft from that station. They battle with sleet and hail and wind long before (and long after) they've battled with the enemy. But they can only do that because of a group of ground crew, men whose names never strike the headlines.

Where the cruel wind howls and bites like a mad dog, these men work. Though their fingers are blue with cold, though their clothes are stiff with frozen rain, they swarm over the aircraft, cleaning, tightening, adjusting, fitting: with almost loving care.

I would like to tell you about the radio mechanics. You don't hear much about them; more because the job they do is one of the things we don't talk about. They are highly skilled men. They are doing a job that has much to do with the successful defence of this island. But no glamour surrounds them. They are hidden away, many of them, in isolated areas. They do not have the fellowship of the mess. They sleep at odd hours. But they do their job magnificently. They take great pride in it. They know its importance. They know that, each day, they have done something to help to win the war. In that knowledge they are happy. They are well content.

Let me take you up to a fighter station during the season when cross-channel sweeps are being made. On the days when these are at their height, the squadrons take off three or four times. That means heavy work for the ground crews. It means constant and careful checking of engine and airframe. But these men do not complain. If the aircraft they service are in action—it is their fight. If their pilot does a victory roll as he comes in for a landing—it is their victory.

They have a peculiar sense of possession. It is their aircraft—their pilot—their crew—their war—their victory.

Let me tell you of another incident. Recently, one of our bomber squadrons was converted from twin-engine bombers to heavy, four-engined types. The air crew had made the change in record time—just half the time taken by any other squadron. They completed their conversion, a very few days before the first thousand bomber raid on Cologne. But while the air crew was completing its job, the ground crew had accomplished an even greater task. Faced with new aircraft there were hundreds of minor additions and modifications that had to be made. Fitters, riggers, engine mechanics, armourers, even clerks turned in. They worked night and day. They had as little as four hours sleep one night. At times there were as many as thirty men working on one aircraft. But, when the Commander-in-Chief gave the order that sent another thousand bombers into the air, THAT squadron was ready. It sent out the largest number of aircraft it had ever done. It dropped four times the weight of bombs, that it had ever dropped. Every aircraft functioned perfectly.

You didn't read about those ground crew in the stories that were headlined all over the world because: **THEY TOIL WITHOUT GLORY.**

But the men who flew the giant bombers knew what they had done. They did not spare their praise. And I can tell you, the Wing Commander of that squadron knows he has the finest ground crew now serving in the British Isles.

They serve with little praise, no medals, no glory. Yet there is bravery where chance it falls.

Take for instance, the bravery of Flight Sergeant Lummis who was working with gasoline in a hangar at Trenton, Ontario. Suddenly a full can of gasoline burst into flame. Calmly, Flight Sergeant Lummis carried it towards the doors of the hangar. Ahead of him was the expanse of the aerodrome; behind him a hangar crammed with precious aircraft. The heat was intense; and Lummis, his hands and face burned, was forced to set down his blazing load. For an instant he looked back—saw that hangar filled with valuable planes. Again he picked it up, the searing hot flames licking over his face and chest, blistering his hands, and carried it hundreds of feet beyond the hangar—to safety. In time Flight Sergeant Lummis was awarded the George Medal. And remember, decorations are hard to get in Canada.

This is the hour—(as I told you it is two o'clock in the morning here) at which our bombers may be expected to arrive over the spot, in Germany, which has been designated; target for tonight.

At this very moment German people may be dashing madly to the shelters as more than one thousand aircraft sound over their heads. Their night may be made hideous with the shriek of descending bombs; the bursting of incendiaries; the explosions of the anti-aircraft batteries.

And if (at this very moment) a German war factory is disintegrating under the weight of heavy bombs; if a submarine base is heaving from its foundations—give praise to the flying crew certainly. But save a few—or more than a few—of your words of praise for the ground crew—the men who make such gigantic raids possible.

Save some of your cheers for them.

Each time you read in your papers of a bombing attack; or of a vicious fighter battle; or the sinking of a submarine remember the ground crew. Each time I leave an air station (usually at night) my heart goes out to these men: to whom I now pay tribute.

Let me assure their relatives that their efforts to win the war are as important as any other. They shall not go unrecognized. Let your prayers be for them too, for in so doing, you pray for the safety of them that fly. The ground crew pursue a noble calling, and:

They toil without glory!

APPENDIX C

> The following article was written in 1946 and published in *The Ottawa Citizen* in four instalments, the first of which appeared on 18 June 1946. It is reproduced with the permission of *The Ottawa Citizen*.

Unite the Fighting Forces
By Air Marshal H. Edwards C.B.

Now that the blast of war has blown elsewhere the average citizen feels disposed to forget all about wars and anything that may have a bearing on them. War always leaves behind an unsavory aroma which most of us try to ignore by forgetfulness and while the professional sailor, soldier or airman struggle to offset the public lack of interest against an experienced efficiency, apathy sets in which in turn impinges on the forces themselves to multiply the evils that exist either in reality or in the imagination.

Wars there have always been in recorded history. At the termination of each there always prevailed a pious hope that it would be the last. Contrary to such hope another one has followed and in their succession each has become more and more furious and intense in dimensions and inventions that leave no doubt in anybody's mind that sooner or later one thing or the other must happen—peace in perpetuity or extermination. The days have passed when the warrior returned from the chivalrous contest to fatten for the next and tell glamourous tales of what was once a gentleman's business reserved for the few. Everyone in this era is involved in prevailing wars either killing, being killed or paying the cost of the struggle. His or her interest in peacetime cannot diminish if for no other reason regard is to be had for the purse strings. Further, wars are unhappily succeeding one another with greater frequency—only twenty-one years between the last two[138]—so that of all important national questions you and your family cannot be unconcerned with the nation's defence.

* * *

In May 1940, a general alarm was sounded when the enemy was on the doorstep of Britain and not so very far from us. We all regretted the lack of interest in the defence of ourselves and many swore it must never happen again. We engineered a commendable escape but certain precepts and changes emerged.

Across the horizons of the fighting services there has arisen a very important cloud of doubt. Throughout the long lives of the army and navy and in the shorter one of the air force a compelling and purposeful tradition has grown, a spirited tradition of pride in themselves based on rivalry and competition not only among each other but also among the several units or organizations that comprise the whole.

This tradition, though mainly gainful to the smaller units, has frequently brought about a state of isolation of one service from the other, a state which, in its worst form, created a separation which threatened disaster. As one war succeeds its predecessor the task of the three services becomes more and more a joint undertaking demanding more and more an advancement arm-in-arm, and more and more interdependence.

Gone are the days when the navy alone and unaided could keep the seas. We see, instead, the devastating spectacle of a gigantic naval battle being fought and decided without either side getting close enough to shoot at each other. We see, and have seen, the dependence of the air force on land and sea bases. Despite claims of the air exponent, the air force must still come to earth and admittedly it is helpless there. Hitler abandoned his air force and admitted defeat thereby. General Marshall in his revealing report pays great and ample tribute to the air force for its great share in the victories of his armies but it took the persuading genius of General Eisenhower to steer all the forces in Europe to a common course.

All this seems to provoke a suspicion that a combined and successful leadership in war might be equally successful in peace and in preparation for what may never come. Would it be better to continue to progress along the tested and proven lines that only a war can strain or would it be better to go back to the old system? Let us look around.

---

[138] I.e. between the First and Second World Wars.

APPENDIX C

This article has no great concern with speculation as to the future of peace and war except, so to speak, to salute the arrival of the United Nations and the atomic bomb: the former with a fervent blessing; the latter with alarm. Its purpose is to look upon the services as they are and to discuss their controlling organization, and to give, as far as possible, a description of the advantages and drawbacks of each of the systems—existing and proposed.

* * *

Let us consider the existing system first that is, where we have our warriors in three separate parcels with wrapping string drawn fairly tight. Each marches along in its own way bearing its own burdens of administration, each with its own machinery to carry out its work.

Each has a chief of staff and a similar chain of responsible officers down the line doing much the same thing but in the naval way or the army or the air force way as the case might be.

Each has its own accounting organization, its own medical service, its own supply and purchasing branch. Each has its own radio branch, its printing and stationery branch. The Air Force flies aircraft in fairly strong doses; the Navy flies nearly as many and both have highly costly maintenance personnel to look after them.

In sum, it would seem that there is a serious duplication which if removed would effect savings attractive to the taxpayer.

But are there no advantages? Certainly there are.

To start with there is morale: the thing that makes people do things without thought of personal risk or gain.

There is identity. "I belong to the finest navy in the world." Similar rousing identifications are not inspired in an unidentified mob. Morale is hard to foster, harder still in peacetime to maintain. One thing is certain—the roots of high morale spring from identity. Little more than modesty comes from anonymity. Any scheme of change should never disregard this most important of considerations.

* * *

The unification purist takes the view that the best way to bring about the desirable changes would be to take revolutionary measures, tear down the whole structure and start again from scratch. Unification would begin by putting everyone into one "common defence" service. Everybody would wear the same type of uniform with slight variations to suit climates and conditions, would conform to the same laws and regulations; and the several branches would come under the control and command of one man in the different territorial sub-divisions.

The purist would therefore implement by law what has hitherto been done by desire and self-subordination. Except in few and jealously safeguarded circumstances, no officer of one of the services can exercise command over another. By this method the commander of a force whether on land, sea or in the air, could "order" anyone in that force to do his bidding rather than "invite" him. This must sound as ridiculous to the layman as it does to the "common defence" purist. While there is an outlet whereby a combined force of all the services can act under one head, it is not an automatic process but requires declaration and preparation beforehand.

At the top there are, at present, three heads, three chiefs of staff all aiming at the same target but from a different angle. True, they bind themselves into a committee but the best that ever seems to come from a committee is a compromise and seldom a clear-cut decision. Would one man, in an inevitably dictatorial military service, not be better able to make decisions than three? It seems to have worked well in wartime in the field as we have seen.

And who should this head man be?

I have heard that a similar discussion is raging in the military circles of the United States where there are only two separate services while Canada, like Britain, has three. The basic cause seems to be the insertion of the air-war into what was once a state of tranquil and chivalrous reciprocity.

The British argument started way back in World War One. Except among a group of young, red hot enthusiasts, aeroplanes were a nuisance at the start but soon became indispensable to both army and navy. The air started an interservice war which caused the authorities, in true British style, to call in General Smuts who, but shortly before was their bitterest enemy, to sort things out. In a fine history-making document he told a terrible tale and argued the air force into being a separate service. Then as now, he could find no way of banging official heads together and so make the services see eye to eye; they were pulled farther apart. Can we put them even closer together again and make them stick with consequent saving to our bank account? And without loss to fighting efficiency? Or an increase of it?

The out-and-out unificationist holds that morale can be engendered in a single service just as easily as it can in three separate ones. I think it could; given plenty of time. It could certainly be bred into a single service over the long haul and what a happy day that would be. The rivalry now present

APPENDIX C

within the services themselves is clear proof of that—the tank man thinks little of the infantry man and vice versa. The pilot shows friendly scorn of the navigator who boasts that it is he who gets the pilot there and so on. Would rivalry within a single service produce the indispensable morale that three separate ones now create and would a single service not do away with expensive duplication to say nothing of unified direction and control?

* * *

As far as Canada is concerned there is nothing new about unification or amalgamation of the services. As long ago as 1924 a department of national defence was formed under one minister and one chief of staff. It had before it a plan to use one set of auxiliary branches to service all three.

No one who has looked into the history of this idea can doubt that it was a failure. Due largely to preponderance of numbers in the army, the other two—the navy and the air force—were absorbed and not unified or amalgamated. They were squelched into a system unsuited to their needs and purposes, a system that had long been antiquated and obsolete. On the grounds that what was good for the army was good enough for anyone else, the navy and air force had to conform to a strange standard that would bear no adaptation to their intimate problems. They found themselves on a combined seniority list that controlled, or attempted to control, promotion among at least two of the services so that one by promotion could not get ahead of the other. The inevitable consequence was that no one liked the scheme and did everything possible to defeat it. Final separation came again at the outbreak of the last war.[139] Looking back I feel that failure did not lie in the plan itself but in the conflict of opinion as to its application. Perhaps some suspicion and jealousy had crept in, but whatever the cause when the starting bell of war clanged, the services rode away from one another in three different directions and with them either their own piece of the central organization or else created new ones.

That may have been a mistake but we can bank on it that the people of that day acted with good reason, as subsequent events give us good cause to believe. Anyone with a question in his mind can look at the record.

There is nothing quite so sweet as the lamb and the lion together in slumber provided the small one is not inside the other. That is the fear of the navy and the air force—to be gobbled up by the bigger brother whose teeth are old but whose appetite still is good.

---

[139] I.e. the Second World War.

Sheer weight of numbers used to be the criterion of power. Is it so today? The heavy bomber is manned by six of a crew. Measure its potency against three hundred men with rifles or machine guns or whatever they can carry. The counting of heads has no bearing on relative merit in the gladiatorial arena of today. The fears of the two smaller services are more than likely baseless, but until they are removed by the assurance of deeds there will always remain a suspicion.

All that, from the national point of view means nothing. No nation can afford a fighting force as big as it would like, although it may be the cheapest form of insurance that it can buy. What any nation expects is the best attainable for its money, so, consequently, the personal views and ambitions of anybody and everybody should, and indeed, must be subordinated to what is best for the whole.

We have now pretty well travelled the whole mesh of complexities. Let us see if we can get somewhere nearer the pith. Disregarding all subsidiary considerations and divesting the subject of all explanatory wrappings there are, immediately, two main conundrums: to put command and determination in the hands of a single person; and secondly to have one set of common services and servants instead of three.

To say that it would be too much for one man to cope with, draws the eye to the responsibilities of a Prime Minister, the President of a large republic or to the Premier of Russia. Organization is directed manpower. One Minister of National Defence, therefore, should be enough. He could, in times of stress, have three parliamentary assistants to represent and specialize in the affairs of the three services; but in any event there should be three deputy ministers, all of equal status and salary—civil servants who would deal with the day by day non-warlike occupations of the department. Attached to them would be a necessary civilian staff.

At this point we come to the most difficult problem. There would be a single chief of staff over all three services. To remove the disquieting elements of such an appointment from any one of the services the post should frequently revolve amongst the three of them and to take away any thought of the smaller being absorbed by the larger, the smallest in numbers, be it army, navy or air force, should be selected as the one from whose ranks the first appointment should be made. Thereafter at short intervals of two years or so each service would have it in turn in the reversed order of total numbers. Under this man would come three subordinate chiefs: the chief of the army staff, the chief of the naval staff and the chief of the air staff.

By this plan one man would advise the minister instead of three (usually with conflicting opinions), and each service would have its own head who is a specialist in its functions. One man would coordinate the work and avoid duplication. It might be said that the top man would most likely favour the service from which he sprang, I think the contrary would be more probable.

* * *

To amalgamate or unite the subordinate branches the same formula could be applied. To simplify the process we might consider how it could be done by any one of them. Let us take perhaps the most difficult of the lot—the medical branch. Each service has a medical branch, each branch has a director of medical services, each has separate hospitals, convalescent homes and no doubt some kind of a research department. To put them all together should require no more difficulty than assembling the top men provided we kept the sting of absorption out of it. If we apply the same rules of fair treatment, and rotation of top men within short periods of time, to this metamorphosis not only would a saving in money be achieved but greater efficiency should result. Indeed this particular branch might go farther and amalgamate itself with other medical departments of the government such as veterans affairs, national health and Indian affairs, with consequent efficiencies and savings among the lot.

Such a radical step of joining civilians and soldiers in a peacetime occupation might sound strange but in modern war it is hard to say which of them bears more of the battle. Further, in peacetime the service medical officer normally gets insufficient medical practice to keep him skilled in the science and art of his profession since the number of patients daily falling to his care are in such small numbers and simple of disposal; any difficult cases are given other treatment. That might equally apply to the other government departments mentioned.

In all the fighting forces the published figures give a grand total to be ultimately some 51,000 of all ranks in the permanent forces spread as they will be across the Dominion. At the high estimate of three per cent the anticipated number of hospital cases at any one time would be 1,530. For such small numbers it is hard to justify the variety and number of services hospitals existing.

Consider another branch. The accountant and pay branches of the navy and air force follow an organization essentially the same. The army system is quite different. If the army could find it convenient to adopt the scheme of the other two, unification of all three should present no difficulty and with the fair process of equality of advancement, the personal problem could be removed.

This could be made to apply to many other of the ancillary services and by mutually co-operative spirit of give and take should lead to considerable economy and efficiency.

* * *

Up to now only the immediate situation has entered our considerations. What might be done over the long haul? If the foregoing discussion is acceptable and the necessity of a single service really exists, as it seems to do, how best can it be brought onto a permanent basis? It took the air force no more than a scant ten years to breed out the army and navy elements that first composed it. A change of uniform distinct from the other two; an air force atmosphere and a different way of doing things.

First, all three must sink their identity and their names into the pool of a new one—a common defence force. The Royal Canadian Defence Force or some such name. Officers and enlisted men would, as new entries, join such a force and not one of its former components. The uniform would be different and distinct and common to all, allowance being made for climate and special working conditions as now pay would be equal for equal service and qualification—a matter that has caused much bitterness in the past. Common regulations and laws of discipline would apply equally to all, thus giving the power of command to competent authority over anybody, anywhere.

Specialists there would necessarily be as now. Each person would join for service as a mechanic, a stoker, a medical officer, aircrew or a cook as the case may be. There would, as now, be specialist schools for technical training; but only one staff college and one pre-entry college.

I feel sure that the many people who have devoted almost a lifetime of painstaking care and energy to the particular service of their choice will find in this discourse something of heresy and undesirable change. They will say that it will be hard to replace the pride in his service and repugnant to see it shorn of its glory. They will contend that as identity vanished so would esprit de corps and morale. Perhaps it would, though I doubt it because the entity he now serves would still be a component to which he might still bear loyalty and through it in turn to a higher entity. In such a comparison we might view the empire or the U.N.

Again he might think his side might suffer individually but I think he will agree that in the course of time the best man would come to the top.

APPENDIX D

Letter from A/M John Plant to Bea Edwards

**LE CHATEAU
VENEUX - LES - SABLONS (S. & M.)
FRANCE
Tél: 18 à Moret**

29 Feb. 52

Dear Bea:

Please let me send you my sympathy and at the same time, even in a small way, share your great sorrow. To me Gus was always much more than a mere senior Air Force officer, he was in many ways more like a father. From him I learned much about the ways of men; from him I learned a philosophy on loyalty—that it spreads downwards as well as upwards, for when I have been in trouble he has helped me, when I have been successful, he has praised me.

Like all who had the good fortune to serve with him, I shall always regard him as the greatest of the Air Force. I shall always remember him as a man whose unselfish loyalty and perseverance was indeed the motto of the R.C.A.F—Per Ardua ad Astra. To him, more than to any other person goes credit for the position of the R.C.A.F. today.

I cannot help but recall that my first arrival in Ottawa was the evening of the departure of the King & Queen. In the mess at Rockliffe that evening there was an atmosphere of rejoicing. A job had been done. It had been done well. The R.C.A.F. on its first major public appearance in Canada had done well—as well as it had done in London at the King's coronation. It has not always done as well since, but in more recent years the officers who were trained by Gus have had an opportunity to pass on some of the things he taught them and so on its three last parades—the presentation of the gates at Trenton, the trooping of the colours at Ottawa and the recent reception of the Royal Couple at Trenton—the Edwards' standard of smartness, precision and cleanliness has been achieved by the R.C.A.F.

It was Group Captain Edwards who brought into being the RCAF medical service. Air Commodore Edwards established the R.C.A.F. pay and accounts branch. By his judicious posting, for training purposes, of Wilf Curtis, AVM Edwards as AMP produced the present CAS under whose guidance we have prospered. In the face of opposition, in some cases from his own officers, Air Marshal Edwards succeeded in creating a Canadian Bomber Group with Canadian squadrons and stations commanded by Canadian officers. He provided us too with Canadian fighter squadrons, coastal command squadrons and transport squadrons. Had it not been for all these things which he did, the R.C.A.F. might still be an off-shoot of the Army. Certainly we would not have officers of senior rank who can speak with some authority and with a voice of some experience on operational matters.

I could write pages on the Edwards saga. What sort of a man was he? To describe him to you, who knew him best of anyone in the world might be wrong.

However I do remember him, as do all of us who served close to him, as a warm-hearted man capable of deep emotion, tolerant of our human weaknesses, impatient at our stupidity, but willing always to hear our point of view, willing to change his own mind if our arguments were valid and well founded.

All of us who mourn with you today can say with all sincerity—"<u>this was a man.</u>"

Please accept my most heartfelt sympathy, though I feel my words can express so little.

John Plant

APPENDIX E

ROYAL CANADIAN AIR FORCE
Organization, Operations and Rank Structure in 1942–43

ORGANIZATION
Minister of National Defence for Air: Hon. Charles G. (Chubby) Power
Chief of the Air Staff (CAS): Air Marshal Lloyd S. (Bread) Breadner

The Air Council:
Originally formed in November 1938 with four members, membership increased as the RCAF expanded. Its function was to coordinate policy, operations, administration, management, and training. The CAS was President of the Council with membership consisting of the Minister and directors of various branches of the service each with the title of "Air Member," e.g. Air Member for Personnel (AMP), Air Member for Organization (AMO), Air Member for Training (AMT), etc.

OPERATIONS
There were two main areas of Operations: in Canada, the Home War Establishment, which included the British Commonwealth Air Training Plan (BCATP); and outside Canada, RCAF Overseas. Overseas operations, with headquarters in London, England, covered the United Kingdom, and the Middle and Far East. While Air Marshal Harold (Gus) Edwards held the post of Air Officer Commanding in Chief RCAF Overseas, he reported directly to the Chief of the Air Staff at headquarters in Ottawa.

RANKS
Officers

A/M	Air Marshal		
A/V/M	Air Vice Marshal		
A/C	Air Commodore		
G/C	Group Captain	**Women's Division**	
W/C	Wing Commander	Wg Off	Wing Officer
S/L	Squadron Leader	Sqn Off	Squadron Officer
F/L	Flight Lieutenant	Flt Off	Flight Officer
F/O	Flying Officer	SO	Section Officer
P/O	Pilot Officer	ASO	Assistant Section Officer

Other Ranks

WO1	Warrant Officer Class 1	WO1	Warrant Officer Class 1
WO2	Warrant Officer Class 2	WO2	Warrant Officer Class 2
FS	Flight Sergeant	FS	Flight Sergeant
Sgt	Sergeant	Sgt	Sergeant
Cpl	Corporal	Cpl	Corporal
LAC	Leading Aircraftman	LAW	Leading Airwoman
AC1	Aircraftman Class 1	AW1	Airwoman Class 1
AC2	Aircraftman Class 2	AW2	Airwoman Class 2

APPENDIX F

CAREER SUMMARY OF AIR MARSHAL HAROLD EDWARDS

Date	Rank and Posting
14 December 1915	Aviator Cadet (Able Seaman) in Royal Canadian Naval Volunteer Reserve
25 February 1916	Flight Sub Lieutenant—Royal Naval Air Service—Flight training in England
6 August 1916	Fighter Pilot 3 (Naval) Wing—Luxeuil-les-Bains, France
14 April 1917	Shot down returning from Freiburg raid and taken prisoner (escapes twice, once for ten days, but is recaptured)
1 April 1918	Flight Lieutenant—Royal Air Force
December 1918	Repatriation Officer—Berlin
January 1919	Embarkation Officer—Warnemünde, Germany
12 April 1919	RAF 47 Squadron "C" Flight—Krasnodar, South Russia
End of March 1920	Evacuated from Novorossisk, South Russia
5 July 1920	Demobilized in England
9 September 1920	Flight Lieutenant—Canadian Air Force Flight training—Camp Borden
15 October 1920	Staff Officer—Headquarters, Ottawa
September 1923	Staff Course—Royal Military College
December 1923	Flight training—Camp Borden

February 1924	Adjutant and operational pilot—Winnipeg (and OIC Victoria Beach)
1 April 1924	Flight Lieutenant—Royal Canadian Air Force
20 September 1926	Liaison Officer—Air Ministry London
29 September 1926	Promoted Squadron Leader
3 October 1927	Royal Naval College—Greenwich
1 January 1929	Staff Officer—Headquarters, Ottawa
1 September 1934	Commanding Officer RCAF Station—Dartmouth
1 April 1936	Promoted Wing Commander
12 May 1937	Heads RCAF contingent to coronation of King George VI
25 February 1938	Senior Staff Officer—Headquarters, Ottawa
10 April 1939	Promoted Group Captain
1 February 1940	Promoted Air Commodore
1940–41	Air Member for Personnel
5 August 1941	Promoted Air Vice Marshal
25 November 1941	Air Officer-in-Chief, RCAF Overseas
20 June 1942	Promoted Air Marshal
16 July 1943	Air Officer Commanding-in-Chief, RCAF Overseas
1 January 1944	Special duties—Headquarters, Ottawa
29 September 1944	Retired

Honours and Awards

Companion, Order of the Bath (Mil)

1914–18	General Service Medal, Victory Medal
1939–45	Star, Africa Star, Defence Medal, Canadian Volunteer Services Medal and Clasp, War Medal
1935	Jubilee Medal
1937	Coronation Medal

APPENDIX F

1920	Order of St. Anne w/sword and bow (Russia)
	Order of St. Stanislaus w/sword and bow (Russia)
1947	*Officier de la Légion d'Honneur* (France)
	Croix de Guerre avec Palme (France)
1948	The Military Order of the White Lion "for Victory" —The Star—1st Class (Czechoslovakia)
1948	Legion of Merit, Degree of Commander (United States of America)

APPENDIX G

ABBREVIATIONS

AC2	Aircraftman Second Class
A/C	Air Commodore
A/C/M	Air Chief Marshal
AFHQ	Air Force Headquarters
AFU	Air Fighting Unit
A/M	Air Marshal
AMP	Air Member for Personnel
AO-in-C	Air Officer-in-Chief
AOC-in-C	Air Officer Commanding-in-Chief
A/V/M	Air Vice Marshal
BCATP	British Commonwealth Air Training Plan
B/Gen	Brigadier General
CAF	Canadian Air Force
CAS	Chief of the Air Staff
CF	Canadian Forces
CIA	Central Intelligence Agency
CO	Commanding Officer
Cpl	Corporal
Col	Colonel
DAOC-in-C	Deputy Air Officer Commanding-in-Chief
DOC	District Officer Commanding
FBI	Federal Bureau of Investigation

APPENDIX G

F/L	Flight Lieutenant
F/M	Field Marshal
F/O	Flying Officer
FS	Flight Sergeant
F/S/L	Flight Sub Lieutenant
G/C	Group Captain
GOC	General Officer Commanding
HCU	Heavy Conversion Unit
HQ	Headquarters
JATP	Joint Air Training Plan
LAC	Leading Aircraftman
LAW	Leading Airwoman
L/Gen	Lieutenant General
M/Gen	Major General
MRAF	Marshal of the Royal Air Force
NCO	Non-Commissioned Officer
NMC	National Military Cemetery
OIC	Officer in Charge
OR	Orderly Room
OTU	Operational Training Unit
PA	Personal Assistant
P/O	Pilot Officer
PRC	Personnel Reception Centre
RAF	Royal Air Force
RAAF	Royal Australian Air Force
RCAF	Royal Canadian Air Force
RCAMC	Royal Canadian Army Medical Corps
RCMP	Royal Canadian Mounted Police
RCN	Royal Canadian Navy
RCNVR	Royal Canadian Naval Volunteer Reserve
RFC	Royal Flying Corps

RN	Royal Navy
RNAS	Royal Naval Air Service
RNZAF	Royal New Zealand Air Force
Sgt	Sergeant
S/L	Squadron Leader
S/O	Section Officer
UNRRA	United Nations Relief and Rehabilitation Administration
USAF	United States Air Force
USAAF	United States Army Air Force
USN	United States Navy
USSR	Union of Soviet Socialist Republics
WAAF	Women's Auxiliary Air Force
WAG	Wireless Air Gunner
W/C	Wing Commander
WD	RCAF Women's Division

ABOUT THE AUTHOR

Suzanne K. (Sue) Edwards was born and brought up in Ottawa. Following high schools in Vancouver and Montreal, she had a brief sojourn at McGill University where, after two years, this Royal Institution for the Advancement of Learning decided, quite rightly, she and the university would both be better off following separate paths.

For many years she lived and worked in Montreal, with her career culminating in the establishment and direction of a company that specialized in the management of associations and conferences, both in Canada and abroad. She also became interested in wood sculpture and later made a full-time commitment to life as a sculptress, returning once again to the business world in Toronto during the 1990s.

Sue retired to Nova Scotia in 1997 where she seeks the ever elusive goal of lowering her handicap at the Digby Pines Golf Club.

To order more copies of

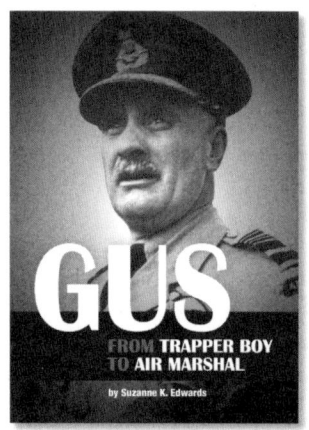

Contact:
General Store Publishing House
499 O'Brien Road, Box 415
Renfrew, ON Canada
K7V 4A6

1-800-465-6072
Fax: (613) 432-7184

www.gsph.com

VISA and MASTERCARD accepted